CLIFT NOTES
Intelligence and the Nation's Security

A. Denis Clift

Second Edition
Edited by James S. Major

For Kathy Hogan
with great
friendship,

Deni Clift

March 7, 2014

The Joint Military Intelligence College supports and
encourages research on intelligence issues that
distills lessons and improves support to policy-level
and operational consumers.

Clift Notes: Intelligence and the Nation's Security

First edition January 2000
Second edition August 2002

This book is a publication of the Joint Military Intelligence College Writing Center. It presents selected speeches and writings of A. Denis Clift, President of the Joint Military Intelligence College. The views expressed are those of the author and do not necessarily reflect the official policy or position of the Department of Defense or the United States Government.

This book is prepared for the use of U.S. Government officials, and the format, coverage, and content are designed to meet their specific requirements. U.S. Government officials can obtain additional copies of this book directly or through liaison channels from the Defense Intelligence Agency.

The Office of the Secretary of Defense (Public Affairs) has approved this document for unrestricted public release.

Library of Congress Catalog Number   **2002107020**
ISBN   **0-9656195-5-9**

FOREWORD

In 1996, Denis Clift in his typically generous fashion shared with me speeches he had recently delivered as President of the Joint Military Intelligence College during an official mission to Bucharest and to the Annual Meeting of the Society for Military History. I urged him to expand on such writing, adding that his was a light that had been too long under a bushel.

In the speeches and essays presented in *Clift Notes: Intelligence and the Nation's Security*, the wisdom and the vision of a gifted thinker, writer, practitioner, and leader shine forth. He examines the origins, evolution, and structure of intelligence in America, its place in the nation's defense and national security construct, and its responsibilities and achievements in the workings and life of our remarkable democracy.

Within this framework, he traces the evolution of defense intelligence, the importance of intelligence education, and the birth, steadily growing role, contributions, and resulting increase in stature of the Joint Military Intelligence College. Looking beyond his fences, he applauds the growing teaching and study of intelligence at colleges and universities across the country. He reminds that past intelligence advances and successes, from code breaking to satellite making, have drawn on the genius of the broadest cross-section of the nation's citizens, that it is essential that young Americans from across the nation continue to offer their talents to the calling of intelligence, to service to their nation.

The author, as these writings reflect, serves as a case in point. Upon his graduation from Stanford University in 1958, he had a letter in hand from the Executive Editor of *Newsweek* wishing him good luck in the Navy, asking him to be in touch upon his return, telling him that he was one who had been tentatively selected for a job. Those four years of naval service would, instead, launch him on a career, now in its fifth decade, that has taken him to the very highest levels of national security responsibilities, with ever-expanding contributions to the defense, foreign-policy, intelligence, and academic workings of the nation.

Samuel Vaughan Wilson
President Emeritus
Hampden-Sydney College

EDITOR'S PREFACE TO THE SECOND EDITION

by James S. Major
Director, Joint Military Intelligence College Writing Center

In the preface to the first edition of this book, I wrote that "challenges loom on the horizon, from the proliferation of weapons of mass destruction to the ever-increasing threat of domestic and international terrorism. Intelligence has never been more important to decisionmakers and policymakers than in these perilous times." In light of the terrorist attacks on the World Trade Center and the Pentagon less than two years later, those words resonate with understatement. Now our nation's leaders—executive and legislative alike—stand united in their resolve to conquer terrorism. And the Intelligence Community will be an essential element in that fight. We have arrived at a point in this nation's post-Cold War history where the United States is threatened not by the military might of a monolithic enemy but by challenges from far-flung nations and disparate factions. These are indeed perilous times.

This edition contains seven new chapters, speeches given by the President of the Joint Military Intelligence College in wide-ranging venues: the World Affairs Council in San Antonio, Texas; the U.S. Coast Guard Academy at New London, Connecticut; the Merchant Marine Academy at Kings Point, New York; the Kennedy School at Harvard University; the Miller Center at the University of Virginia; Trinity College in Washington, DC; and an International Security Studies conference at Yale University.

While the subject matter of this book invites wide readership, it is intended foremost as a book of readings for students and faculty at the Joint Military Intelligence College as well as for other academic institutions that include intelligence studies as part of their curriculum. To that end, the book is subdivided into sections to facilitate reading by major subject area. A common thread woven throughout the updated chapters is the challenge faced by the United States Intelligence Community in dealing with a complex new threat—not only from domestic terrorism, but also from increasingly sophisticated information technologies capable of inflicting serious damage on our infrastructure by attacks in cyberspace.

The subtitle of this book is *Intelligence and the Nation's Security*. Intelligence is a vital component in safeguarding United States national security. Whether it is a tool in "The Commander's Kit" (chapter 9) or a partner in strategic negotiations "With Presidents at the Summit" (chapter 20), intelligence contributes immeasurably to the security of this nation. The collected essays and speeches of Denis Clift illustrate that point clearly, from the perspective of a man who has been there and who is focused on the future.

James S. Major
Washington, DC
May 2002

EDITOR'S ACKNOWLEDGMENTS

No work of this nature is possible without the cooperation of other organizations and individuals. We are grateful to the following for their permission to reprint items previously published by them:

- *American Intelligence Journal,* a publication of the National Military Intelligence Association, www.nmia.org. Special thanks to Zhi M. Hamby-Nye.
- *Defense Intelligence Journal,* published by the Joint Military Intelligence College Foundation, and its editor Bill Manthorpe.
- Harvard University and its Program on Information Resources Policy. Special thanks to Dr. Tony Oettinger.
- Mrs. John T. Hughes, for her permission to publish "The San Cristobal Trapezoid," copyright 1992 by John T. Hughes.
- *Joint Force Quarterly,* published for the Chairman of the Joint Chiefs of Staff by the Institute for National Strategic Studies, National Defense University.

Dr. Russ Swenson, Director of the Joint Military Intelligence College Office of Applied Research and the driving force behind the College's new Center for Strategic Intelligence Research, provided counsel, advice, and assistance at many junctures during the process.

Ms. Jessica M. Steinruck provided her usual efficient administrative support in preparing the manuscript and ensuring that I had proper updates for all new material.

The Production Services Division (ISP-1) who supports the Joint Military Intelligence College, worked side-by-side with us throughout the project to help make this a professional second edition.

As always, my wife Joan Major earned my eternal gratitude for her occasional sanity checks and for her moral support throughout the project.

CONTENTS

CLIFT NOTES

INTELLIGENCE AND THE NATION'S SECURITY

PART ONE

INTELLIGENCE IN HISTORY AND IN ACTION

CHAPTER 1
INTELLIGENCE EDUCATION FOR
JOINT WARFIGHTING

In this essay, first published in an edited version in the Spring 1999 issue of Joint Force Quarterly, *the author documents the growing contributions of the Joint Military Intelligence College at the turn of the century. The College, he writes, is preparing the next generation of intelligence leaders in a joint service academic environment for roles and responsibilities that are part of* Joint Vision 2010. *He traces the history of the College from the time of its establishment by Department of Defense Directive as the Defense Intelligence School in 1962. He charts the College's increased degree-granting authority with Congressional legislation for the Master of Science of Strategic Intelligence in 1980 and for the Bachelor of Science in Intelligence in 1997. He describes the increasingly important research contributions both by faculty and by students, adding that one of the College's greatest strengths lies in the fact that intelligence research and teaching are conducted up to the highest levels of security classification.*

The end product of the intelligence effort must be the real-time, fully fused picture-the amalgamation of national, theater, and tactical collection from all the military services and intelligence agencies. But in addition to depicting an adversary's position, and as the Chairman's Joint Vision 2010 properly envisions, this picture should also accurately portray the location and status of friendly forces. The result is a "Common Operational Picture" that provides the commander a high-confidence view of both friend and foe.

Vice Admiral Dennis C. Blair, U.S. Navy
"Intelligence in Partnership" Conference
Joint Military Intelligence College
June 1997

In June 1998, with the accreditation of the Bachelor of Science in Intelligence (BSI) degree, the Joint Military Intelligence College opened a new chapter of expanded service to the defense, intelligence, and broader national security communities. As the nation's only accredited academic institution offering the BSI degree and the Master of Science of Strategic Intelligence (MSSI) degree, the College is preparing the next generation of intelligence leaders in a joint service academic environment for the roles and the responsibilities that are part of Joint Vision 2010.

To educate in intelligence is to examine the machinery of leadership and decisionmaking—national, theater, and tactical—that intelligence fuels and to examine the prospecting, the drilling, the refining, the distribution, and the performance of that fuel in the cyber era. Winston Churchill had an enduring belief in the importance of intelligence. He drew on the work of British and other secret services throughout his career. Soon after becoming wartime Prime Minister, he ordered an examination of the role intelligence was playing in operational and strategic decisions, resulting in a revitalization of the British intelligence system.[1]

Joseph Stalin distrusted intelligence. He rejected reports from several sources of imminent German invasion in 1941, showering at least one with expletives and labeling them disinformation. Some 30 years later, his successor as Soviet head of state, former KBG chief Yuri Andropov, would retain control of the KGB as General Secretary. The Politburo agenda would swell with KGB issues coming forward for favorable decision, and the General Secretary would stay closely involved in the secret service's covert links with foreign terrorist organizations.[2]

President Eisenhower, in the words of his staff secretary Brigadier General Andrew Goodpaster, from the time of the Battle of the Bulge on, was deeply impressed by the value of intelligence, its limitations and incompleteness, and its role in the making of strategy. An imagery analyst commenting on Eisenhower's use of satellite photography, has said: "After he saw CORONA photos of how the Vietnamese were beginning to penetrate Laos, he told us about the difficulties of fighting a war under such circumstances. He compared it to the way Tito outfoxed the Germans in World War II."[3] In the 1960s, "Presidents Kennedy and Johnson each affirmed repeatedly that he was not going to be the President who lost Vietnam and the rest of Southeast Asia. Told by CIA that 'you can't win in Vietnam,' they might well have told themselves, 'I can't not win in Vietnam.'"[4]

To understand how a leader draws on and assesses intelligence is to begin to understand a single facet of that leader's thinking. To delve deeper, in his research at the Joint Military Intelligence College faculty member Daniel S. Gressang has taken as his starting point the underlying importance to intelligence of understanding a leader's thinking so as to be able to predict behavior and intent. While the traditional focus of such study is on the intent of a foreign adversary, Gressang has also examined the impact that the characterizations and verbal labels used by senior U.S. policymakers for a given issue have had on the intelligence officers and intelligence organizations. From this, he has assessed the risk that is inherent in the transfer of that policymaker's mindset to the intelligence bureaucracy with resulting bias and distortion, however well-intentioned, in intelligence tasking, collection, reporting, and analysis.[5]

During their year of graduate study at the Joint Military Intelligence College, officers and senior noncommissioned officers from each of the Services and civilians from across the intelligence and law enforcement communities consider such issues with faculty and meet with military leaders and senior policymakers as part of their study of the dynamics and the tensions between intelligence and policy, the structure of the national security process, and the impact of personalities and group dynamics—not included in the wiring diagrams—on the process. "The worst decisions were often the unanimous ones," Admiral William J. Crowe, U.S. Navy (Retired), former Chairman, Joint Chiefs of Staff, told one class this year, "because no one questioned the group's assumptions." "Intelligence is like air," former National Security Adviser Anthony Lake observed. "You don't realize you are using it until you don't have it."

National Security Structure and Policy is one of nine core courses in the Joint Military Intelligence College's 14-course postgraduate curriculum that also requires the research and writing of a master's thesis for award of the MSSI degree. Other core courses include 21st Century Intelligence: National Military Strategy; 21st Century Intelligence: The Emerging International Security Environment; Strategic Warning & Threat Management; Intelligence Collection: Evidence for Analysis; Intelligence Research and Analytic Methods; Intelligence Analysis: Continuity and Change; Information Technologies in the Cyber Era; and MSSI Thesis Seminar.

35th YEAR

The Joint Military Intelligence College was established by Department of Defense directive in 1962 as the Defense Intelligence School, merging the former Army and Navy Intelligence Schools. The school was to operate under the direction of the Director, Defense Intelligence Agency (DIA), and was attached to DIA for administrative support. A Board of Visitors, appointed by the Secretary of Defense, was established to provide findings and recommendations on the work of the institution. In 1980, the Congress authorized the school to award the Master of Science of Strategic Intelligence degree. The degree was accredited by the Commission on Higher Education of the Middle States Association of Colleges and Schools in 1982, and the school was rechartered that year as the Defense Intelligence College with the two-fold mission of education and research.

A decade later, in the era of joint doctrine, the College adopted its current name. In 1997, the Congress authorized the College to award a second degree, the Bachelor of Science in Intelligence (BSI). The College's accreditation was reaffirmed by the Commission on Higher Education in June 1998 to include the new BSI degree.

The College's main campus is housed in the Defense Intelligence Analysis Center, Bolling Air Force Base, Washington, DC, with a satellite campus at the National Security Agency (NSA). The student body averages between 430 and 450 a year, including fulltime students in the postgraduate and undergraduate programs and part-time students in the weekend and evening programs, the Master's program for Reserves, and the postgraduate program at the NSA campus.

To meet the requirements of the sponsoring Services, departments, and agencies, the College is educating future intelligence, defense, and national security leaders, graduates who will be full partners with their policy, planning, and operations counterparts; graduates prepared to anticipate and tailor the intelligence required at the national, theater and tactical levels. In his address to the Class of '98 this past March, former Supreme Allied Commander Europe General George Joulwan, U.S. Army (Retired), a member of the College's Board of Visitors, said that today's commander looks to intelligence to be the lead player and a principal player from start to finish in any crisis or combat operation. From his own in-theater experience, he repeatedly stressed the necessity of intelligence's lead, given the dynamics of U.S. national security requirements.

A. Denis Clift

In preparing its graduates for their onward careers, in preparing them to play their parts in shaping the real-time, fully fused picture—the lead-player role in the development of Vice Admiral Blair's Common Operational Picture providing the commander a high-confidence view of both friend and foe—the College draws on the teaching tools of case methodology, gaming, and simulation. War-game elective courses are designed within the context of the settings of major war games hosted by the several military staff and war colleges with whom the Joint Military Intelligence College has a working relationship—the National Defense University's National War College, the Air University, and the U.S. Marine Corps Command and Staff College.

In March 1998, 16 graduate students—a Navy Lieutenant and Army and Air Force Captains—played the role of J-2s and Deputy J-2s in the Army War College's capstone Strategic Crisis Exercise '98. The students devoted several weeks in the Joint Military Intelligence College's elective Joint Intelligence Exercise course preparing for their interaction with more senior counterparts at Carlisle. They joined the exercise in full stride, manning the intelligence cells, providing regular briefings, and participating throughout in discussions of options with exercise decisionmakers. At the request of the Army War College, 36 JMIC students are scheduled to participate in Strategic Crisis Exercise '99.

In future gaming and exercises, the College is planning to expand the capability of its students to participate not only on-scene but also from remote locations, replicating the growing, information-age, real-world demands on the flow of intelligence in crisis and conflict.

> Virtually everything we do in intelligence, surveillance and reconnaissance (ISR) or fully integrated command, control, communications, computers and ISR (C4ISR) today is performed on sets of interlocking functional architectures. . . . If these architectures don't function, or function in unpredictably corrupted modes, our confidence in our competence and capability to control events is degraded or destroyed. [6]

And as Admiral Studeman, a JMIC alumnus, proceeds to underline, the consequences of such failure are dire on the modern battlefield.

In part to facilitate cyber-era participation in gaming and exercises, the College has fitted out and is now operating a technology laboratory and, as a result of the curriculum review completed in 1997, has added the new core course Information Technologies in the Cyber Era. Students work in a computer/software environment mirroring state-of-the-art environments throughout the Intelligence Community. The College is exploring with students the interlocking architectures and how they facilitate worldwide collaboration in collections, analysis, and dissemination. Further, exploring the opening world of computer deception, the College is encouraging critiques of system strengths, weaknesses, and vulnerabilities. If there is a single truth in this fast moving-era, it is that each year's new students bring greater and greater cyber-space knowledge and skills to their studies and research.

RESEARCH

Writing on the relationship between research and teaching, Wilhelm von Humboldt, founder of Berlin University, said:

> Both teacher and student have their justification in the common pursuit of knowledge. . . . The goals of science and scholarship are worked toward most effectively through the synthesis of teacher's and the students' dispositions. . . . Not only do such students profit when taught by scholars who are themselves engaged in creative endeavors; scholarship itself is enriched when the younger generation consciously, if naively, questions it.[7]

Teaching and research at the College are conducted up to the highest levels of security classification—one of the College's great strengths—with all students, faculty, and staff holding the appropriate clearances. Academic freedom is central to the life of the College. Research by both students and faculty is being produced at both the classified and unclassified levels and is making a direct contribution to the national security interests of the United States and to the theory, doctrine, and methodology of intelligence.

While graduate students have an absolute choice in their selection of subject for their Master's theses, they have for their consideration a growing menu of recommended topics from the Services, Commands, and agencies of the Intelligence Community. When Master's theses have been written, approved, and the degree awarded, titles and summaries of the works are posted on Intelink for information and accessing by the user community. To cite one recent example, a thesis on Japan's capabilities and limitations as a peacekeeping national brought a letter from the Office of the Secretary of Defense commending the quality of the work and requesting similar research on 31 other nations.

Faculty not only guide such research but also collaborate with students on synergistic research products. In 1997, the College published the volume *Intelligence for Multilateral Decision and Action,* a 600-page work examining intelligence in the era of coalition warfare, United Nations peacekeeping and peacemaking, and international refugee crises. Dr. Perry Pickert, Colonel, U.S. Marine Corps Reserve, was the senior editor, distilling essays from 22 Master's theses written by graduate students from the Army, Navy, Air Force, Marine Corps, Coast Guard, State Department, and Defense Intelligence Agency.[8]

Some of the chapter titles give the flavor of the work: Evolution of the UN Department of Peacekeeping Operations; Intelligence and the International Atomic Energy Agency; Intelligence Support to Refugee Operations: Who's the Expert?; and From Iraq to North Korea: The Role of Counterproliferation Mindset. *Intelligence for Multilateral Decision and Action* is being included in course work at the Joint Military Intelligence College and a growing number of colleges and universities across the country, for example, the Industrial College of the Armed Forces, Harvard, and the Patterson School of Diplomacy and International Commerce, University of Kentucky.

A growing number of works by students and faculty are appearing in the Director of Central Intelligence's quarterly journal *Studies in Intelligence* and the Joint Military Intelligence College Foundation's *Defense Intelligence Journal*. Research also appears in the JMIC Discussion Papers and Occasional Papers series. The next work to be published is a book by faculty member Mark G. Marshall on imagery analysis.[9]

THE BACHELOR'S DEGREE

The noncommissioned officer corps of the U.S. Armed Forces is the envy of militaries around the world. Within the U.S. Intelligence Community, as the size of the Armed Forces continues to reduce in numbers, NCOs increasingly are manning national-level and theater-level positions previously held by commissioned officers. Many of these NCOs, as well as their intelligence-technician civilian counterparts, have acquired considerable college credits during their careers but do not yet have a baccalaureate degree. Another of the Joint Military Intelligence College's strengths and contributions is the educational program it affords talented, highly motivated NCOs, culminating in accredited undergraduate and graduate degrees in their professional field of intelligence.

The BSI is a fourth-year, senior year, degree-completion program. It is a demanding program, beginning with admissions. Applicants must have completed three undergraduate years of college work: a minimum of 80 semester hours of undergraduate studies, with at least 20 credits in upper division classes; with a minimum of 30 of those credits earned in the classrooms of a regionally accredited college, and with the satisfaction of sufficient General Education Requirements in such fields as math and the sciences. A minimum of 2.5 cumulative grade point average is required, and a writing sample is part of the application process. During the four-quarter academic year leading to the degree, the BSI students take 19 courses ranging across the spectrum of intelligence studies, including a culminating senior seminar in intelligence with its requirements for a major research paper.

As word of the BSI program spreads, it is generating considerable interest. The number of applicants is rising. There is an ongoing dialogue between the admissions office and potential applicants, with the number of NCOs and intelligence technicians who are registering in college courses to bring themselves to the BSI's three-year admissions standard on the rise. It is a program of importance to the readers of the *Joint Force Quarterly* for the opportunity it may offer those serving under their leadership.

OUTCOMES ASSESSMENT

The April 1998 Commission on Higher Education Evaluation Team's report, which would lead to the College's reaffirmation of accreditation to include the bachelor's degree, opened with the following words:

> The Joint Military Intelligence College (JMIC) exhibits the principles and practices that the Middle States Association (MSA) considers characteristics of excellence in institutions of higher education. Particularly noteworthy is the

clear sense of mission and purpose which permeates the College and the dedication of its faculty, administration, and staff. It has been recognized that the "Joint Military Intelligence College is a national asset performing a national service." The team concurs.[10]

This positive assessment serves most importantly as a reminder of the excellence in teaching and the excellence in research that must be attained with each incoming class, with the coming of each new academic year. It serves as a reminder that one of the key characteristics of excellence is the manner in which a college conducts institutional research and outcomes assessment. How the graduates view the quality and value of the education they have received and how the sponsoring and receiving Services, departments, and agencies view the performance of the graduates are questions central to the work of the institution.

As members of the graduating Class of 1998 depart—for assignments such as the Second Marine Expeditionary Force, G-2; U.S. Strategic Command; Headquarters Army Central, Saudi Arabia, G-2; Joint Intelligence Center Pacific; and the White House Situation Room—they complete an exit survey seeking their detailed comments on the year just completed at the College. As officers, NCOs and civilian professionals climb in their careers—distinguished alumni such as Rear Admiral Thomas R. Wilson, U.S. Navy, Director of Intelligence, J-2, Joint Staff, nominated in April 1999 as Director, Defense Intelligence Agency with the rank of Vice Admiral, and Lieutenant General Michael V. Hayden, U.S. Air Force, former Deputy Chief of Staff, U.S. Forces Korea, and currently, Director, National Security Agency—the College is reaching out through new lines of communication, the new association of graduates, for example, to stay in touch and to benefit from their counsel. Such steps are in addition to the formal surveys the College conducts with its graduates and with sponsoring receiving organizations and commands. Hopefully, this essay on the growth and direction of the College will serve, in part, to open new lines of communication with the *Joint Force Quarterly* readership, for example, your recommendations on priority issues warranting formal research.

On 25 June 1998, U.S. Representative Ike Skelton (D-MO) was the speaker of honor at the Joint Military Intelligence College's "Leading Intelligence in the 21st Century" Conference. In his address, he said:

> We must be prepared for an array of unwelcome eventualities if we are to protect our security and uphold our values. Thus, we maintain sizable and powerful military forces equipped with sophisticated weapons. Thus, we commission our ablest citizens and educate them at institutions such as this to guard the peace and to be prepared to wage war should war become necessary.[11]

His words serve to shape our future work.

CHAPTER 2
FROM ROE, SIMS, AND THOMAS TO YOU

In his first speech to the students and faculty of the Joint Military Intelligence College after having assumed the presidency in 1994, the author recounts his first contacts with the fledgling Defense Intelligence Agency in 1961, and the growth of the defense intelligence mission over the more than 30 subsequent years. He identifies the College as a center of excellence for the education of intelligence professionals in a joint environment. He relates historical examples of intelligence used by George Washington, for whom Roe worked, and by Assistant Secretary of the Navy Theodore Roosevelt, who received detailed reports from Lieutenant William S. Sims, U.S. Naval Attaché to Paris. He cites important contributions to the literature of intelligence, including an essay by Brigadier General Chuck Thomas on intelligence in DESERT STORM. He urges the students to turn their education at the College to maximum professional advantage.

Students and faculty of the Joint Military Intelligence College, colleagues and friends. Our meeting together this morning marks the real beginning of my new role as President of the Joint Military Intelligence College.

I count it a distinct honor to have been named President of the College. I am dedicated to working with each of you studying here to ensure that your education is better than that of your predecessors and to working with each of you serving in the College on faculty and staff—to ensure that the roots we are striking grow deeper and deeper and the institution we are nurturing continues to climb as the preeminent center for the education of military intelligence professionals.

Thirty-six years ago, as a Navy Ensign, I was in intelligence school, but not here. Neither the Defense Intelligence Agency nor the College had yet been conceived. I was at the Naval Air Station, Alameda, preparing for my first tour at the Fleet Intelligence Center, Pacific (FICPAC). This was at the height of the Cold War, when our work at FICPAC focused on the USSR and the Soviet Navy.

My navy years would include two Antarctic expeditions—not a job, but an adventure. In 1961, I would receive orders back to Washington and to the Office of Naval Intelligence (ONI) at the height of the Berlin Crisis. This was also the year of the creation of DIA. Up on the fifth floor of the Pentagon we were engaged in guerrilla warfare with the new defense agency. ONI had a proud history going back to the 1880s; we did not need this new upstart taking over our spaces.

DIA: 32 YEARS OF EXCELLENCE IN DEFENSE OF THE NATION

As we meet today, DIA is in its 32nd year and, earlier this year, we had the pleasure of marking the 10th anniversary of the Defense Intelligence Analysis Center. Those ceremonies included the presentation by Germany's Ambassador to the United States, Ambassador Immo Stabreit, of segments of the Iron Curtain. The Ambassador stated:

> The gift from the Federal Republic of Germany of a portion of the Iron Curtain honors the triumph of human spirit. It honors the important contributions made by the Defense Intelligence Agency during the Cold War, and underscores the vital mission of the generations who follow, in defense of freedom.[1]

As you study the Intelligence Community structure, you should learn that Soviet Foreign Minister Andrei Gromyko inadvertently had a hand in the creation of DIA. As Lyman Kirkpatrick would report in his book *The Real CIA*, an important factor

> was the denunciation of the United States intelligence activities in Berlin on the part of Soviet Foreign Minister Andrei Gromyko, in Geneva in 1959. The violence and ferocity of Gromyko's attack and his allegations that United States intelligence work created a dangerous situation in Berlin resulted in the President personally taking much more direct interest in United States intelligence activities.[5]

Kirkpatrick would be tasked by President Eisenhower to head a Joint Study Group to examine the future structure of foreign intelligence activities of the United States. The study group had the good sense to draft much of its final report on the liner SS *United States* en route from Southampton to New York. That report, in late 1960, would recommend the creation of the Defense Intelligence Agency, a recommendation that Eisenhower would pass to his successor, President Kennedy. The DIA came into being in the first year of the Kennedy administration.

Now the Cold War is over. The passage of time has been swift, the course of history remarkable, since this center's dedication in 1984. The two streamers on the DIA flag—two Secretary of Defense Meritorious Unit Awards pinned to the flag in October 1986 and July 1991—attest to the dedication and achievements of the intelligence professionals who have served and are serving in the defense of freedom. The 1986 streamer, pinned on by Secretary of Defense Caspar Weinberger, honors the intelligence provided to the Naval and Air Force component commanders during the Libyan counterterrorist operations, the intelligence provided to policymakers and tactical commanders during the TWA Flight 847 hijacking, the *Achille Lauro* hijacking, and the Philippine crisis. The 1991 streamer, pinned on by Chairman of the Joint Chiefs of Staff General Colin Powell, honors the consistently outstanding and dedicated intelligence support to the National Command Authority and field commanders throughout Operations DESERT SHIELD and DESERT STORM.

The substantive contributions of defense intelligence to the commander in the field in that conflict moved with greater reliability and effectiveness as the result of the Joint Intelligence Center (JIC), created by DIA in the Pentagon and the JIC Forward in Riyadh. The Congress recognized these institutional advances with the passage of the National Defense Authorization Act for Fiscal Years 1992 and 1993, directing the Secretary of Defense to consolidate existing single-service current intelligence centers in the greater

Washington area into a single, joint intelligence center for the support of military operations. This is now a National Military Joint Intelligence Center managed by the Defense Intelligence Agency in its capacity as the intelligence staff activity of the Chairman, Joint Chiefs of Staff.

JMIC: A CENTER OF EXCELLENCE

A day or two after I took the office of President, I was discussing the dramatic changes that are unfolding in the world and in the business of military intelligence with Lieutenant General Linc Faurer, President of the Joint Military Intelligence College Foundation. General Faurer asked if I would put down in writing the thoughts I had just expressed about the role of the College. This is what I underlined in a letter dated 28 October:

> The Joint Military Intelligence College is a center of excellence for the education of intelligence professionals who will be called upon to provide foreign military and military-related intelligence as part of military operations in peacetime, crisis and combat; force planning and weapon systems acquisition; and defense policymaking.

> Today's Joint Military Intelligence College graduate serves in an era of widespread geopolitical change. It is an era in which joint doctrine guides the roles and deployment of operating forces; timely two-way flow of accurate intelligence from the national level, through theater Joint Intelligence Centers and Joint Task Forces to deployed tactical-level forces, is central to mission accomplishment; intelligence requirements in joint and combined military operations extend beyond U.S. forces to support for allied, coalition, and United Nations forces.

> More broadly, the Joint Military Intelligence College is educating future leaders of the intelligence and national security community; leaders who are full partners with their policy, planning, and operations counterparts; leaders able to anticipate and tailor the intelligence required at the national, theater, and tactical levels; leaders who constitute a unique asset to the nation.[2]

Through our array of academic programs at the College, we have in place the courses and the teaching that should help to launch you successfully into the professional world and the assignments that I have just outlined. I urge you to go beyond the courses, the core reading, and to steep yourselves in the literature of the world of intelligence, to take advantage of the presence of guest speakers and the perspectives they bring to the world of national security.

Those of you studying in the College this year, writing theses as part of the Master of Science of Strategic Intelligence (MSSI) program, will be making fresh contributions to the world of intelligence at the same time that you draw from the current body of knowledge. Make the most of this; make your thesis the first of your continuing contributions to the world of intelligence.

A. Denis Clift

We have in the College the fledgling *Defense Intelligence Journal*. Since taking this new office, I have already met with Bill Manthorpe, the journal's editor. We are looking at ways to improve the journal to make it most valuable to you, most valuable to the work of the College. Your voices, your writings should play a part in this.

FROM ROE . . .

Recently I came across the following passage in a work by Corey Ford entitled *A Peculiar Service:*

> Roe had arranged to pasture his cattle in Abraham Woodhull's rear meadow which sloped down to Conscience Bay. On his return to the tavern that evening, he would pull out the blank sheet from the ream, conceal it in his shirt, and stroll over to the Woodhull farm to attend his cows. Since it might have attracted attention if they were seen to meet, a wooden box was buried in a corner of the meadow. Roe would drop the paper in this box, and shortly afterward Woodhull would go to the pasture and retrieve it.[3]

As many of you will have realized, Ford was describing the dead drop, the invisible ink, the details of a portion of the spy network George Washington had in place against the British during the Revolutionary War. As Allen Dulles would explain the network:

> From his hometown of Setauket on the north shore of Long Island, Tallmadge recruited a number of acquaintances for his network. Abraham Woodhull [cover name for] (Samuel Culper Senior), using the top floor of his brother-in-law's boardinghouse in New York as a hideaway, prepared the messages intended for Washington which were picked up and carried on horseback by a farmer from Setauket, Austin Rose, who, in turn, handed them over to a boat-man, Caleb Brewster, who took them across Long Island Sound at night and delivered them to Tallmadge [cover name for] (John Bolton), who then relayed them to George Washington.[4]

. . . SIMS . . .

Move forward from the Revolutionary War to the turn of this century, to the work being done by U.S. attachés about 100 years ago.

Long before attaining the rank of Admiral in his distinguished career, Lieutenant William S. Sims was appointed in 1897 as U.S. Naval Attaché in Paris. He would visit Russia and make an extended tour of the principal naval bases of Europe. His reports would be requested by the Assistant Secretary of the Navy, Theodore Roosevelt. Sims' reports focused on the methods used by the countries he visited in their warship construction and gunnery practice. His extended observations convinced him that American gunnery was far less effective than that of the foreign fleets, and his detailed reports so advised Washington.

I have also learned from our colleagues in the Office of Naval Intelligence that Naval Attaché Sims had a sense of humor. He reported on the French method of training carrier pigeons, recommending that the U.S. Navy should cross-breed pigeons with parrots—so that the birds could vocalize their messages. This drew a reproof from the Navy Department.

... AND THOMAS ...

Closer to your future responsibilities as you study in this College is Brigadier General Chuck Thomas's essay, "Inside a J-2 Joint Intelligence Center: Supporting DESERT STORM," in the Winter 1991 *Studies in Intelligence.* Your goal as your careers progress should be to contribute to your profession at the same time that you are serving in your profession.

... TO YOU: OPPORTUNITIES TO CONTRIBUTE

In the late 1970s, when I was serving as Vice President Walter Mondale's Assistant for National Security Affairs, I was one of a handful of Americans privileged to read the President's Daily Brief, the most important daily intelligence summary in the world, prepared by the Director of Central Intelligence (DCI) for the President. The more I read it, the more I thought it was inadequate, terrible on occasion. I sent a polite, classified blast off to the seventh floor of CIA headquarters, proposing changes in content, changes in format, ways to better tailor such information for the President of the United States. CIA listened; we met. In March 1980, the DCI would write the Vice President thanking me for the role I had played in the new and revised PDB. I survived that assault on CIA. Share your good ideas with the rest of us in the College and the Community.

Earlier in my career, in 1974, President Gerald Ford had appointed me to head the National Security Council's senior staff for the Soviet Union and Eastern and Western Europe. I had the good sense to interview and bring aboard as one of my assistants a talented young CIA analyst by the name of Robert M. Gates. Bob and I would have numerous discussions about the interface between policy and intelligence, the problems and the avenues open to the solution of those problems. As his career continued to shoot skyward, Bob Gates would publish some excellent pieces on policy and intelligence in CIA's classified quarterly *Studies in Intelligence.* I cite, for example, "An Opportunity Unfulfilled: The Use and Perceptions of Intelligence Analysis at the White House," in the Winter 1980 issue.

As President of the College, I have the privilege to continue to serve as a U.S. Commissioner on the U.S.-Russian Joint Commission on Prisoners of War/Missing in Action, a commission created by the Presidents of the United States and Russia in 1992 with the humanitarian goal of accounting for those still unaccounted for—both U.S. and Russian—from World War II, the Cold War, Korea, and Vietnam. This work has taken me on a remarkable odyssey across the former USSR—from the Kremlin, to Kazakhstan, to a 1958 crash site on a mountain slope in Armenia, to the cruiser Petropavlovsk in Vladivostok, to Lafortova Prison, where I kept one eye on the exits.

A. Denis Clift

In September 1992, my fellow commissioners and I were visiting the regional headquarters of the MVD in Khabarovsk. Our meeting was to be on the ninth floor. The elevator stopped somewhere between the 7th and 8th floors. The lights went out. I thought, "Hmmm . . . maybe they've decided this is as far as it goes for the Chief of Staff of DIA." Our Russian escort started yelling from inside the elevator. Then, the sound of footsteps, voices, and a woman calling out, "How many of you are there?" There was an in-the-dark head count.

- "Eight!"
- "That's too many," the voice called back.
- "We know," we yelled in English and Russian. "Get us out of here."

And I will end on that intelligence lesson. Do not tell people what they already know. Learn how to operate your intelligence elevator, how to deliver accurate, reliable intelligence when and where needed, and how best to help guide your consumer to the desired goal.

While you are learning, while you are contributing, I also urge you to take professional pleasure and satisfaction from your service to your nation. Hubert Humphrey was fond of pointing out that our founding fathers had spoken of life, liberty, and the pursuit of happiness. Enjoy yourself in this important business.

CHAPTER 3
THE SAN CRISTOBAL TRAPEZOID

Following the author's move from The White House staff to defense intelligence in 1981, he was named DIA's Assistant Deputy Director for External Affairs, serving with then-Deputy Director John T. Hughes. Following Hughes' retirement in 1984, Clift replaced him as Deputy Director. He urged Hughes to document his extraordinary role in the Cuban Missile Crisis and volunteered to do both the additional research required and the writing. The result is "The San Cristobal Trapezoid," co-authored with Hughes and published in the first unclassified edition of Studies in Intelligence *shortly after Hughes death in 1992. The work would receive the Director of Central Intelligence's Sherman Kent Award for that year's best contribution to the literature of intelligence. Written in the first-person of Hughes, it recounts the role of intelligence prior to, during, and after the crisis. Reading like a novel, it is an enormously instructive insight into the inner workings of the Intelligence Community during national crisis, the intelligence-policy interface, and the importance of both strategic warning—which had failed—and all-source tactical intelligence. The essay climaxes with Hughes' nationally televised briefing on 6 February 1963.*

Aerial photos give crisp hard information, like the dawn after long darkness.

— Arthur Lundahl, Director of the
National Photographic Interpretation Center

A courier stepped forward to meet me as I reached the Pentagon's River Entrance. I remember the moment: 7:30 a.m., 8 February 1963, a wintry morning brightness just emerging. "Mr. John Hughes?" "Yes," I said. "I've been asked to deliver this to you." He handed me a manila envelope, then departed. The return address, in block letters, read "The White House."

My office was nearby inside the Pentagon in the Joint Staff spaces next to the National Military Command Center, almost directly beneath the office of the Secretary of Defense. I opened the letter. It was from the President.

Dear Mr. Hughes:

I thought you did an excellent job on television in explaining our surveillance in Cuba. I understand it was done on short notice. I want you to know how much I appreciate your efforts. With best wishes.

Sincerely,

John Kennedy

Cuba. For the past seven months, the U.S. Intelligence Community had riveted its attention on that island nation. Its topography, road network, cities, military garrisons,

A. Denis Clift

storage depots, deployed ground-force units, airports and airbases, seaports, merchant shipping, and naval units had been photographed, categorized, and studied. U.S. reconnaissance also zeroed in on Soviet merchant ships, fighter aircraft, surface-to-air-missile (SAM) units, missile patrol boats, and rocket forces.

As photointerpreters, my colleagues and I could recall the key features of the intermediate-range and medium-range ballistic missile (IRBM and MRBM) sites the Soviets had been rushing to complete in October 1962: the missile-servicing buildings, the nuclear warhead storage bunkers, the oxidizer vehicles, propellant vehicles, missile shelter tents, and the missiles. San Julian, Holgui, Neuvitas, Mariel, Sagua La Grande, Remedios, and San Cristobal were names that took on a special meaning after the discovery of the missiles and bombers, the peaking of the crisis, Soviet withdrawal, and my briefing to the nation on network TV on 6 February 1963, two days before the President's letter arrived.

As Special Assistant to Lieutenant General Joseph F. Carroll, Director of the Defense Intelligence Agency (DIA), I was responsible for providing reconnaissance intelligence support during the crisis to Secretary of Defense Robert McNamara, Deputy Secretary Roswell Gilpatric, Chairman of the Joint Chiefs of Staff (JCS) General Maxwell Taylor, and the Joint Chiefs. There had been intensive coordination with Arthur Lundahl, Director of the National Photographic Interpretation Center (NPIC). In his capacity, he was responsible for providing critical national intelligence support to the President, Director of Central Intelligence (DCI) John McCone, and the Executive Committee of the National Security Council.

Building on the CIA's initial U-2 reconnaissance flights in the summer and early autumn of 1962, the Department of Defense would eventually fly more than 400 military reconnaissance missions over Cuba during the crisis. Targeting information for each photo mission had to be developed for the JCS Joint Reconnaissance Center (JRC) to coordinate the operations and allow for policy review by the Secretary, the Deputy Secretary, and the White House, and then be delivered to the reconnaissance units that would fly the missions. The highest priority was to move that film from the returning aircraft through the photo labs, through analysis, to the policy level of government—a 24-hour-a-day operation, with intense time pressures and a crucial need for accuracy.

In his introduction to Robert F. Kennedy's memoir of the Cuban missile crisis, *Thirteen Days*, McNamara wrote:

> The performance of the U.S. Government during that critical period was more effective than at any other time during my seven years' service as Secretary of Defense. The agencies of government—the State Department, the civilian and military leaders of the Defense Department, the CIA, the White House Staff, and the UN Mission—worked together smoothly and harmoniously.[1]

The entire intelligence-operations team for U.S. reconnaissance against Cuba demonstrated a sense of urgency and national mission that epitomized this effort.

TACTICAL DATA

Intelligence did not perform flawlessly during the crisis. The Intelligence Community had not provided clear warning of the Soviet Union's intention to place offensive nuclear weapons in Cuba. Indeed, the debate over Khrushchev's motives and the USSR's strategic intentions continues. The community did, however, provide tactical intelligence on the USSR's rapid deployment of missile and bomber forces in Cuba. As the crisis mounted, tactical warning and targeting data were developed and steadily updated in support of strike options being developed by the JCS and the NSC Executive Committee. Targets included the MRBM and IRBM missile installations, the IL-28/BEAGLE bombers, the 24 SA-2 SAM sites, the MiG-21 fighters, and other ground, air, and naval targets.

The intelligence flowing from the reconnaissance missions provided the irrefutable evidence the U.S. required to document to the world the basis for its response, as well as the targeting data that would have been needed if the crisis touched off an armed conflict. It tracked the surge of Soviet military personnel to some 22,000 by the end of October 1962, and then the ebb in those numbers to some 17,000 as the troops manning the offensive weapons departed.

STRATEGIC WARNING

Strategic warning is the most important component of effective intelligence. Perhaps the greatest barrier to developing effective strategic indications and warning for decisionmaking is the tendency of the human mind to assume that the status quo will continue. The Cuban missile crisis and many other conflicts of the postwar era, including the Arab-Israeli Yom Kippur war and the Falklands conflict, confirm that nations generally do not credit their potential opponents with the will to take unexpected acts. We did not believe the Soviets would do so in 1962.

I was part of a team assisting General Carroll in his responsibilities as a member of the U.S. Intelligence Board (USIB), the top policy forum of the Intelligence Community, whose membership included the DCI and the Deputy Director of Central Intelligence, the Director of DIA, the Department of State's Director of Intelligence and Research, the Director of Naval Intelligence, the Army and Air Force Assistant Chiefs of Staff for Intelligence, the Director of the National Security Agency, the Assistant General Manager for Administration of the Atomic Energy Commission, and the Assistant to the Director of the FBI. Each person brought the intelligence strengths of his respective organization to the table. It was the Board's primary duty to produce the formal National Intelligence Estimates (NIEs) and Special National Intelligence Estimates (SNIEs) on key international issues and events for consideration by the NSC. With the memory of the Bay of Pigs disaster still fresh, and with the politically charged U.S. concern over Fidel Castro's consolidation of communist power in Cuba and the growing Soviet military presence there, the USIB focused on Cuba in its estimates. At the same time, the Intelligence Community tracked and recorded the entry of Soviet weapons by type and capability.

A. Denis Clift

TWO NIES

NIE 85-2-62, *The Situation and Prospects in Cuba*, was issued by the Board on 1 August 1962. It underlined Castro's political primacy, the loyalty of the Cuban armed forces to Castro and his brother Raul, the provision of Soviet Bloc military equipment and training to Cuban forces, and the deepening commitment of the Soviet Union to preserve and strengthen the Castro regime.[2]

As of 1 July 1962, the monitoring of Soviet military deliveries indicated that there were 160 tanks, 770 field artillery and antitank guns, 560 antiaircraft guns, 35 jet fighters, 24 helicopters, and 3,800 military vehicles of various types in Cuba.[3] On 27 July, Castro announced that Cuba would soon have new defenses against the United States. On 29 August, as the weaponry continued to roll off Soviet ships in Cuban ports, a CIA U-2 photographed the first SA-2 SAMs. Human intelligence sources in Cuba were reporting the sighting of rockets on the island. We concluded that the rockets were not MRBMs/IRBMs.

On 19 September 1962, in NIE 85-3-62, *The Military Buildup in Cuba*, the Intelligence Community reiterated its belief that the USSR would not introduce offensive strategic weapons into Cuba. Its key conclusion stated:

> The USSR could derive considerable military advantage from the establish-ment of Soviet MRBMs and IRBMs in Cuba, or from the establishment of a submarine base there. As between these two, the establishment of a submarine base would be the more likely. Either development, however, would be incom-patible with Soviet practice to date and with Soviet policy as we presently esti-mate it. It would indicate a far greater willingness to increase the level of risk in U.S.-Soviet relations than the USSR has displayed thus far, and conse-quently to other areas and other problems in East-West relations.[4]

DCI McCone personally was not persuaded that the Soviet buildup was essentially defensive. Fate, however, would have him in Europe on an extended honeymoon when the crisis began. His messages to the President from Europe in mid-September advising that the evidence pointed to Soviet preparations for introducing offensive weapons into Cuba could not compete with the contrary judgment of the formal NIEs that the missiles would be for defensive purposes.

Following the discovery of the defensive SAMs in late August, the President warned Khrushchev that the U.S. would not permit the introduction of offensive weapons. The Soviet leader's responses through several channels from Moscow to Washington repeated the official Soviet position that only defensive weapons were being introduced into Cuba. In his news conference on 13 September 1962, the President delivered a clear statement of the U.S. position on Cuba and on the possibility of Soviet offensive weapons being deployed there.

SOVIET BUILDUP

The Intelligence Community continued to monitor the rapid buildup and assess its implications. From July to 1 November 1962, the number of tanks would grow from 160 to 345; the field artillery and antitank guns from 770 to 1,320; the antiaircraft guns from 560 to 710; the jet fighters from 35 to 101; the helicopters from 24 to 70 or more; the military vehicles from 3,800 to between 7,500 and 10,000. And through late August, September, and early October we continued to identify new categories of weaponry: the construction of 24 SAM sites with 500 missiles by 1 November; the introduction of some 24 to 32 Free Rocket Over Ground (FROG) rockets; the installation of four cruise missile sites and 160 air defense radars; and the arrival of 12 Soviet KOMAR-class cruise-missile patrol boats at Cuban ports.[5]

U-2 MISSIONS

From 1956 on, I had participated in the Intelligence Community's tasking of the U-2 by contributing the Army's and DIA's intelligence collection requirements to the flight planners of the operational missions. I had helped analyze the photographic intelligence from the U-2 flights over the Soviet Union from 1956 to 1960. Its advanced photographic gear complemented the extraordinary capabilities of the U-2 as an aircraft. The U-2 carried the HR-73B camera system, a big, high-technology camera with a 36-inch focal-length lens able to capture considerable detail from altitudes of 14 miles. The camera load was two 6,500-foot rolls of 9-1/2-inch film. Each mission could produce more than 4,000 frames of film, with vertical, single-frame ground coverage of 5.7 x 5.7 nautical miles.

Following the flight of 29 August 1962, CIA launched additional U-2 missions on 5, 17, 26, and 29 September and on 5 and 7 October. Working through an interagency committee, collection requirements were formulated that would shape the flight profile of each mission. The work of reading the film from each mission took place in NPIC in an atmosphere of intense analytical debate throughout September and early October. These U-2 missions established an excellent baseline for judging the nature and pace of the Soviet military buildup.

The success of our efforts owed much to the brilliant leadership of Art Lundahl, who was internationally recognized for his contributions to photographic interpretation and photogrammetric engineering. His dedication to improving the nation's reconnaissance capabilities and his professional standards shaped the work of all who were a part of his crisis team.

SA-2 CONTROVERSY

One issue for the photointerpreters was the intended role of the Soviet SA-2 GUIDELINE SAM, which had been operational with Soviet air defense forces since the late 1950s. The 30-foot-long SA-2 had a solid-propellant booster and a kerosene-based second-stage sustainer, and it could sprint to Mach 3 carrying a 280-pound high-explosive warhead with a proximity fuse to a range of 30 miles. Radio guidance from ground-based target acquisition radar fed steering commands to the missile's control fins. We assessed it as reliable and accurate.

The U-2 missions through 5 September revealed a disproportionate buildup of SA-2 launch sites in western Cuba. One school of thought contended that this deployment pattern was not particularly worrisome, given that Havana and the larger part of the Cuban population were in that region. Further, most of the sites were along Cuba's periphery, where one might expect such missiles arrayed in a national air-defense network.

Another line of analysis held that the disproportionate concentration of SA-2s in the west meant that the Soviets and the Cubans had important military equipment there requiring greater protection. The photointerpreters pushed on with their analysis, somewhat hampered by a policy-level decision following the 5 October mission to avoid the western sector on future U-2 missions because of administration concerns that an SA-2 might shoot down a U-2, thereby escalating the crisis.

Analysis was not based exclusively on photo interpretation. One of my DIA colleagues, Colonel John Wright, directed the work of a center in DIA that collated intelligence from all sources. The center evaluated the photography together with other sources, including reports from refugees and agents in Cuba. These reports continued to warn of large rockets, possibly missiles, arriving in Cuba and of suspicious military activity in western Cuba.

FOCUS ON SAN CRISTOBAL

Colonel Wright and his staff became increasingly interested in the SA-2 sites near San Cristobal, in the western part of the island. Most important, the U-2 photography indicated that these sites formed the outline of a trapezoid. This suggested that the sites were forming a "point defense" to protect some extremely important weapons emplacements or installations. This deployment pattern was similar to those identified near ballistic-missile launch sites in the Soviet homeland. The stationing of these SA-2s, together with human-source reporting of the missiles in western Cuba, strongly suggested that there were offensive Soviet ballistic missiles to be found within the San Cristobal trapezoid.

SHIFT IN RESPONSIBILITY

The President's advisers largely agreed that the new evidence warranted resuming U-2 missions over western Cuba. New requirements were issued for photographic reconnaissance of the San Cristobal area. Because of continuing concern over the international repercussions should one of the U-2s be shot down, it was decided that future U-2 missions should be flown by the Air Force. If any questions about the flights should arise, they would be acknowledged as military reconnaissance missions.

The 4080th Strategic Wing of the Strategic Air Command, based at Laughlin Air Force Base in Del Rio, Texas, was given the assignment. The next flight was set for 14 October, with major Rudolph Anderson, USAF, as the pilot. The mission went flawlessly, and copies of the photography were sent by courier to NPIC, Navy analysts, the Strategic Air Command (SAC), and other key commands.

EVIDENCE OF MRBMS

Photointerpreters at NPIC called me at the Pentagon on 15 October. MRBMs had been found and confirmed. I called General Carroll to tell him what I had just heard and that I was on my way to NPIC. He asked me to give him another call as soon as I had personally reviewed the evidence.

After a quick look at three or four of the frames, I called General Carroll back and told him that the film showed ballistic-missile carriers, associated equipment, and support trucks. The U-2 camera had caught an MRBM convoy just as it was preparing to pull into the cover of a wooded area.

That evening General Carroll, my colleague John McLauchlin, and I reported directly to Deputy Secretary Gilpatric. He asked me the same question that the President would ask Art Lundahl the following morning. It was the same question that would be asked by each of the select senior U.S. officials being informed of the discovery as they looked at the tiny objects and patterns on our photographs of the Cuban countryside: "Are you sure that these are Soviet MRBMs?" I answered, "I am convinced they are." The next morning, Lundahl told the President he was "as sure of this as a photointerpreter can be sure of anything."

STRATEGIC INTELLIGENCE

The urgent work of the Executive Committee would begin on the morning of 16 October. While the world remained ignorant of the mounting crisis, those supporting the President and the Executive Committee were aware of the responsibility and trust that had been given us. The President needed absolute confirmation of the presence and numbers of MRBMs and any other offensive weapons that the Soviets had in place in Cuba. He needed time to marshal U.S. ground, sea, and air forces and to consider the options for their use should military action be required. He also needed time to decide how best to confront Khrushchev with the evidence, and he had to plan how to implement the U.S. response. Secrecy was essential. More documentary evidence was required.

U-2s from SAC were moved to Florida. Between 15 and 22 October, they flew 20 missions over Cuba to search the entire island. These reconnaissance flights helped us to understand what the Soviets were up to and what stage of weapons deployment they had reached. This information enabled the Intelligence Community to give the President and his advisers its best judgment as to whether the missiles were operational and, if not, when they would most likely become operational.

A. Denis Clift

As a result of highly classified and urgent work, the community would determine that the first of the MRBMs would become operational on 28 October. While U.S. intelligence had not provided strategic warning that the Soviets would introduce such weapons, intelligence had discovered the weapons before they became operational, giving the President an advantage in planning his response.

Analysis of U-2 photography went on around the clock, with few, even in the Intelligence Community, given access to the intelligence. As new photography became available, General Carroll and I would brief the Secretary and then take the same findings to the Chairman and the Joint Chiefs to prepare the Defense representatives for the continuing deliberations of the Executive Committee. Our photointerpreters pored over earlier U-2 photography of the geographic locations where we were now discovering the offensive weapons. These comparisons enabled us to determine when the Soviets had begun construction, a process which confirmed the clandestine and time-urgent design of the Soviet operation.

SEABORNE SHIPMENTS

With the deployment of the missiles in Cuba now established, we began to reexamine earlier photointelligence to determine how they had arrived. From September to mid-October, the navy had photographed several Soviet merchant ships en route to Cuba, including the *Poltava* and the *Omsk*, riding high in the water and with unusually long cargo hatches. It was apparent that these merchant vessels must have been transporting a high-volume cargo that was not particularly heavy. We then realized that they had, in fact, been delivering missiles that were to be offloaded at night.

SS-4s AND SS-5s

The photography of the 17 October U-2 mission revealed a major new development: the construction of a fixed IRBM site at Guanajay, just west of Havana. While the mobile MRBM posed a serious threat, its range was limited to targets in the southern United States.

We had studied the SS-4 MRBM since before its first appearance on parade in Moscow the year before. It had an overall length of just over 73 feet with warhead attached. It had a support crew of 24 men, and it was serviced by a dozen vehicles. The SS-4 had sufficient fuel and thrust to deliver a 1-megaton nuclear warhead on short notice up to 1,000 miles, a range that threatened the southeastern U.S. in an arc extending from Savannah, Georgia, to New Orleans, Louisiana.

The SS-5 IRBM, by contrast, had a range of over 2,200 miles, and it could hit any target in the continental U.S. except Seattle, Spokane, and other cities in Washington state. It was clear that we were not facing a temporary expeditionary force in Cuba. The SS-5 required complex permanent launch sites, with troop quarters, missile shelters, warhead bunkers, and a large logistic train.

We had monitored the development and testing of the SS-5 SKEAN since the late 1950s. Operational in 1961, the SS-5 was the newest of the Soviet Union's IRBMs and the product of its intensive strategic rocket program. The SS-5's warhead yield also was estimated at 1 megaton, but it had better inertial guidance than the SS-4.

FOUR KEY SITES

Continuing intelligence analysis provided irrefutable evidence that the Soviets were pushing ahead simultaneously with the installation of ballistic missiles at four separate locations: MRBMs at San Cristobal and Sagua La Grande, and IRBMs at Guanajay and Remedios. Soviet construction was progressing at a breakneck pace; photointelligence from successive U-2 missions indicated that sites were rapidly approaching operational status. Their construction workers were experiencing some difficulties as was evident from earth scarring and deep tire ruts produced by heavy transporters in the soft soil of the semitropical countryside.

The Soviets and Cubans were working almost continuously to set up 24 MRBM launchers plus 18 reserves for a total of 42 SS-4 MRBM nuclear missiles, as well as three fixed IRBM launch sites, each with four launchers. If these sites were completed, their missiles would significantly affect the strategic balance.

CRATOLOGY

The U-2 mission of 15 October discovered a third dimension to the impending nuclear threat. In late September, U.S. maritime surveillance had spotted a merchant ship bound for Cuba carrying a number of large crates on its deck. To deduce their content, U.S. photointerpreters had to resort to the fledgling "science" of cratology.

Unique dimensions, shapes, volumes, and other features of the apparently innocuous-looking crates allowed analysts to determine with some precision by mid-October that the crates contained disassembled IL-28/BEAGLE bomber aircraft. The U-2 photographed 21 of these crates, one with the top open and the BEAGLE fuselage exposed, at San Julian Airfield on 15 October. This was our first sighting of part of the total force of 42 bombers the Soviet Union was delivering to the San Julian and Holuin Airfields.

MEETING WITH GROMYKO

At the White House, the Executive Committee weighed the new evidence in its deliberations on the best course of action to recommend to the President. On 18 October, the President proceeded with an office call by Soviet Foreign Minister Gromyko, an appointment that had been made many weeks before. Without tipping his hand about the U.S. discovery of the Soviet MRBMs, IRBMs, and bombers in Cuba, President Kennedy underscored to Gromyko the unacceptability of Soviet offensive nuclear weapons on the island. Gromyko responded with assurances that the weapons being introduced were strictly defensive.

SNIE's JUDGMENTS

The Executive Committee soon narrowed the options to airstrikes against the missile sites and bomber bases versus a naval blockade of the island. On 20 October, the Intelligence Community published its views on the implications of the committee's options in SNIE-11-19-62, *Major Consequences of Certain U.S. Courses of Action on Cuba.*

SNIE 11-19-62 was cautious about the likely results of either a selective or a total blockade of Cuba. It argued that nuclear warheads could be delivered covertly aboard aircraft or submarines evading the blockade, that the Soviet missiles already in Cuba would still be poised to strike, that it would not weaken Castro's regime, and that either a selective or total blockade would give the Soviet Union time to mobilize world pressure against the United States. The SNIE judged that neither type of blockade would necessarily escalate to war, either in Cuba or elsewhere, and that the Soviets would not be driven to immediate military retaliation.

The estimate also judged that, whatever the nature of any U.S. military action against Cuba, it would not be likely to provoke Khrushchev and his colleagues into launching all-out nuclear war. The authors wrote:

> We believe that there would probably be a difference between Soviet reaction to all-out invasion and Soviet reaction to more limited U.S. use of force against selective objectives in Cuba. We believe that the Soviets would be somewhat less likely to retaliate with military force in areas outside of Cuba in response to speedy, effective invasion than in response to more limited forms of military action against Cuba. We recognize that such an estimate cannot be made with very great assurance and do not rule out the possibility of Soviet retaliation outside of Cuba in case of invasion. But we believe that a rapid occupation of Cuba would be more likely to make the Soviets pause in opening new theaters of conflict than limited action or action which drags out.[6]

THE PRESIDENT'S DECISION

Proponents of the alternate options of U.S. response continued to argue with the Executive Committee until the President had chosen a course which he had judged would not push Khrushchev beyond the brink. It would demonstrate U.S. resolve, and it would provide the President and his advisers the time and the leverage they required in their communications with Khrushchev to demand that the USSR withdraw its missiles and bombers from Cuba.

President Kennedy's report to the American people on the Soviet missile and bomber buildup in Cuba was delivered from the White House Oval Office at 7:00 p.m., 22 October, one week after the discovery of the MRBMs at San Cristobal. I was with Navy photointerpreters in Suitland, Maryland. We listened to the President's somber, electrifying words. As stated in the second of his announced actions, the President had ordered low-level surveillance photo missions by Navy and Air Force tactical reconnaissance squadrons to begin the following morning.

Given the array of MiG-21 fighters, antiaircraft guns, and SAM defenses that would confront our reconnaissance planes, tactical intelligence support was vital to their success. In turn, their success would be essential to the President's strategy. As we worked to prepare for the following day's briefing, there was a profound sense of urgency.

LOW-LEVEL MISSIONS

Shortly after dawn on 23 October, Navy pilots of Light Photographic Squadron 62 and Air Force pilots of the 363rd Tactical Reconnaissance Wing took off on the first low-level photo missions over Cuba. Later that day, the President issued Proclamation 3504: *Interdiction of the Delivery of Offensive Weapons to Cuba.* It stated that as of 2:00 p.m., 24 October, forces under his command had instructions to intercept any vessel or craft proceeding toward Cuba and to interdict the delivery of surface-to-surface missiles, bombers, bombs, air-to-surface rockets and guided missiles, warheads, mechanical and electrical equipment for such weapons, and any other materials subsequently designated by the Secretary of Defense.

Our aerial reconnaissance of Cuba took a quantum leap both in volume and in precision of detail with the low-level missions. The Navy and Marine Corps pilots assigned to Light Photographic Squadron 62 (VP-62) were flying the single-engine reconnaissance RF-8A version of the F-8 Crusader fighter. It carried five cameras. The Air Force pilots of the 363rd Tactical Reconnaissance Wing were flying the RF-101 reconnaissance version of the F-101 Voodoo fighter.

The RF-101's reconnaissance eyes were the KA-53 aerial reconnaissance cameras with black-and-white and color emulsion 5-inch aerial roll film loaded in 250-foot film cassettes, cameras with shutter speeds up to 1/3,000th of a second. The combination of planes and cameras in these Navy and Air Force tactical units was as remarkable in its sophistication as was the technology aboard the U-2s.

The RF-8As and RF-101s covered their targets 500 feet off the ground at speeds of 600 mph. With this speed and altitude, the Soviets and Cubans had no warning, only the sonic roar as the reconnaissance planes flew by on flight profiles that brought them in low over the Gulf of Mexico with a pop-up over the target. At the successful conclusion of each mission, the VP-62 pilots would paint another dead chicken on the fuselages of their Crusaders to symbolize Castro's chickens coming home to roost.[7]

The reconnaissance photography these pilots were delivering was spectacular. It was clear, large-scale documentation. It permitted us to gain full understanding of the MRBMs that would be operational by the 28th and to track the continuing intensive construction of

A. Denis Clift

the IRBM sites. The photography provided our combat-mission planners with the precise detail they required in the event the President were to order a strike against the island.

As soon as each low-level mission delivered its film to the squadron and wing photo labs, it was developed and flown to Washington and to other photographic analysis centers.

THE JRC

The nerve center for the U.S. reconnaissance effort was the Joint Reconnaissance Center (JRC) in the Pentagon, under the direction of then-Colonel Ralph D. Steakley, USAF. The JRC had been created to provide the JCS, the Office of the Secretary of Defense, the Department of State, and the White House with a focal point for policy decisions on the U.S. reconnaissance missions being undertaken worldwide long before the Cuban missile crisis. The Intelligence Community, the Unified and Specified Commands, and others would identify reconnaissance requirements. The JRC would clear mission plans through the appropriate policy level of the government, and, with approval received, authorize the reconnaissance missions.

We fed our reconnaissance targeting requirements to Steakley. He had assigned liaison officers from the Center to the Tactical Air Command and SAC. The JRC and the operational planners of the Air Force and Navy drew up detailed flight plans to fulfill the latest intelligence requirements. The work proceeded around the clock. Steakley had a cot in his office, where he lived throughout the crisis. He was under relentless operational pressure. He had received a telephone call from President Kennedy's secretary with the message, "The President has directed that you not be away from your phone for more than three rings." Secretary McNamara had made it clear that he personally wanted to be certain that each mission flown was in accordance with a determined plan and a predetermined approval cycle. Steakley was regularly summoned to the White House to brief the President on the planned flights.

The President and the Executive Committee were seeing explicit details of the Soviet nuclear offensive buildup. They were following the advances of the MRBMs and IRBMs toward operational status with each day's low-level reconnaissance take. The missions, as the President knew, were dangerous and might escalate the crisis beyond the control of either side.

A BAD DAY

On 27 October, an Air Force RB-47 flying maritime surveillance missions against Soviet shipping crashed on takeoff from Bermuda with the loss of all four crew members. That same day a Soviet SA-2 GUIDELINE missile brought down a U-2 over Cuba flown by Major Rudolf Anderson, the pilot of the U-2 flight on 14 October that had filmed the discovery of the Soviet MRBMs. Anderson was killed, and the pressure to retaliate intensified.

AN EFFECTIVE CYCLE

We felt this pressure in our support to Secretary McNamara and the JCS. The work cycle began with the delivery of hundreds of feet of new photography in Washington, usually each evening, which had to be analyzed around the clock. I would arrive at either the Pentagon or NPIC early each morning to review the findings and to prepare to brief McNamara and the JCS, usually before the start of the morning Executive Committee sessions at the White House. Current intelligence for targeting of SAM sites was fed to the military planners for inclusion in the target folders. There was a growing consensus that the U.S. would have to act.

The gravity of the situation was confirmed by the results of the low-level reconnaissance missions. The JRC worked with Air Force and Navy planners in drawing up the final flight plans. The pilots agreed that flight tracks for each mission were flyable, and that they were the best tracks to achieve coverage of the requested targets. This success was matched by the cycle we had developed of film processing, readout, and feedback to both the national level and the operators. The results of each day's reconnaissance were available to feed into the following day's planning and execution.

WHITE HOUSE STATEMENT

On 26 October, the President approved the release of a statement updating the American people on the status of the Soviet missile sites. It reported that development of the IRBM sites was continuing, with bulldozers and cranes observed clearing new areas within the sites. It noted that MRBMs had been observed, with cabling running from missile-ready tents to nearby power generators. And it concluded that the Soviets were trying to camouflage their efforts at the sites.

The USSR's measured response to the quarantine was of critical importance to the President's restrained approach to the crisis. No ships with prohibited or even questionable cargoes had tried to run the blockade. The shootdown of Major Anderson had brought the U.S. to the brink of a retaliatory strike against military targets in Cuba, but the President remained determined to force Soviet compliance with U.S. demands on terms short of war. Intelligence had given him the information he needed to catch Khrushchev red-handed. There could be no question of the validity of the U.S. charges. But the President knew he was running out of time: The MRBMs would become operational on 28 October.

MESSAGES FROM KHRUSHCHEV

On 26 October, Khrushchev sent President Kennedy first one message, then another. The first couched the Soviet Union's conditions for the withdrawal of its missiles and bombers from Cuba in terms of a requirement for an end to the U.S. blockade and for a promise from the U.S. that it would not invade Cuba. The second Khrushchev letter added another, far more difficult demand:

You are worried over Cuba. You say that it worries you because it lies at a distance of 90 miles across the sea from the shores of the United States. However, Turkey lies next to us. Our sentinels are pacing up and down watching each other. Do you believe that you have the right to demand security for your country and the removal of such weapons that you qualify as offensive, while not recognizing this right for us?

This is why I make this proposal: We agree to remove those weapons from Cuba which you regard as offensive weapons. We agree to do this and to state this commitment in the United Nations. Our representatives will make a statement to the effect that the United States, on its part, bearing in mind the anxiety and concern of the Soviet state, will evacuate its analogous weapons from Turkey. Let us reach an understanding on what time you and we need to put this into effect.[8]

THE U.S. REPLIES

While the U.S. missiles would eventually be withdrawn from Turkey, at the peak of the Cuban missile crisis the President rejected including them or any mention of them in the terms that would be set for the withdrawal of the Soviet missiles from Cuba. In the midst of the Executive Committee meeting on 27 October on the next step to be taken by the U.S., Attorney General Robert Kennedy proposed that the U.S. reply to Khrushchev's first letter and not to the second. He actually drafted the reply, stating the terms we were willing to accept, plucking them from several often-disparate Soviet messages. They were the terms on which the settlement ultimately was based.[9]

The President's reply of 27 October opened on a positive note, welcoming Khrushchev's "desire to seek a prompt solution to the problem." The President then stressed that if there were to be a solution, work had to cease on the missile bases, and the offensive weapons in Cuba had to be rendered inoperable and removed, with supervision of the removal under appropriate UN arrangements. The U.S. in turn would lift the quarantine and would assure the Soviet Union that it would not invade Cuba. The President then hinted at future U.S. willingness to consider the missiles in Turkey, without explicitly so stating: "The effect of such a settlement," he wrote, "on easing world tensions would enable us to work toward a more general arrangement regarding 'other armaments,' as proposed in your second letter which you made public." The President closed his reply by again stressing the imperative of an immediate Soviet halt to work on the MRBMs and IRBMs and rendering the weapons inoperable.[10]

Attorney General Kennedy handed over a copy of the President's reply to Soviet Ambassador Dobrynin, stressing the President's belief that the substance of the Soviet response to this message would dictate swiftly whether the two superpowers would resolve the crisis or escalate to war.

On 28 October 1962, Khrushchev agreed to President Kennedy's terms: Work would stop on the missile sites, and the weapons would be dismantled and withdrawn. The word arrived quickly as we continued to support preparations for U.S. military action. There was tremendous exhilaration. The Intelligence Community and the military shifted gears, moving to the responsibility of monitoring Soviet dismantlement and withdrawal.

MONITORING THE WITHDRAWAL

New orders from Moscow to the Soviet missile and bomber forces in Cuba were dispatched immediately. As early as 29 October, low-level reconnaissance flights brought back evidence that the MRBM missile erectors were no longer in their missile-ready firing positions. We would monitor every step of the Soviet withdrawal through photography, reports from human sources, ship-to-ship inspections, air-to-ship surveillance, and other sources and methods. Weather permitting, the Navy RF-8As and Air Force RF-101s flew across Cuba on daily missions collecting thousands of frames of up-to-the-minute evidence for examination by the photointerpreters, analysts, and the senior levels of government.

Early on, the Soviets started to break up the IRBM sites—sites which would never meet their planned 15 December operational date, chosen to coincide with Khrushchev's planned address to the United Nations. Bulldozers tore up the missiles' concrete launch pads and smashed through missile-support facilities. Each of the sites was systematically monitored. The status of the support equipment, propellant trailers, nuclear weapons-handling vans, and communications vans was also an intelligence indicator. We tracked their withdrawal from the missile sites to the ports and onto a succession of Soviet merchant ships. The reconnaissance cameras documented Soviet personnel boarding ships for the voyage back across the Atlantic.

The Navy quarantine remained in effect, examining any inbound ships and, in a new phase, inspecting outbound ships to determine their cargoes. The Soviets complied with orders to strip away canvas covering each of the missiles in their canisters, with each clearly in the open, riding as deck cargo. They also complied with orders to break open the wooden crates containing the IL-28 bomber wings and fuselages, permitting us to count each and to confirm their departure.

Quarantine commander Admiral Ward reported that while the business was deadly serious and while the U.S. forces insisted on full, precise compliance with all demands, there was no sign of Soviet hostility.

STATUS REPORTS

On 2 November, President Kennedy provided his first formal status report on the dismantling of the Soviet missile bases in Cuba in an address to the nation. He reported that careful examination of aerial photography and other information was confirming the destruction of the missile bases and preparation of the missiles for return to the USSR. He said that U.S. surveillance would continue to track the withdrawal closely and that this unilateral inspection and monitoring would continue until the U.S. arranged for international inspection of the cargoes and overall withdrawal.

A. Denis Clift

By the time of his news conference on 20 November, the President had received sufficient intelligence to be able to report that the missile sites had all been dismantled, that the missiles and associated equipment had departed Cuba aboard Soviet ships, that U.S. inspection at sea had confirmed that the numbers departing included all known missiles, and that Khrushchev had informed him earlier that day that the IL-28 bombers would all be withdrawn from Cuba within 30 days. Following this Soviet compliance with U.S. demands, the President announced that he had ordered the lifting of the quarantine. He went on to stress that close surveillance of Cuba would continue, bearing in mind that Castro had still not agreed to allow UN inspectors to verify the removal of all offensive weapons or to set safeguards in place to prevent their reintroduction.

In his news conference of 12 December, the President had to repeat his position of 20 November, stating that, while the U.S. continued to press for on-site inspection, he would take every step necessary through continuing close daily surveillance to ensure that no missiles or offensive weapons were reintroduced.

PAYING TRIBUTE

With the quarantine lifted, the President flew to Florida on 26 November to pay tribute to the reconnaissance wings and squadrons. At Homestead Air Force Base, the President presented Outstanding Unit Awards to the 4080th Strategic Reconnaissance Wing and the 363rd Tactical Reconnaissance Wing. He saluted the work of the pilots and their ground crews:

> I may say, gentleman, that you take excellent pictures, and I've seen a good many of them. And beginning with the photographs which were taken on the weekend in the middle of October, which first gave us conclusive proof of the buildup of offensive weapons in Cuba, through the days that have followed to the present time, the work of these two units has contributed as much to the security of the U.S. as any units in our history, and any group of men in our history.[11]

He then flew to Key West, to Boca Chica Naval Air Station, to present Unit Citations to Navy Light Photographic Squadron 62 and Marine Light Photographic Squadron VMC-J2.

On 28 November, SAC Commander in Chief General Thomas Power awarded the Distinguished Flying Cross to 10 U-2 pilots of the 4080th. Admiral Robert Dennison, USN, presented the same decoration to 25 pilots of the Navy, Marine Corps, and Air Force tactical reconnaissance units. The next day the planes' cameras were again in action over Cuba.

MONITORING CONTINUES

The reconnaissance missions of November enabled us to monitor the disassembly and crating of the IL-28 bombers at San Julian and Holguin Airfields and the departure of the crates from Cuba, just as we had earlier monitored the destruction of the IRBM sites at

Guanajay and Remedios and the departure of the MRBM missiles from San Cristobal and Sagua La Grande. The first missions of 1963 also enabled us to continue to monitor the status of the Soviets' considerable remaining defensive installations, weaponry, and personnel, ostensibly in place to protect against the threat of invasion.

The number of Soviet troops had swollen to between 22,000 and 23,000 on Cuba at the peak of the crisis. With the departure of the missile and bomber forces, we could now identify some 17,000 troops still on the island. Our order of battle in early 1963 showed that Soviet military equipment in Cuba included 24 SAM sites with 500 missiles; 104 MiG fighters, including 24 of the new MiG-21 jets capable of Mach 2 performance; 200 air defense radars; 12 KOMAR-class missile patrol boats; upwards of 100 helicopters; four cruise-missile sites with 150 cruise missiles; more than 700 antiaircraft guns; 24 to 32 FROG rockets; 7,500 to 10,000 military support vehicles; more than 1,300 pieces of field artillery and antitank guns; and some 400 tanks.[12]

Taken together, this weaponry would have given the Soviets a layered set of ground, sea, and air defenses for their missile sites and bomber bases. And there could be little doubt that the remaining weapons were defensive in character. While the Intelligence Community assessed the MiG-21 as being capable of carrying a nuclear weapon, we knew that was not the fighter's intended mission. With a nuclear weapon aboard, the MiG-21 would have a combat radius of little more than 200 miles restricted to clear weather, daytime missions. Of prime importance, our analysis of each new batch of reconnaissance photography showed absolutely no evidence of the types of security facilities that one could expect with confidence that the Soviets would have in place if there were still any nuclear weapons stored on the island.

We were confident of the complete withdrawal based on the comprehensive character of our reconnaissance and monitoring in late 1962 and early 1963.

REFUTING RUMORS

When the U.S. Congress reconvened in late January 1963, our hard evidence on the defensive nature of the Soviet forces in Cuba remained largely classified. The public debate was feeding rumors that Soviet nuclear offensive capabilities remained in Cuba, that missiles were hidden in caves, and that the MiG-21s and KOMAR patrol boats could deliver nuclear weapons. Such rumors were pouring in from anti-Castro Cuban refugees, and they were fueled by those still angry that the President had not invaded the island and done away with the communist regime.

Following his Congressional testimony on 5 February, DCI McCone issued a formal unclassified statement in the name of the USIB reviewing the entire Soviet buildup and the departure of the missiles: "We are convinced beyond reasonable doubt, as has been stated by the Department of Defense, that all offensive missiles and bombers known to be in Cuba were withdrawn soon thereafter. . . . Reconnaissance has not detected the presence of offensive missiles or bombers in Cuba since that time." Referring to the alleged storage of missiles in caves, McCone said, "All statements alleging the presence of offensive weapons are meticulously checked. So far the findings have been negative. Absolute assurance on these matters, however, could only come from continuing penetrating on-site inspection."[13] The statement still did not defuse the issue.

In my appearance with Secretary McNamara before the House Subcommittee on Defense Appropriations on 6 February, the Secretary reviewed each phase of the Soviet buildup since the spring of 1962. To set the stage for my classified presentation to the subcommittee of the most important photography, the Secretary described the role of reconnaissance in some detail. Immediately after my presentation, the President decided that the photographic evidence had to be declassified and shared with the American people.

BRIEFING THE NATION

Shortly before noon, Secretary McNamara informed me that I was to present the briefing to the nation that evening on national television from 5:00 to 7:00 p.m. I was to make the presentation in the State Department Auditorium to an audience of journalists and photographers assigned to the White House, State Department, and Defense Department. The briefing requested by the President included photos, charts, and tables that would document clearly the discovery of the Soviet ballistic missiles, their assembly and operational readiness, and their dismantlement and removal from the island. The photos were selected from among the best available and reflected the superb quality of the photography regularly provided by our reconnaissance jets.

Secretary McNamara told me that he would introduce the presentation and take the follow-on questions. He asked to see the text of my briefing and was surprised when I told him that there was no written text because I had committed the briefing to memory, and that the sequence of the photography and charts would shape and pace the presentation. The Secretary directed his military assistant, Colonel George Brown, USAF, who would go on to become Chairman of the Joint Chiefs of Staff, to take me under his charge for the remainder of the day and ensure that I was at the State Department by 4:00 p.m.

By 3:30 p.m., we were ready. The graphics had been checked and rechecked, classifications removed or covered, and some descriptive annotations added. Colonel Brown and I arrived at the State Department at 4:00 p.m. The auditorium was larger than I had expected, and the viewing screen—at least 12 feet by 8 feet—towered above the stage. This screen would enhance and display the photography to maximum advantage. To tell the story effectively, however, I had to be able to point to photographic details that would be well beyond reach. I contacted my special assistant, Captain Billy R. Cooper, USAF, at the Pentagon about the problem, and he was more than equal to the challenge. He grabbed a roll of tape, securely joined two long fishing poles, and rushed to his car. I had this tailor-made pointer in hand and was set and ready to go at 5:00 p.m.

The air was charged in the auditorium. The press was out in full force and McNamara was to the point:

> Good afternoon, ladies and gentlemen. In recent days questions have been raised in the press and elsewhere regarding the presence of offensive weapons systems in Cuba. I believe beyond any reasonable doubt that all such weapons

systems have been removed from the island and none have been reintroduced. It is our purpose to show you this afternoon the evidence on which we base that conclusion.

Since 1 July, over 400 reconnaissance flights have been flown over the island of Cuba by U.S. military aircraft. These reconnaissance flights provided the essential basis for the national decisions taken with respect to Cuba in October. They provided the basis for the military preparations necessary to support those decisions. They provided the evidence we were able to present to the world to document the basis and the rationale of our action.

The reconnaissance flights recorded the removal of the offensive weapon systems from Cuba, and they continued to provide the foundation for our conclusion that such weapons systems have not been reintroduced into the island.

Mr. John Hughes, the Special Assistant to General Carroll, the Director of DIA, will present to you a detailed photographic review of the introduction of Soviet military personnel and equipment into Cuba, with particular emphasis on the introduction and removal of the offensive weapons systems.

After Mr. Hughes completes his review, I will summarize very briefly our current estimates of the Soviet military strength in Cuba.

Mr. Hughes.

I began my briefing.

EDITOR'S NOTE

At the time of the Cuban Missile Crisis, I was a 20-year-old college senior anticipating my future as an Army officer, fully expecting that the immediate future might include a tour of duty in Cuba. I would watch John Hughes' briefing that night on national television, and would marvel at the photographic evidence being revealed to the nation. Twenty years later, I would be assigned to the Pentagon office of John T. Hughes, then the Deputy Director for External Affairs of the Defense Intelligence Agency, as Hughes' Executive Officer, responsible for overseeing the myriad operational and administrative details swirling about this man and his office.

Eight months into my tour, President Ronald Reagan chose John Hughes to give another special presentation to the nation—this time on another hot-spot: Nicaragua. With déjà vu apparent, the site for the briefing was to be the State Department Auditorium with the giant screen, and again, Hughes would need a long pointer to reach every part of the enormous projected images. This time it was his Deputy, Colonel Al Jones, who pulled from his desk a sectional bamboo fishing pole, which Hughes assembled on-site for the briefing. If one looks closely at the pictures of John Hughes that appeared on the front pages of the *New York Times* and the *Washington Post* that Wednesday, 10 March 1982, one can make out the ridges separating the sections of the bamboo fishing pointer.

JSM

CHAPTER 4
THE KNOTTED STICK OF HISTORY

In this 1996 banquet address to the Society for Military History, the author states that "Good intelligence history is the staff in our hand, a knotted stick fashioned from the branch of an oak, the strongest and stoutest of trees, aiding us in our navigation of the land through peace, crisis, and war." He relates some of his own encounters with history, as Editor of the United States Naval Institute Proceedings; *as staff member at the 1978 Camp David Summit involving President Carter, Prime Minister Menachem Begin, and President Anwar Sadat; and draws from his current experiences as a Commissioner on the U.S.-Russia Joint Commission on Prisoners of War/Missing in Action. He captures exchanges between President Harry Truman and OSS Director William J. Donovan, leading up to the National Security Act of 1947. He reminds of the perils posed to national security by what former Director of Central Intelligence Robert Gates calls "Washington's historical amnesia." He commends the value of intelligence-related historical research by students in the Master's program at the Joint Military Intelligence College.*

"This is the patent age of new inventions
For killing bodies, and for saving souls,
All propagated with the best intentions."

With this verse from Lord Byron, Graham Greene turned to history to frame his novel *The Quiet American* for the reader, a novel set in Saigon in the 1950s when the French were fighting to hold their empire in the Far East.[1]

My first role as a historian, or more correctly as one dabbling in history, dates back to the late 1930s. Lord Byron was not on my lips. I am told—and you will take due note that I can confirm none of this—that the occasional sitter who used to harness me up and take me out for airings had a friend who worked for President and Mrs. Roosevelt in their apartment just a block away from ours, an apartment overlooking New York City's Washington Square. Social invitations received there were placed in a silver punch bowl near the front hallway. During the ladies' midmorning coffee chats, I was deposited on the front hall floor, the punch bowl between my outstretched legs, to shuffle the President and Mrs. Roosevelt's incoming cards and letters.

WITH PRESIDENTS TO THE SUMMIT

Forty years later, I would add to this sense of history. From 7 September through 17 September 1978, I would be sequestered in the Catoctin Mountains—the site of Roosevelt's beloved Shangri-La—a staff member at the Camp David Summit with President Carter, Prime Minister Begin, and President Sadat. The place of the Camp David Summit in history, and its impact on the Middle East peace process, on U.S. security, and on international stability, continue to be assessed. Clearly the summit will stand as an enduring

A. Denis Clift

page in diplomatic achievement. It was an event made far more remarkable by the historical appreciation and the contributions to history that radiated from the Egyptian and Israeli leaders.

Anwar Sadat had pointed the way with his visit to Jerusalem in November 1977. I had gained an even earlier appreciation of his statesmanship during his meeting with President Ford in Salzburg two years earlier. Our host for the state dinner on that occasion had been Chancellor Bruno Kreisky. When Sadat rose, he delivered his lengthy extemporaneous response to the Chancellor's toast in German, a tongue he had learned during the era of his opposition to British rule of his country.

The Israeli team at Camp David—led by Menachem Begin, the guerrilla fighter for independence—included Minister of Defense Ezer Weizman, today the President of Israel. In the shade of the Maryland mountainside, Weizman—the former fighter pilot and Commander of the Israeli Air Force—would tell us of days earlier still in World War II when he was delivering fuel to British airfields and ferrying new vehicles for the British army in the desert. "The desert has its own rules of life and war; in those wide spaces," he would write, "battle is waged as near as possible to the roads, to the main routes. There is a striking paradox: The desert covers an enormous area, but control of its central routes is enough to dominate it all."[2]

The Israeli Foreign Minister, Moshe Dayan, was a charismatic, legendary warrior who exuded the spirit of his nation. Between the long, intense negotiating sessions he would speak of his love of archeology, his passion for each new uncovering of antiquities in his Land of the Book. He would give me a copy of his work *Living with the Bible* in which he had written, "The people closest to me were the founders of our nation, the patriarchs Abraham, Isaac and Jacob. They wandered the length and breadth of the land with a staff in their hand, a knotted stick fashioned from the branch of an oak, the strongest and stoutest of trees."[3]

On the final early evening of the summit, I was with a colleague in Laurel Lodge. The rumble of thunder built to a Wagnerian finale. Prime Minister Begin and an aide entered the lodge and joined us. "Begin shook our hands warmly; he was still absorbing the splendid meaning of his actions that day. 'For years,' he said, 'all the time I was in the Opposition, they said "Don't elect him; he will bring war." 'Last year I was contemplating retirement, and now I am bringing peace.' "[4]

THE SEARCH FOR PRISONERS OF WAR AND MISSING IN ACTION

For the past four years, I have been serving as a commissioner on the U.S.-Russia Joint Commission on Prisoners of War/Missing in Action, a commission created by the Presidents of the United States and the Russian Federation to help determine the fates of those still unaccounted from World War II, Korea, the Cold War, and Vietnam. Until his death last December, the Russian side of the Commission was chaired by Colonel General Dmitriy

Volkogonov, a historian whose works on Lenin and Stalin brought international acclaim and national controversy, a historian whose perspective contributed immeasurably to the humanitarian goals of the commission. Volkogonov was completing work on a new volume when he died, a study of the Soviet General Secretaries. During a flight from Moscow to Washington in 1994, I was telling him of my meetings with Leonid Brezhnev in the 1970s. Volkogonov listened, spinning a pen somewhat impatiently between his fingers. "Brezhnev was not an idiot," he said, when I had finished, "he was an absolute idiot!"

In the work of the Commission, pages of history have miraculously appeared and come into focus before our eyes. We have walked rocky slopes in Armenia where fragments of wreckage from a C-130 shot down in September 1958 still lie. We have interviewed the pilots who attacked the plane, the air defense commander who gave them their orders, villagers who witnessed the fiery crash. We have received gun camera photographs of the attack, of the plane disintegrating, from former Soviet military archives.

In April 1993, I would rise in the Oval Hall of the Kremlin to criticize the KGB's successor organization, the SVRR, for not sharing more of its archives with the Commission, given that the Cold War aircraft losses we were investigating had occurred in areas where the Border Guards would have had responsibility. Half holding my breath as we left the meeting, I asked Ambassador Mac Toon, the U.S. Co-Chairman, how many souls he thought had criticized the KGB in that setting and exited vertically on their own two feet.

In December 1993, the Russians introduced me to a retired KGB sailor who had heard the Commission's appeal for information and who had traveled to Moscow from the Ukraine. The sailor, Vasili Saiko, had been serving in the Pacific 42 years before, in 1952, and had witnessed the shootdown of an American RB-29 from the deck of his border guard cutter. The cutter had been dispatched to the crash site north of Hokkaido, and Saiko had pulled the corpse of an American aviator from the sea. He told me that as the cutter had returned to port, he had lifted the corner of the tarpaulin and had eased a ring from one of the dead American's fingers. As he spoke, he reached into a pocket, withdrew the ring, and passed it over to me—a United States Naval Academy ring, class of '50, in mint condition with a script capital D on its face and the name John Robertson Dunham engraved on the inside band. Mr. Saiko told us there had been no other signs of crew or survivors, that all that had remained of the aircraft was one severed wheel, nondescript flotsam, and aviation gasoline bubbling to the surface.

Saiko's appearance before the Commission led to a more intensive search of Border Guard Archives, the discovery of a roughly drawn map of a cemetery on Yuri Island, and a statement of burial witnessed by three Border Guard officers. On their second expedition in 1994, a U.S.-Russian team unearthed the coffin, and the remains were flown to Hawaii, where they were identified. Captain John Robertson Dunham, United States Air Force, was lain to rest in Arlington National Cemetery on 1 August 1995, with a B-52 passing low overhead in final honors.

Before I leave the work of the Commission, I should note that another of my Russian colleagues is General Major Anatolii Volkov. A classic bear of a man, General Volkov is an

A. Denis Clift

engaging officer, a study in deep selection. In 1993, as a young colonel, he handpicked and then led a line of tanks onto a bridge of the Moscow River, where they proceeded to shell the Russian Parliament. Soon thereafter he was promoted to general—herein lies the historian's challenge.

PROCEEDINGS OF HISTORY

Years earlier, I would work closely with historians writing on the lives and the contributions of important figures in U.S. military history, and on the major events shaping that history. From 1963-1966, I was Editor of the *United States Naval Institute Proceedings,* a journal that has made unique and enduring contributions to history for well over 100 years. I had joined the *Proceedings* as an assistant editor the year before, and the September 1962 issue was the first I had put a pencil to—what a privilege—what an issue. The lead essay was Marine Colonel R. D. Heinl, Jr.'s "The Right to Fight," a chapter from his about-to-be-published history of the Marine Corps, *Soldiers of the Sea*—a chapter powerfully written, capturing the Corps' harsh, victorious fight for its very existence following World War II, a fight in the halls of Washington, a chapter reminding in a far broader sense of the wisdom of the founding fathers' Executive and Legislative checks and balances. Heinl would write:

> The national reaction to General Vandergrift's statement was instantaneous and favorable; that of the White House was equally instantaneous but in the opposite direction. The Commandant had dealt S.2044 a body blow-a kick to the groin, some thought—and when Congress adjourned in August, the merger bill was unacted on.[5]

That same issue carried Rear Admiral Kemp Tolley's "The Strange Assignment of USS *Lanikai.*" Tolley recounted his mission in late 1941, on orders from the President, to commission the schooner *Lanikai* in the Philippines and sail her into the path of the Japanese Fleet. He had come to believe that mission was designed to provoke the Japanese into sinking her and triggering U.S. entry into World War II. The *Lanikai* finally dropped anchor in Perth, Australia on 18 March 1942-82 days out of Manila. "My God! What are you doing here?" cried Rear Admiral William Purnell, Chief of Staff to Commander Southwest Pacific. "You're supposed to be dead!"[6]

There were excellent historians at the Naval Academy in the early 1960s, as there are now. One of my friends in those days was Professor Bob Seager, who had just finished mining a rich trunk load of prime documents and was proofing the galleys of his biography of President Tyler, entitled *And Tyler Too.* Bob would soon depart for the University of Maine to become, in his words, "Captain of my own sinking ship," as chairman of Maine's History Department. There was no chance in those days of his becoming chair at the Naval Academy. That seat was taken by the distinguished Professor E. B. Potter.

One of the last articles I had the pleasure of editing before leaving the Naval Institute for the London School of Economics was Ned Potter's biography of Fleet Admiral Chester William Nimitz, who had passed away just months before in early 1966. The chronology of Admiral Nimitz's career and life made for splendid professional reading. Ned Potter's biography went far beyond that. He wrote that Nimitz as Commander in Chief of the Pacific Fleet in early 1942 had three questions tacked over his desk

"which he expected his subordinates to be prepared to answer about any problem: 1. Is the proposed operation likely to succeed? 2. What might be the consequences of failure? 3. Is it in the realm of practicability of material and suppliers?"[7]

In his retirement, Nimitz would co-author with Potter *Sea Power: A Naval History.* And, Potter wrote, at the outset of the project Nimitz gave his five-star admiral's advice on the writing of such history. "Officers understandably resent having their operations publicly criticized by civilians," said Nimitz. "My suggestion to you is this: Give all the facts, as accurately, objectively, and fairly as you can, but don't draw conclusions. Let the reader do that. Let the facts speak for themselves."[8]

TRUMAN AND THE NATIONAL SECURITY ACT OF 1947

Fleet Admiral Nimitz had become Chief of Naval Operations by the time President Harry S. Truman had rolled up his sleeves to get on with the epochal work of shaping a new national security structure to prevent another Pearl Harbor, a structure equal to the demands of the nuclear era. I have always taken great pleasure in Truman's manner, his way of delivering himself. I remember once during my White House staffing years sending a note up the line to one far more senior reminding of how Truman had handled one particularly difficult question at a White House Press Conference: "Come on, fellows; you don't think I'm dumb enough to try to answer that one, do you?"—or words to that effect.

President Truman had been confronted early on with the challenge of handling the reins and guiding a chariot being pulled by independent military, diplomatic, and intelligence steeds. In crossing the Atlantic to the Potsdam conference, he had admired the advances in communications support for the President aboard the cruiser USS *Augusta.* The first Lieutenant's office had been reconfigured as the Advance Map Room, corresponding to the Map Room in the White House. "Here," Truman would write, "messages were received and transmitted in virtually the same volume and with the same dispatch as the White House itself. For all practical purposes the Advance Map Room was the White House during the time the *Augusta* was underway."[9] At the same time, there was too much to do, and he chafed at the time consumed in the nine-day passage. The first Presidential aircraft, the *Guess Where II,* had now been replaced by the *Sacred Cow,* which had preceded Truman to Europe and supported him during the summit. As Potsdam drew to a close, he wrote his mother and his sister: "I'd rather fly. . . . I could be home a week sooner. But they all yell their heads off when I talk of flying."[10]

President Truman got on with the work that would emerge as the National Security Act of 1947. The voices he would hear, the words he would receive, have a familiar ring as the nation now debates the future structure and shape of the Intelligence Community 50 years later. In his memorandum to the President of 13 September 1945, OSS Director William J. Donovan would write:

A. Denis Clift

1. I understand that it has been, or will be, suggested to you that certain of the primary functions of this organization—more particularly, secret intelligence, counter-espionage, and the evaluation and synthesis of intelligence—that these functions be severed and transferred to separate agencies. I hope that in the national interest, and in your own interest as the Chief Executive, that you will not permit this to be done.

2. Whatever agency has the duty of intelligence should have it as a complete whole. To do otherwise would be to add chaos to existing confusion in the intelligence field. The various functions that have been integrated are the essential functions in intelligence. One is dependent upon the other. [signed Donovan][11]

I suggest this evening that one could redo the signature block and redate it 1996!

In *Donovan and the CIA*, Thomas Troy's history of the establishment of the Central Intelligence Agency, the classic intragovernmental skirmishes over the future of intelligence, the personality clashes, the separate options, unfold. Troy captures the role played by Deputy Director of Naval Intelligence Rear Admiral Sidney Souers—fellow Missourian, owner of Piggly-Wiggly, eager to return to his business in St. Louis—in drafting the letter Truman would sign to the Secretaries of State, War, and Navy, establishing the Central Intelligence Group as OSS's successor, the forerunner of CIA.[12]

The definitive history of the National Security Act of 1947 necessarily will be the work of a future generation. The language of the act is the source of study, wonder, and emulation abroad. It is the bedrock from which the U.S. Government proceeds even today in its assessment of how best to shape and assign the Intelligence Community for the work of the new century.

I have returned quite recently from a visit abroad, which included an address to the National Defense College in Bucharest. I would note that there is a fascination and an admiration for all things American in Romania today. One evening my hosts insisted that I watch the Oscar awards with them on their newly liberated television. They knew every movie. They knew each actor and actress—and I pretended that I did, too! At the request of my Romanian hosts, the subject of my address to their National Defense College was "civilian control over U.S. intelligence," a foreign concept of the greatest importance to them as they work to build a genuine democracy, but a concept central to the National Security Act of 1947.

TOWARD A CURE FOR HISTORICAL AMNESIA

Robert Gates, the former Director of Central Intelligence, is fond of saying that there is a historical amnesia in Washington. I am sure most of you would agree. The examples are countless. They are both deplorable and hysterical. Senator John Warner was alert to this syndrome as is clear in his "Additional Views," a paper accompanying the *Report of the*

Commission on the Roles and Capabilities of the United States Intelligence Community, published on 1 March 1996. Senator Warner writes:

> In the Spring of 1994, when I drafted the legislation creating this Commission, the Intelligence Community was "under siege" from certain Members of Congress and others in the wake of the Aldrich Ames spy case and the revelations surrounding the NRO Headquarters controversy. Members of Congress were advocating "slash and burn" of the intelligence budget. One even proposed the abolition of the CIA, preferring to merge its functions into other government agencies. It was clear that a "cooling off" period was essential. Time was needed to ensure that our vital intelligence capabilities were not sacrificed as an overreaction to the problems—though very serious—of the day.[13]

In the work of the Commission in its broadest sense, cooler heads have prevailed. Its very first finding underlines the vital contributions intelligence has made and is making to U.S. security, the need for a strong intelligence capability in the future. This work now feeds into the ongoing review of the community by the Executive Branch and the House and Senate Intelligence Oversight Committees.

As this debate unfolds, as the role of intelligence—its importance undiminished—continues to evolve in each succeeding decade, it is imperative that historians subject both the organization of U.S. intelligence and its role to an ever more thorough examination. It is imperative that writings on the history of intelligence cut through the fog of political amnesia to provide a beacon both for the leaders of the nation and the operational commanders in the field.

One of the truly fine officers and historians I have had the pleasure of knowing is Colonel John A. Cash, United States Army. I recently reread his book entitled *Seven Firefights in Vietnam.* Cash, then a major, was author of four of the seven firefights. He had been in the action, and the power and precision of his writing in "Gunship Mission, 5 May 1968" takes you there to witness and learn. John Cash wrote:

> Following 500 meters to the rear and slightly to the right, Major Hunt began lining up on the target axis, even before Payne had made his break, for it was his job at this point to protect the exposed underside of Payne's ship from enemy fire. His copilot, Warrant Officer Davis, fired the flexguns, adjusting the bullet strikes into the base of the pagoda in much the same fashion as one would direct a stream of water from a garden hose. Hunt fired his rockets in two 2-round volleys, guiding on the bullet strikes, while Rexer and Sullivan fired their door guns at enemy weapons flashes and likely positions along the flanks and forward of the target area.[14]

In his Foreword to this work, Brigadier General Hal Peterson, Chief of Military History, commented on the purpose of such writing, "a preliminary record of the achievements of men who served their nation well, a preface to a full military history of the war that is already in preparation."[15] As a nation, we attach importance to the writing of military

A. Denis Clift

history. In administration after administration—again, recalling Bob Gates' thoughts on political amnesia—too often we do not attach importance to its being read.

In 1954, as a copyboy for the New York *Daily News*, I had the thrill of riding up Broadway in a ticker tape parade, riding in an open press truck immediately in front of Lieutenant Genevieve de Galard Terraube, the angel of Dien Bien Phu. To believe Robert McNamara's memoir *In Retrospect*, that half-hour truck ride put me on near equal footing in terms of historical knowledge with some of the leaders who would shape American policy toward Indochina in the early 1960s:

> I had never visited Indochina [McNamara wrote], nor did I understand or appreciate its history, language, culture, or values. The same must be said, to varying degrees, about President Kennedy, Secretary of State Dean Rusk, National Security Advisor McGeorge Bundy, military adviser Maxwell Taylor, and many others. When it came to Vietnam, we found ourselves setting policy for a region that was terra incognita.[16]

Others in the government did know the history, language, culture, and values of the region, but they were not being listened to, at least not initially. In Panel 1F of this Conference, Intelligence Perspectives on the Vietnam War, Hal Ford's paper, "An Analyst's View: Why Were CIA Analysts so Pessimistic About Vietnam?" offers an excellent examination of this period—an examination including the analysts' appreciation of the implications of the "Viet Minh's smashing 1954 victory over the French at Dien Bien Phu and the end of French rule."[17]

In the Joint Military Intelligence College (JMIC), which I am privileged to lead, many of our graduate students are contributing most importantly to the history of intelligence through their research and their writing. The publishing house Frank Cass of London has just brought out Army Captain Ronnie E. Ford's book *Tet 1968: Understanding the Surprise,* a work based on his JMIC Master's thesis, work that contributes further to our documenting of intelligence, our examination of its role during the Vietnam conflict. In his introduction, Captain Ford writes:

> The Communist surprise was achieved not because Allied intelligence failed to collect enough enemy attack indicators, but because the Americans were simply incapable of believing the indicators they had. The indicators were discounted because U.S. and South Vietnamese analysts were not able to fuse them properly with the significance they implied. In short, intelligence knew all about the enemy, but failed to understand him. They knew the facts, but did not understand their meaning.[18]

At the JMIC, the Joint History Office of the Chairman of the Joint Chiefs of Staff presents the Fleet Admiral Chester W. Nimitz Archival Research Award each year to the graduate student whose thesis reflects the most outstanding archival research in a military historical field. At our September 1995 commencement exercises, the Nimitz Award was presented to Air Force Captain Bradford J. Shwedo for his thesis entitled *Patton's ULTRA System and its Employment on the European Battlefield.*

General Patton valued intelligence and used intelligence. His G-2, Brigadier General Oscar W. Koch, would write in 1971: "In Patton's commands, intelligence was always viewed as big business and treated accordingly. Although working, by necessity, in the shadows, it always had its place in the sun. It was never viewed as subordinate to any other staff activity. G-2 was never the forgotten man."[19]

What General Koch could not discuss when his memoirs were published in 1971 was the place of ULTRA in Patton's intelligence calculus. Even mention of ULTRA was classified then. A quarter century later, Captain Shwedo captures the place of ULTRA, the value Patton attached to the intercepts from the German wireless Enigma machine, the care taken by his G-2 to segregate these intercepts from the rest of the Command's all-source intelligence, to avoid becoming a captive of the intercepts, to use one against the other in measuring the enemy's intentions.[20]

I believe Fleet Admiral Nimitz would be delighted to know that his name is associated with Captain Shwedo's research. The facts on Patton's use of ULTRA are presented as accurately, objectively, and fairly as possible. The facts speak for themselves. Projected from the past, they provide invaluable lessons, guidelines, direction for the future. Good intelligence history is the staff in our hand, a knotted stick fashioned from the branch of an oak, the strongest and stoutest of trees, aiding us in our navigation of the land through peace, crisis, and war.

CHAPTER 5
THE DINKUM OIL

In a 1997 address to the Patterson School of Diplomacy and International Commerce at the University of Kentucky, the author looks at the parallel demands on those who do their work well in the fields of journalism and intelligence—the need to uncover the real low-down, the real stuff, "the dinkum oil." He discusses the need for a professional intelligence literature, changes occurring in the contemporary literature of the profession, and the fresh contributions today's young intelligence professionals are making to the method, vocabulary, body of doctrine, and fundamental theory of the intelligence discipline.

"Intelligence has become, in our own recent memory, an exacting, highly skilled profession, and an honorable one," Sherman Kent wrote in 1955. But, he added, "As long as this discipline lacks a literature, its method, its vocabulary, its body of doctrine, and even its fundamental theory run the risk of never reaching full maturity."[1]

Kent, one of the great figures in the history of the Central Intelligence Agency, former Yale historian, and Chairman of the Board of National Estimates from 1952 to 1967, founded the journal *Studies in Intelligence* to speed and assist the reality of works he described as "the institutional mind and memory of our discipline."[2] On the occasion of his retirement in 1968, he returned to the importance of the written word in an essay in *Studies* entitled "Valediction," in which he recalled a lecture on grand strategy given by Bernard Brodie at the National War College in 1947:

> The speech came to a climax when Mr. Brodie identified a couple of strategic decisions of World War II which he held in low esteem and indicated that they might not have been made if Americans had devoted more time to thinking and writing about strategy. The moral was pointed and purposefully so: Strategy is your business; why don't you systematize your thinking about it and perpetuate your reflections in a professional literature?[3]

THE NEED FOR A PROFESSIONAL LITERATURE

In the communications age, there is still one nagging, underlying requirement in the development of a literature, and that is the need for writers. At the same time that Sherman Kent was in his zenith at CIA, Professor Chilton R. Bush was pioneering in the education of future writers and communicators at Stanford University. Bush—"Chick" Bush—had joined the Stanford faculty in 1934, following nine years at the University of Wisconsin, and headed the Department of Communication and Journalism from 1945 until his death in 1972. "We don't train a man for a vocation," he once said. "We train him to be a well-informed, responsible member of the community. The purpose of the academic program is mainly motivational."[4]

A. Denis Clift

For Bush, the writer's place was out in the world, not in the classroom, and he loved to send his students into the field—to the criminal courts for their first murder trials, to internships with the *San Francisco News*. He was the author of several books, and he dedicated *Newspaper Reporting of Public Affairs*, the standard in its field, to "Professors Dick Chase, Frank Clarvoe, Paul Edwards, Spud Hamilton, Pete Lee, Dick Macfarlane, Charley Massey, Baron Muller, and Harvey Wing of the *San Francisco News* who have helped to make some fine reporters of the eager material in Journalism 183."[5]

At the beginning of Chapter One, Bush identified the three basic rules: "1. Know news. 2. Know where to get it. 3. Go get it." He wrote of the skills and attitudes needed by a good reporter of public affairs: the need to be gregarious, to develop a good working relationship with the stenographers, the clerks and, yes, the officials in high places; the need to have curiosity; the need to be enthusiastic, however dull the day or task at hand; the need to answer for the reader those significant questions about the event that naturally arise in the reader's mind; the need to have a critical sense, to develop a habit of verifying information given him by checking it against his own sense of the probabilities; the need to be resourceful, to locate another source or sources when information is denied from the most obvious or logical source; the need to respect confidences; and the need to be a literary craftsman, to be able to write well in the idiom.[6]

It is not clear that Sherman Kent and Chilton Bush ever met, ever discussed this over a sherry, but it is certain that Kent would have applauded every facet of such teaching.

GETTING TO THE DINKUM OIL

In day-to-day news, the good reporter knows that the reader needs answers starting with the who, what, where, when, and why of every story's lead. We absorb such writing and take it for granted, whether it is coverage of one of man's great ascents: "The explorers of Apollo 8 took their places in history alongside Columbus and Magellan today, when they landed their spacecraft in the South Pacific three days after completing man's first flight around the moon,"[7] or one of man's great descents: "Two young British men who said they did it 'just for kicks' accomplished something yesterday no one has ever done before—they parachuted from the 86th floor observation deck of the Empire State Building. . . . 'The only thing that could go wrong was the landing area; would we get mugged when we landed?'"[8]

Reporting of the Spanish Civil War, as computed through the eyes, mind, and hands of Ernest Hemingway, became an enduring blend of reconnaissance, reporting, and literature:

> Across the river the enemy had just taken the bridgehead and the last troops had swum across the river after the pontoon bridge was blown. Shells were coming in now from the little town of Amposta across the river and registering aimlessly in the open country and along the road. You would hear the double boom of the guns and then the whirling, cloth-ripping, incoming rush, and dirt would fountain brownly up among the grapevines. The war had a pointless, undangerous dumbness that it has when the guns first come into action before there is proper observation and the shooting is accurately controlled, and I

walked down along a railroad track to find a place to watch what General Franco's men were doing across the river.[9]

Reporting of the Finns' annihilation of the Russian 44th Division in January 1940 in the battle of Suomussalmi through the professional touch of Matthew Halton, correspondent for the *Toronto Star,* was at the same time a vivid description of carnage frozen in the Arctic winter, of Finns moving as lone wolves and in ghost patrols of twos and threes and sixes and dozens invisible in their whites, and an expert's four-part assessment of what had gone wrong for the Russians, including:

> The armaments of the Russians were as good as any in the world, but they were in the hands of poor troops and incredibly misused. They had fine anti-tank guns—but the Finns had no tanks. They had superb anti-aircraft guns—and the Finns had hardly any aircraft. They had thousands of excellent motor-trucks—but they were almost useless in the deep snows. They had horse-drawn wagons that were immobile once they were off the few main roads—while the Finns had narrow sleds that could go almost anywhere. They had excellent mobile field kitchens—on wheels; as soon as the Finns captured any of these they immediately put them on sleds.[10]

As emphasized time and again in Halton's reporting, the Russians had bad intelligence; they thought Finland would fall without a struggle. Such writing, such reporting, such literature is what the Australians would call "the dinkum oil," the real low-down, the real stuff.

CONTEMPORARY LITERATURE OF THE PROFESSION

In a tribute to Sherman Kent on the occasion of the 25th anniversary issue of *Studies in Intelligence,* Harold Ford wrote: "Our calling needs character. It also needs characters. In the best sense, Sherm Kent has both."[11] Without a doubt, Kent would have added: "Our literature needs character. It also needs characters." In the best sense, 1997 is proving to be a year for both.

In *A Spy for All Seasons*, Duane R. "Dewey" Clarridge has published his memoirs on 33 years in CIA's clandestine services. In his Foreword, he sets two goals for his work: First, to pay his legal bills and to help underwrite a fund for other officers in the service who find themselves in need of an attorney as a result of problems arising from their professional work, and second, to "provide a more fulsome and accurate description to the public of what a clandestine services case officer really does."[12] Writing with conviction and patriotic pride, he recounts a swashbuckler's career ranging from Nepal and India, the Middle East, Southwest Asia, and Europe to Central and South America—and Washington, DC. To protect sources and methods, by his own account, he occasionally "blurs" geographic locations, dates, and people. On unnumbered page 11 of the work, it is stated:

> Note: The CIA's Publications Review Board has reviewed the manuscript for this book to assist the author in eliminating classified information and poses no

security objections to its publication. This review, however, should not be construed as an official release of information, confirmation of its accuracy, or an endorsement of the author's views.[13]

The work's incredible detail on clandestine operations—Central American operations little more than a decade old, for example—the author's advisory on "blurring" and CIA's explanation to avoid misunderstanding combine to make the book an important addition to the literature. Dewey Clarridge's triumphs, his grudges, his portrayal of policies and events, are grist for debate within and without the profession. The detail he brings to the contemporary clandestine services—reporting by an American on the U.S. system, with no security objections posed by his parent service—marks the turning of a new chapter in the literature.

Dewey Clarridge shares with his readers the approach that he took to his service. On returning from his first overseas assignment in Nepal, he writes: "The young CIA officer who had left the States in 1957 as a 'clerk' was returning a bit over two years later as an uncontestable case officer, albeit self-taught. Opportunity does indeed create the man."[14] Further on in his career, Clarridge philosophized on a tour in Rome in terms that could well have been learned at Chick Bush's knee:

> I believe in calculated risk taking, which comes from weighing all the pros and cons and making an intelligence go/no-go decision, applying a large dose of common sense. There is a world of difference between this measured analysis and taking a risk that is in effect a gamble. I never felt that I was reckless or irresponsible. I simply knew that excessive caution was paralyzing, and that if you waited for everything to be perfect, you'd never do anything. Moreover, from experience, I knew that my technique worked.[15]

On a tour still later as Chief of the European Division of CIA's Directorate of Operations, he wrote:

> I was saddled with an overabundance of yuppie spies who cared more about their retirement plan and health insurance benefits than about protecting democracy. For them CIA was just a job. . . . Many junior officers lacked writing skills. I had no more than a handful of officers whose educational credentials put them on an equal footing with their European counterparts.[16]

In his peroration, the final sentences of the book's concluding paragraph, he writes: "I have often thought during my career that I should have been paying the Agency for the privilege of serving in the clandestine services. Perhaps, even more to the point, never during my thirty-three years at the CIA did I awake in the morning and not want to go to work; I couldn't wait to get there."[17]

While Dewey Clarridge laments the current decline of the clandestine services, his work, in fact, should be of fascination—a full-color recruiting poster—for the young man or young woman interested in intelligence as a possible, worthy career. He opens a window on the life of an overseas case officer, on the classic personnel frictions facing anyone anywhere rising rapidly in the ranks, on the place of the CIA in the worlds of intelligence and national security, on Washington's checks-and-balances tangle, and on the pride that comes from service to nation. Those seeking talented new recruits to such service would do well to sow this contribution to the literature electronically and in hardcopy bound editions across the land.

MEETING THE CHALLENGES OF A NEW ERA

Service to nation in the professional world of intelligence goes far beyond the work of CIA's clandestine services. The 1990s are a decade—the beginning of a new era—in which refugee crises, multinational operations, peacekeeping, and coalition warfare have joined strategic deterrence and large-scale conventional warfare as the responsibilities of the United States Armed Forces together with the Intelligence Community. We have entered an era in which global problems—proliferation of weapons of mass destruction, international terrorism, crime, narcotics trafficking, and threats to our information superstructure—climb higher on the national agenda. It is an era in which the Chairman of the Joint Chiefs of Staff in his planning guidance looks to U.S. Armed Forces that will be largely based in the United States but also permanently stationed overseas, Armed Forces that will be working with foreign militaries honoring our commitments, strengthening our capabilities—forces operating as joint forces participating in coalition and multinational operations. The challenges of this new era have brought intelligence into full partnership with both planning and operations. It is an era, in turn, challenging the best minds in the discipline to anticipate new intelligence needs and to meet revolutionary intelligence requirements.

Perry L. Pickert also served in the CIA, as an intelligence analyst from 1979 to 1986. Dr. Pickert—a Ph.D. from the Fletcher School of Law and Diplomacy, Tufts University, and a Juris Doctorate from George Mason University School of Law—is a Colonel in the U.S. Marine Corps Reserve, with service as an intelligence officer, as a counterintelligence team commander, and as an operations officer of a civil affairs group. In 1986, he joined the State Department to work on United Nations and other international organization issues. From 1994-1996 he served on the faculty of the Joint Military Intelligence College as a visiting professor in the department of intelligence collection.

At the College, Perry Pickert joined with other faculty members advising the active duty and civilian professionals working toward their Master of Science of Strategic Intelligence degrees on thesis topics covering a broad new front: analysis of the enhanced UN role in world politics, intelligence in UN decisionmaking, support to peacekeeping operations, nuclear nonproliferation, the future of U.S. intelligence in multilateral environments, and Congressional oversight. In 1996, he undertook a review of relevant theses and distilled more than 20 of them into essays published this June in the Joint Military Intelligence College volume *Intelligence for Multilateral Decision and Action*. In his Introduction to that volume, Pickert wrote:

> The direct American intelligence participation and support in the context of
> multilateral institutions required rethinking basic assumptions about the nature

of the intelligence process in a Hobbesean world of state against state in preparation for the next war. . . . Intelligence sharing is always a two-way street with
dim lighting and few road signs. Ambiguity and an imperative to move forward
have generated opportunities for original research. [18]

The work's essays are grouped into chapters and include the preparedness of the U.S.
Armed Forces to conduct peacekeeping in a UN context, intelligence in a UN context, an
examination of the role of intelligence in recent peace operations, African and Japanese
contributions to peacekeeping, nonproliferation, the UN's role in resolving the Korean
conflict, Congressional oversight relating to intelligence support to UN peacekeeping, and
future issues. In one essay, Lieutenant Robert Allen, U.S. Navy, traces the coming of
intelligence to the UN Department of Peacekeeping Operations, the opening of the UN
Situation Center in 1993. In another, Captain James Edwards, U.S. Army, examines the
lessons to be learned in refugee operations from the capabilities of the UN High
Commissioner for Refugees—the collection, analysis and dissemination performed by its
Center for Documentation and Research, the center's refugee world—REFWORLD—
database.

Captain Audrey Hudgins, U.S. Army, performs pathfinding research on decisions
resulting in a new flow of intelligence to the International Atomic Energy Agency (IAEA),
writing:

> The experience in Iraq proved that the IAEA is capable of handling intelli-
> gence information. As a result, the U.S. Intelligence Community and the IAEA
> have extended this cooperation to other regions of the world, namely North
> Korea and Iran. The usefulness of intelligence can be seen in the IAEA's han-
> dling of North Korea. Hans Blix, IAEA Director General, traveled to Pyongy-
> ang to make final arrangements for the IAEA's first inspection required under
> the provisions of the safeguards agreement. At that time, the IAEA apparently
> utilized information provided by the U.S. Intelligence Community to challenge
> the veracity of North Korea's nuclear declaration. During a recent IAEA mis-
> sion to Iran, Iranian officials asked the Agency to identify locations they
> wished to visit. On the basis of intelligence and other information from mem-
> ber states, IAEA officials picked a number of sites, all of which were visited.
> Future negotiations with other countries might also be aided by the interna-
> tional use of intelligence. The number of clandestine programs that exist
> throughout the world remains to be seen, but it has become clear that neither
> the IAEA nor the U.S. Intelligence Community can accomplish in isolation the
> objectives called for by the common interests. The IAEA verification regime is
> best supported by the employment of foreign intelligence information, as the
> Iraq experience has proved.[19]

In parallel with the publication of this new college book, Major Stewart Bentley, U.S.
Army, has had a revision of his Joint Military Intelligence College Master's thesis on the
role of the Dutch resistance and its cooperation with OSS in World War II—a work entitled
Orange Blood and Silver Wings: The Role of the Dutch Resistance During Operation

MARKET GARDEN—accepted by *Studies in Intelligence* for the CIA 50th Anniversary issue. This carefully researched intelligence history is rich in detail and bears importance messages for future operations.

Talented, highly motivated young professionals are making fresh contributions to the method, vocabulary, body of doctrine, and fundamental theory of the intelligence discipline. They are researching and writing well. They are contributing to the literature. They are producing the dinkum oil.

CHAPTER 6
SAFECRACKERS: THE PAST, PRESENT, AND FUTURE
OF U.S. INTELLIGENCE

The intelligence professional's most complex challenge is to describe the threat, bound its capabilities, and forecast its intentions. We can learn, the author told his audience in this 1998 speech delivered at the Georgia Institute of Technology, from the lessons of historical intelligence successes—the lessons of the arts of illusion and deception, of avoiding mindset, and of inducing mindset in others. History documents the struggles and the achievements, the technological ingenuity, and the breakthroughs of those Americans who cracked KGB ciphers, who placed the first photographic satellites in orbit, and who handled well-placed spies and double agents. Now, when the United States faces new and emerging threats—the threats of rogue nations, terrorism, and weapons of mass destruction—the coming generation of intelligence professionals must be drawn from the broadest cross-section and embody the fullest range of talent of the American people. That generation will be the "safecrackers" of the 21st century.

In this information age, the term "virtual reality" is subject to a variety of interpretations:

> In England recently, a man ran a red light, and a police camera took a picture of his car in the intersection. The police sent the man a citation, along with a picture of his car. The man wrote out a check, took a picture of it and sent the photograph of the check to [the] police. The police ... sent back a photograph of a pair of handcuffs. The man paid the fine promptly.[1]

There are other realities. Fifty-one years ago this July, President Harry S. Truman signed the National Security Act of 1947 into law creating the defense, intelligence, and foreign policy framework that provides today for the security of the United States. Later in his tenure as President, Truman inscribed a photo portrait that hangs in the sunny, marbled first-floor hallway of Central Intelligence Agency headquarters: "To the CIA," he wrote, "—a necessity to the President of the United States—from one who knows."

THE THREAT REMAINS

From the late 1940s through the early 1990s, the CIA—to be joined by the National Security Agency and the Defense Intelligence Agency—and the broader U.S. Intelligence Community developed and deployed the people, the tools, and the tradecraft required for strategic deterrence, conventional conflict, and political action in the Cold War era. In 1998, the NATO-Warsaw Pact rivalry is history, but the requirement continues for intelligence on foreign strategic nuclear weapons systems, for intelligence on foreign conventional force structures and capabilities, and for intelligence on the political direction and intentions of other nations. These standing needs for intelligence—incredibly demanding in and of themselves—have been joined by new ranks of requirements to meet a new era, an era in which a new, emerging, supplanting layer of lawlessness is spreading, often at cyberspace speed, across the globe.

"As the new millennium approaches," Secretary of Defense William S. Cohen wrote in November 1997, "the United States faces a heightened prospect that regional aggressors, third-rate armies, terrorist cells, and even religious cults will wield disproportionate power by using—or even threatening to use—nuclear, biological, or chemical weapons against our troops in the field and our people at home." [2]

On 28 January 1998, Director of Central Intelligence George Tenet, Director of the Defense Intelligence Agency Lieutenant General Patrick M. Hughes, and Assistant Secretary of State for Intelligence and Research Phyllis Oakley testified before the Senate Select Committee on Intelligence concerning the issue of threats to the national security. Each identified the proliferation of biological, chemical, and nuclear weapons—the spread of weapons of mass destruction—as the most serious threat to the nation.

The multi-dimensional challenge for intelligence professionals in this new era ranges on one plane from the fathoming of the terrorist's mind to the fathoming of the designs of entire rogue nations. Much earlier in this century, the terrorist in Joseph Conrad's *The Secret Agent* gave us a glimpse into one such mind:

> I have always dreamed of a band of men absolute in their resolve to discard all scruples in the choice of means, strong enough to give themselves frankly the name of destroyers, and free from the taint of that resigned pessimism which rots the world. No pity for anything on earth, including themselves, and death enlisted for good and all in the service of humanity—that's what I would have liked to see. [3]

The Venezuelan-born terrorist Ilyich Ramirez Sanchez was better known as Carlos the Jackal. His two best known "trademarks were to become a fearsome expertise with firearms—his favorite method of killing was a bullet between the eyes—and a thorough indifference to human life." [4] Last year, during the triple-murder trial leading to his life sentencing in a courtroom in Paris, he mouthed his own fierce beliefs: "The world is my domain," he said. . . . "I loudly and clearly claim moral responsibility with Palestinian groups and personal responsibility for all acts of war carried out by the PFLP [Popular Front for the Liberation of Palestine]. And I am proud of this." [5]

Richard Butler, head of the UN Special Commission monitoring Iraq, has in recent remarks captured a fraction of the challenges posed by today's rogue nations:

> The Iraqis have, according to Butler, "never" provided a credible explanation of what has happened to between 40 and 70 missile warheads that were filled with chemical or biological weapons. [6] "They lied for four and a half years about the very existence of a biological weapons program. They just flat out denied that they had one. When we presented them with evidence to the contrary, they said, oops, sorry. That was a lie." [7] Butler has been quoted as saying

that Iraq had enough biological material such as anthrax and botulin toxin to "blow away Tel Aviv," a major Israeli city.[8]

The intelligence professional must instinctively shift and reshift focus between the plane of a threat's designs and the plane of a threat's practices. Working from an expert knowledge base, the intelligence analyst ideally is able not only to describe the threat, the target, the subject of inquiry but also to bound its capabilities and forecast its intentions—that is, *ideally*. In December 1997, the Director of Central Intelligence's Persian Gulf War Illnesses Task Force published a report entitled "Lessons Learned: Intelligence Support on Chemical and Biological Warfare During the Gulf War and on Veterans' Illnesses Issues." The report presented 19 sets of recommendations, a total of 74 recommendations, all designed to improve the effectiveness of intelligence in future operations.

The report dwelled on the Intelligence Community's shortcomings relating to demolition by U.S. forces of chemical munitions at the Khamisiyah weapons storage site in southern Iraq at the end of the conflict. Prior to the Gulf War, and based on the analytical culture of the late 1980s, analysts had searched for S-shaped bunkers when they looked for suspect chemical weapons storage sites:

> In the years following the war, however, it became clear that S-shaped bunkers were not a reliable signature for the presence of chemical munitions; in many cases the Iraqis had hidden munitions outside bunkers to protect them from Coalition airstrikes. . . . [T]he analytical focus on S-shaped bunkers—in conjunction with incomplete searches that missed the information from the mid-1980s and with different names in multiple databases for the site—led to the exclusion of Khamisiyah from lists in preparation for the war.[9]

The report's recommendations underlined the need to avoid analytical bias, the need to encourage open-minded alternative thinking, the need periodically to review, question, and evaluate assessments based on limited intelligence, to ensure that uncertainties in assessments are clearly articulated, and to have a briefing on Khamisiyah included in a course at the Joint Military Intelligence College—which has been done, and more.

DECEPTION, MINDSET, AND ILLUSION

Learning from the lessons of the Gulf War is of tremendous importance to the United States. To examine the issues bearing on the absence of S-shaped bunkers at Khamisiyah is to examine a single cell among millions forming the body of 21st century intelligence work. To understand that S-shaped bunkers are not necessarily the storage sites for chemical munitions is to ask whether an adversary will then build phony S-shaped bunkers to deceive. The intelligence professional must battle the mind's embrace of bias, its enduring passion for the status quo, its ennui at the very suggestion of the need for an alternative view. The history of war and the history of intelligence provide instructive lessons in the values and the pitfalls of deception, mindset, and illusion.

A. Denis Clift

Writing of his experiences while a Lieutenant Commander in the Royal Navy during World War II, Ewen Montagu recalled a brainstorming session in London after the Allies had North Africa in hand. Sicily was next in line, and the challenge was how to deceive the Germans into reinforcing elsewhere. Montagu asked:

> Why shouldn't we get a body, disguise it as a staff officer, and give him really high-level papers which show clearly that we are going to attack somewhere else. We won't have to drop him on land, as the aircraft might have come down in the sea on the way round into the Med. He would float ashore with the papers in either France or Spain.[10]

With the agreement of surviving relatives, a dear soul who had died of pneumonia was brought into action as Major William Martin, Royal Marines, fitted with uniform, personal papers, and a locked dispatch case containing a personal and most secret letter from General Nye to General Alexander—the very highest level of British command. Martin was launched from the submarine *Seraph* off the coast of Spain. His body was recovered by a fisherman, and his papers were delivered by the Spaniards to the Germans where they moved first to the German Intelligence Service, were judged authentic and sent on to the High Command. German plans were adjusted; the deception had succeeded.

In planning this deception, thinking through its most minute details, Montagu reasoned as follows:

> You are a British Intelligence officer; you have an opposite number in the enemy Intelligence, say (as in the last war), in Berlin; and above him is the German Operational Command. What you, a Briton with a British background, think can be deduced from a document does not matter. It is what *your opposite number,* with his German knowledge and background, will think that matters—what construction *he* will put on the document. Therefore, if you want *him* to think such-and-such a thing, you must give him something which will make *him* (and not *you*) think it. But he may be suspicious and want confirmation; you must think out what inquiries will *he* make (not what inquiries would *you* make) and give him the answers to those inquiries so as to satisfy him. In other words, you must remember that a German does not think and react as an Englishman does, and you must put yourself into his mind.[11]

Knowing what the subject of your interest is thinking, knowing the machinery of that thought process, and acting from the strength of that knowledge is at the heart of intelligence. Just months before Major Martin went to war, the allies had tremendous strength of information and knowledge to help them achieve victory in the crucial North African battle of Alam Halfa. ULTRA intercepts provided Rommel's objectives; a compromised German espionage operation provided a channel for deception reports. Study of captured German maps revealed poor knowledge of the battlefield terrain:

> The allies knew that the sands in and around the Ragil depression would not support armored vehicles. . . . Eighth Army cartographers made a "false-

going" map that showed good hard ground in the Ragil area. The deception was implemented by putting the map in a vehicle deliberately disabled in a minefield. German scouts retrieved the map and delivered it up the chain of command.[12]

Illusion and deception in the world of intelligence are not limited to the battlefield. Moving closer to the present:

When cold war spies wanted to disappear, they went to see Tony Mendez, the master mask-maker, the Central Intelligence Agency's chief of disguise. . . . Mendez worked with Hollywood makeup men and hardened CIA case officers to perfect the craft of creating counterfeit people. He helped create the escape plan, the false identifies and the disguises that got six Americans out of revolutionary Teheran while others were held hostage in 1980. . . . He was the man who helped CIA officers disappear into the world's back alleys. "It's not just the makeup," Mr. Mendez said. "Disguise is not just the face you present. It's the 6,000-year-old secrets, the capability to create illusions. The essence is illusion and deception."[13]

To become proficient in the arts of illusion and deception; to have the discipline allowing at the same time for the avoidance of mindset and the inducement of mindset in others; to have these qualities is to prepare for future effectiveness as an intelligence professional.

SCIENCE AND TECHNOLOGY

Looking beyond these qualities, as the new millennium approaches, to recall, in part, the Secretary of Defense's framework of challenges, science and technology will make contributions of importance—beyond the imaginations of most—to the capabilities and effectiveness of U.S. intelligence. As a point of departure consider two contributions from the past: from the codebreakers, and from the satellite makers.

The National Security Agency's Center for Cryptologic History has documented a remarkable chapter in SIGINT history, the work of the Army's Signal Intelligence Service begun in 1939 and accelerated in World War II—work that would acquire the codename VENONA, work involving the collection and the complex challenge of decoding Soviet diplomatic communications. The NSA documents identify that "Miss Gene Grabeel, a young Signal Intelligence Service employee who had been a school teacher only weeks earlier, started the project."[14] Preliminary analysis indicated that the Soviets had five cryptographic systems in play: for their trade representatives, for their diplomats, for the KGB, and two for the GRU—the first for naval intelligence and the second for the Soviet Army General Staff Intelligence Directorate and attachés abroad.

During 1943, another dedicated young American working the project, Lieutenant Richard Hallock, who had left his archeological research at the University of Chicago for reserve active duty, discovered a weakness in the trade traffic code leading to progress on the other systems. A year later, another analyst broke into the KGB cipher system

A. Denis Clift

SAFECRACKER. It would take several more months before the analysts would be able to read parts of this system—and to realize that they were inside the KGB.[15] By 1946, decoded messages contained the names of U.S. scientists working on the MANHATTAN PROJECT. By 1947, the Army alerted the FBI to mounting signals intelligence evidence pointing to a major Soviet spy operation underway in the United States.

With the Soviets having thus penetrated the United States and having developed their own nuclear weapons capability, U.S. leaders attached increasing urgency to acquiring hard facts about Soviet strategic and conventional military force capabilities—a tall order when dealing with a closed-society target covering one-sixth of the earth's land surface. In the mid-1950s the United States embarked on a photographic-reconnaissance satellite development program—CORONA. The challenges, not to be overly complex when speaking at this institute of technology, were threefold: first to build such a satellite and successfully place it in orbit; second, to have it perform its photographic mission from space; and third, to recover the film from the camera. There would be a dozen failures, four years of tremendous effort, before the first successful mission in 1960.

The public was led to believe that the Thor booster rockets being launched from Vandenberg Air Force Base were part of the unclassified environmental, space-biomedical research DISCOVERER program. During the first, unsuccessful missions, even when the Thors fired successfully and the satellites attained orbit, the cameras malfunctioned. "The system was designed to operate without pressurization . . . and the acetate base film being used was tearing or breaking in the high vacuum existing in space and causing the camera to jam." [16] Film experts and chemists, dedicated Americans working at Eastman Kodak, revolutionized film technology, providing CORONA with a new polyester-based film able to capture the reconnaissance-quality images required while withstanding the rigors of space.

With their photographic missions completed, the film capsules were designed to separate from the satellite and return to earth, deploying a parachute after atmospheric re-entry. The Air Force had the mission of recovering the film capsule by flying recovery aircraft just over the blooming canopy of the descending parachute and snagging the shrouds with a trailing trapeze wire. Here the revolutionary CORONA intelligence system drew on a fresh dimension of American ingenuity and courage. Colonel Philip Rowe, one of the pilots for these flights, would describe the mission as follows:

> An array of grappling hooks and cables hung below and behind the transport to engage the parachute. Hooking the parachute without flying into the canopy or fouling the propellers in the lines required considerable flying skill and preci-sion. . . . A winch equipped with hydraulic brakes stood ready to unwind almost 1,500 feet of cable in barely four seconds as the hooks engaged the parachute. Braking would slow the cable to bring the payload into steady trail behind the plane. Then . . . the winch would wind the cable to draw the para-chute and payload into the cargo bay. It was dangerous work for the cargo han-dlers too . . . The rapidly unwinding cable could become fouled; instant death awaited the crewman caught by that metallic snake.[17]

Owing to the incredible teamwork of thousands, the CORONA photographic satellite program succeeded, with invaluable intelligence contributions during the Cold War. The satellite system, now on display in the Smithsonian's Air and Space Museum, is at the same time a monument to technological advancement and an incredible "you mean that thing really worked?" contraption.

ADDITIONAL HUMAN DIMENSIONS

The human dimension of intelligence has incredibilities greater still. The life and the role of a single individual offer a "tip-of-the-iceberg" example. In December 1997, the Associated Press reported the death at age 83 of Eddie Chapman, "a safecracker who became a valued British double agent during World War II, and the only Briton with the dubious honor of being awarded Germany's Iron Cross."[18] When the Germans overran Great Britain's Channel Islands early in the war they found the near-legendary robber Chapman in jail there. He offered them his services; they took him back to Germany, trained him in sabotage, then slipped him into England in 1942 to blow up an aircraft factory.

Chapman made contact with the British government and reported his mission. The target factory was camouflaged so that German aerial reconnaissance would report its destruction. Chapman was sent back to Germany by the British secret service as a double agent, decorated, and entered into training on the targeting of V-1 buzz bombs and V-2 rockets. He reentered England where he collaborated with his British handlers, feeding the Germans false targeting data. At the end of the war, his prison sentences were suspended. He was dropped by the secret service because of his indiscretions, and lived several years in Algeria before returning once more to England for his final years running a health farm north of London.[19]

The handling of spies and the turning of agents are at the heart of intelligence operations. The challenges they pose, the skills they require, the stresses they place are central to the life of the operator. In the United States, the role of the clandestine services is the subject of continuing scrutiny by the executive, legislative, and judicial branches of government, the media, and the public, balancing on the one hand President Eisenhower's observation that "the American public has always viewed with repugnance everything that smacks of the spy,"[20] and on the other hand the recognition across the nation that such operations correctly managed and overseen are essential to U.S. security.

The intelligence world is not unique, but it has qualities that must be understood and must be part of the vision, the direction, the discipline, and the empathy of the intelligence leader at the approach of the new millennium. Talented, informed, professional leadership is critical to the prospects for effective intelligence, for intelligence successes of core value to the nation in the years ahead. And one need look only at snapshots of two Directors of Central Intelligence who served back-to-back in the 1970s to sense how different each leader, and each leader's message, have been, to reflect on the impact that such swings in leadership must have on those charged with handling the Eddie Chapmans of the world, to reflect on the qualities that future leaders should bring.

A. Denis Clift

In his recent biography of former President and Director of Central Intelligence George Bush, Herbert Parmet wrote:

> George Bush plunged into his work at Langley. A story soon made the rounds describing Bush during a morning meeting with his senior staffers at the beginning of his tenure with the troubled agency. He turned to them, according to accounts that made his career at Langley almost legendary, and said, "What are they trying to do to *us*?" He was, he wanted them to know, one of them. He understood their shattered morale. "He does these things instinctively," said [former DCI William] Colby, who witnessed both the gloom and the Bush factor. It was his sense of leadership. It's his character.[21]

Compare this to the cool, distanced tone of the words that DCI Bush's successor DCI, Stansfield Turner, chose in his memoirs on his years at Langley, discussing a key decision early in his leadership:

> The convulsive reaction to the elimination of 820 positions in the espionage branch reflected the broader concern that human intelligence was being downgraded or pushed aside. In fact, no significant resource or operational authorization that the espionage branch requested was refused. I did, though, give more of my time to the technical systems. . . . Uncovering intentions is the strong point of human espionage, but it is an exaggeration to say that only espionage can do that.[22]

THE COMING GENERATION

There is no argument that effective intelligence is a necessity for the nation. There is argument aplenty as to whether that necessity is being met. To be effective, U.S. intelligence will need informed leaders, and U.S. intelligence will need unquestioned talent and ability in its practitioners.

There is a question as to whether the nation in fulfilling its intelligence responsibilities is benefiting from the true breadth and depth of talent and creativity resident in the American people. The rights of all Americans that ring in opening lines of the Declaration of Independence are as familiar as they are glorious: "We hold these truths to be self-evident, that all Men are created equal, that they are endowed by their creator with certain unalienable Rights, that among these are Life, Liberty and the Pursuit of Happiness." The words shaping accompanying responsibilities, no less important, of all Americans, the words that close the Declaration, are words less-often said: "And for the support of this Declaration, with a firm reliance on the Protection of divine Providence, we mutually pledge to each other our Lives, our Fortunes, and our sacred Honor."

There has been a positive phenomenon at work in the nation in recent times, a growing phenomenon that should contribute to a better fulfillment of our mutual pledge—a phenomenon that should help to ensure that our future needs for effective intelligence are met. At Boston University, Harvard, Georgetown, Kentucky, South Carolina, Texas A&M,

and a steadily growing number of colleges and universities across the United States, course work and courses on intelligence are being included in both undergraduate and graduate curricula.

Intelligence, its history, role, structure, and practice, its value to our democracy, and the opportunities it offers for students weighing future careers, have a formal place in academic examination, no less so, for example, than military science, political science, international commerce, and international affairs. In earlier decades—prior to 1972—a very broad spectrum of young Americans first learned of intelligence, with some entering the field while serving their obligatory tours of duty in the Armed Services. From this large pool, a steady flow of analysts, cryptanalysts, scientists, engineers, visionaries, future clandestine agents, and future leaders entered the Intelligence Community. Tremendous talent still flows from the Services to the community. However, with military service now voluntary and the Armed Forces drawing down in size, the spectrum of Americans is narrowing, and the pool is growing smaller. At the turn of this century, campuses increasingly are becoming an additional point of first learning.

The next generation of intelligence professionals must be drawn from the broadest cross-section and embody the broadest range of talent and capabilities of the American people. In an era of global lawlessness, new minds, fresh approaches must address the interfaces between foreign intelligence and domestic law enforcement, to cite one example, if we as a nation are to meet the challenges to our national security while safeguarding and respecting our Constitution. Just as an earlier generation of Americans cracked the Soviet SAFECRACKER code and pioneered a way to keep the CORONA film from cracking—just as an earlier generation of allies devised effective deception and illusion through the handling of the safecracker double agent and the sending of Major Martin to war—so the cyberspace generation of American intelligence professionals must excel.

The reservoir of talent, the fresh concepts, the means to excel are present in the upcoming generation. It is essential that those entrusted with education and those entrusted with building and staffing the future Intelligence Community, join to examine the best approaches—indeed alternative approaches—to ensuring that this broadest cross-section of Americans understands the role of intelligence, the work of intelligence, and the opportunities intelligence offers as a professional field. As the next in its series of conferences, the Joint Military Intelligence College looks forward a year from now to bringing together representatives from the academic community—from colleges and universities teaching intelligence, from those interested in teaching intelligence—with representatives of the Intelligence Community to consider the course we are setting for ourselves and any compass corrections that might bring us more quickly to our goals.

And for those studying intelligence, looking forward to joining the next generation of intelligence professionals—to joining the world of safecrackers in the 21st century, when your professor quotes, "He was simply a patriot in the sense of a man who believing in the spirituality of a national existence could not bear to see that spirit enslaved,"[23] and when he asks you for identification of the individual's most likely religious, political, or national roots-Iraqi? Croat, Serb, Muslim in Bosnia? Or Belfast IRA?—question the professor's

A. Denis Clift

premise, skirt the mindset trap, sift through alternative possibilities, and, having tapped the growing sources and data banks you are learning to draw from expertly, reply: "None of the above." He was Polish. This was Joseph Conrad writing of his father in the risings against the Russians in 1863.

CLIFT NOTES

INTELLIGENCE AND THE NATION'S SECURITY

PART TWO

INTELLIGENCE IN MILITARY PLANNING AND OPERATIONS

CHAPTER 7
IN HIS OWN TIME, A MAN IS ALWAYS VERY MODERN

Quoting Joseph Conrad's observation that "In his own time a man is always very modern," the author opens this 1995 address to the Naval Postgraduate School with a review of some remarkable intelligence developments over recent decades. He notes that graduates of the Joint Military Intelligence College spearheaded many of the achievements—the blending of state-of-the-art technology with imagination and vision. The author underlines the importance of the College's programs to the education of intelligence professionals—citing the well-established Master of Science of Strategic Intelligence degree and the College's plans for a new Bachelor of Science in Intelligence degree.

One hundred years ago, a magnificent ship of the new, turn-of-the-century United States Navy—the 9,000-ton armored cruiser USS *Brooklyn*—was nearing completion on the construction ways of William Cramp and Sons in Philadelphia. Her trial crew would soon receive a bonus of $350,000 for pushing her to 21.91 knots. On 3 July 1898, off Santiago, Cuba, steaming on just two of her four engines, the *Brooklyn* would overtake the cruisers of Spanish Admiral Cervera one by one, inflicting severe damage as they attempted to flee the American blockade.

The *Brooklyn* may have been a source of inspiration for the U.S. Commissioner of Patents Charles Duell who, in 1899, urged President McKinley to abolish the Patent Office, saying, "Everything that can be invented has been invented."[1] The April 1966 *Naval Institute Proceedings* included a photograph of the cruiser in port, with sailors and top-hatted civilians gazing in admiration at her extreme ram bow, her "hundred foot stacks," and her gleaming white armored sides bristling with 8-inch and 5-inch turreted guns. Beside that photo ran a quote from Joseph Conrad, "In his own time a man is always very modern."

TIME MARCHES ON—AND SO DOES TECHNOLOGY

In fact, the *Brooklyn's* years as a state-of-the-art man of war were sharply numbered. Within five years, the new cruisers were 12,000-tonners; then came the 14,000-ton ten-inch-gunned "Big Ten" ships of the U.S. Armored Cruiser Squadron. Soon, all would be rendered obsolete with the arrival of the *Dreadnought*.[2]

In our own time, as we approach the turn of another century, man is certainly still very modern. With the pace of events on our shrinking planet and in our quickening travels through the universe of cyberspace, however, it is becoming harder and harder to find people such as the Commissioner of Patents or Dr. Dionysus Lardner who, in 1823, said that "Rail travel at high speed is not possible because passengers, unable to breathe, would die of asphyxia."[3]

Instead, increasingly, we are confronted with the challenge of ensuring that the systems we bring into play—even the most modern, commercially available, off-the-shelf systems acquired with relative speed—are not already obsolete on their first day of operation. Throughout this human experience, at the turn of whatever century, the mind has remained the uniquely magnificent instrument for the conception, charting, and provision of our future well-being. Education of the mind is the first step toward attaining and sustaining that well-being-our security, our prosperity, our quality of life, our place as world leader.

THE JMIC AND EMERGING TECHNOLOGY

The Joint Military Intelligence College (JMIC) is unique in offering the nation's only accredited graduate degree in strategic intelligence—the Master of Science of Strategic Intelligence (MSSI)—authorized by statute of the Congress and with full academic accreditation by the Commission on Higher Education of the Middle States Association of Colleges and Schools. The College is entrusted with educating future leaders who are full partners with their policy, planning, and operations counterparts; leaders able to anticipate and deliver the intelligence required at national, theater, and tactical levels; leaders who constitute an important asset to this nation.

Earlier this year, the Chief of Naval Operations, Admiral Mike Boorda, told JMIC students that intelligence has a seat with him at his table from start to finish of all key meetings. That is quite a statement. It is a far cry from the earlier Navy tendency to say "Thanks for the brief, you can leave now" on one side and "Sorry, green door, you are not cleared" on the other. I remember being aboard the carrier *Hancock* on an operational readiness inspection in 1959 and watching as reports that we had just published at the Fleet Intelligence Center Pacific were logged in, then locked away in a safe in mint condition, not read by a single member of the ship's company. To an Ensign, that was somewhat disillusioning, to say the least.

I will dwell in these remarks on the emerging partnership among operators, planners, intelligence officers, communicators, and logisticians, and what underlies that partnership. That partnership is a fact, and it is more than welcome; it is essential. It is as real as the demolition of the wall between the National Military Command Center (NMCC) and the National Military Joint Intelligence Center (NMJIC) in the Pentagon. It is as real as the top priority that four-star theater commanders place on having the Joint Worldwide Intelligence Communications System (JWICS) up and running at their commands.

Rear Admiral Tom Wilson, currently Vice Director for Intelligence on the Joint Staff, former Director of Intelligence for U.S. Atlantic Command, and a graduate of the JMIC Class of '75, offered an excellent glimpse at this new reality in an article on Operation UPHOLD DEMOCRACY in Haiti published earlier this year. He offered a description of the Atlantic Command's (ACOM) data exchange network, ACOM Net. It provides

> the theater with expanded connectivity to all components—Forces Command, Air Combat Command, Atlantic Fleet, and Marine Forces Atlantic—as well as staffs identified for regular training as JTF Commands—namely XVIII Airborne

Corps, III Corps, Eighth Air Force, Twelfth Air Force, Second Fleet, and Second Marine Expeditionary Force. [He described the veritable revolution in extended intelligence connectivity arising from the fact that] from the intelligence perspective the ACOM Net is completely interoperable with the SCI JWICS network. During UPHOLD DEMOCRACY, key operational commanders—such as JTF-180 and TF-185 on USS *Mount Whitney*, JTF-190 in Port au Prince, TF-186 at Pope Air Force Base Fort Bragg, TG-185.2 on USS *Wasp*, and JTF-160 in Guantanamo Bay—ACOM components, and supporting Commands—such as Transportation Command and the Defense Intelligence Agency/National Military Joint Intelligence Center—were linked via SCI VTC, that is to say video teleconferencing at the sensitive-compartmented intelligence level.[4]

The JMIC is educating future leaders in an era in which the emerging partnership between intelligence and operations is a direct result of the experiences—such as UPHOLD DEMOCRACY—and the lessons learned from crisis management and combat since the early 1980s, well before the demise of the Soviet Union and the end of the Cold War. It was in the early 1980s that the Department of Defense and the Intelligence Community came to grips with the fact that the nation's multi-billion dollar intelligence capabilities at the national level were not properly tailored to surge immediately to provide the intelligence required by deployed tactical-level forces.

In the late 1970s, a Navy Captain by the name of William O. Studeman was assigned to ONI. He authored a proposal recommending national-level teams that could deploy on very short notice to provide the initial intelligence link between the national and tactical levels. That proposal was forwarded up the Defense chain, but action was not taken on it.[5] Bill Studeman, however, moved from one important assignment to the next: from Director of Naval Intelligence, to Director of the National Security Agency, to Deputy Director of Central Intelligence. As he did so, he forged important new links, not only between intelligence and operations, but more challenging still, between and among the agencies of the Intelligence Community. Admiral Studeman, JMIC Class of '67, has just been nominated to the College's Board of Visitors.

INTELLIGENCE SUPPORT TO WARFIGHTERS

It would take the grim bombing of the Marine Barracks in Lebanon and the October 1983 findings of the Long Commission—including the recommendation that "the Secretary of Defense establish an all-source fusion center which would tailor and focus all-source intelligence support to U.S. commanders involved in military operations in high threat, conflict, or crisis"[6] —to spark the creation by DIA of the National Military Intelligence Support Teams (NMIST). These three-to-four-member teams were ready to deploy on a few hours notice with suitcase-sized equipment, able to provide the tactical commander in the field or aboard ship with satellite-relayed secure voice, data, and imagery links with the national community. The teams placed first priority on allowing that commander to draw the specific information desired from the national level. At first, NMIST worked in parallel with comparable NSA and CIA teams. Now, all work in concert as the highly advanced National Intelligence Support Teams (NIST) that deploy today.

A. Denis Clift

The flow of more timely, responsive, national-level intelligence also moved to tactical commanders in other new ways through other new channels in the early-to-mid-1980s. The Central American Joint Intelligence Team was formed at the national level to provide fused, all-source, tactical intelligence for use by the Commander in Chief Southern Command. In 1986, in the wake of the Berlin nightclub bombing, all-source operational support packages were prepared at the national level and flown to the F-111s in the United Kingdom and to the Sixth Fleet naval air units aboard the USS *America* and USS *Coral Sea* so that they could participate in the retaliatory strikes on Tripoli.

With the crisis and conflict in the Persian Gulf in 1990-1991, the flow of tailored national-level intelligence reached dramatic new levels. Eleven NMIST teams were deployed. A Department of Defense Joint Intelligence Center (JIC) would be created within the National Military Intelligence Center (NMIC) to shape and manage the two-way flow. A JIC Forward was established in Riyadh to receive the flow at the theater level. While the lessons learned from this crisis and conflict underscored the magnitude of work still ahead to permit the truly effective flow of intelligence down from the theater level to the tactical commander, the results achieved by the intelligence-operations partnership were remarkable. As General Colin Powell, Chairman of the Joint Chiefs of Staff, said at the time: "No combat commander has ever had as full and complete view of his adversary as did our field commander. Intelligence support to Operations DESERT SHIELD and DESERT STORM was a success story."[7]

DESERT STORM was a coalition campaign, the dawning of a new era in which intelligence would flow not only to U.S. and allied forces, but also to coalition partners. It became an era requiring fresh attention to how best to protect sources and methods while providing the intelligence required. The importance of U.S. intelligence to the success of the campaign was confirmed in no uncertain terms by the Defense Minister of France. *The New York Times* reported his surprisingly candid views in an 8 May 1991 article that opened:

> In the first public recognition by France that it was ill-prepared to fight the Persian Gulf war, Defense Minister Pierre Joxe conceded today that French Forces were overwhelmingly dependent on military intelligence provided by the United States. Announcing plans to unite the country's often competing military intelligence bodies into a single branch of the armed forces, he said at a military seminar here: "Without allied intelligence in the war we would have been almost blind." Mr. Joxe urged that intelligence should be as much a part of France's military structure as are its nuclear deterrent, its conventional forces, and its ability to project its power abroad.[8]

TECHNOLOGY AND THE GLOBAL REACH OF INTELLIGENCE

Since the early-to-mid-1980s, the global reach of timely U.S. intelligence, referred to by Minister Joxe, has benefited from the near-real-time links provided by communications satellites and from the accessibility of information in computerized databases. It has also benefited from the surge capabilities of the NMIST. It has been strengthened dramatically by the arrival of the JWICS and a companion, desktop tool for the analyst—the Joint Deployable Intelligence Support System (JDISS).

The JWICS capabilities include video teleconferencing, imagery transfer, electronic data transfer, publishing, and video broadcasting. All this is possible at the highest levels of classification and all interoperable with the Theater Commander in Chief's overall communications network, as Admiral Tom Wilson's essay on UPHOLD DEMOCRACY reported for Atlantic Command. JWICS, first tested in early 1991, was deployed in DESERT STORM and now continues to be installed at more than 125 defense and intelligence locations worldwide.[9]

JWICS now contributes to the defense capabilities of the United States, thanks in large part to the vision of Rear Admiral Ted Sheafer. Admiral Sheafer conducted important work on secure, face-to-face, picture-phone communications when he was serving as the senior intelligence officer of the Atlantic Fleet and Atlantic Command in Norfolk. He continued to develop and expand on this work while Director of Intelligence on the Joint Staff and as Deputy Director of the Defense Intelligence Agency, as well as during his final active-duty tour as Director of Naval Intelligence. Admiral Sheafer is a graduate of the JMIC, Class of '67.

Mr. Steve Schanzer, the Intelligence Community Management Staff's Director of the Intelligence Systems Secretariat—himself the father of the brand new, classified, Intelink information service—has described Admiral Sheafer's work as follows:

> Rear Admiral Sheafer's vision was to bring the indications and warning analyst to the decisionmaker, regardless of location, at any time, on a moment's notice. . . . This led to the introduction of video technology into the I&W process. But the introduction was not, and I emphasize not, technology for its own sake. It was the recognition of the value of the information obtained with the technology. It was the recognition that emerging technology only had value in the context of how it would contribute to the success of the organization. In this case, it was the improvement in the quality, timeliness, and credibility of warning intelligence to senior decisionmakers. [10]

The education that the officers, noncommissioned officers, and civilian professionals are receiving at the JMIC includes an examination of current and emerging systems and technologies. Even more time is devoted to every dimension of the quality of the intelligence that must flow through such systems. The words of a chief executive officer addressing a conference on the education of future engineers are fundamental and instructive. Discussing the leap in the power of computation and its impact on the research and work of engineering, he said: "We need people to understand what's behind the numbers. I've seen some absurd conclusions from people who looked only at the numbers without any other perspective to understand what those numbers meant or why those numbers made sense or didn't make sense."[11] In *The Seven Pillars of Wisdom,* T.E. Lawrence wrote: "Nine-tenths of tactics were certain enough to be teachable in schools; but the irrational tenth was like the kingfisher flashing across the pond, and in it lay the test for generals."[12]

At the College, we are in the business of educating future intelligence experts who will be there with the operational commander and the decisionmaker. Those experts expect to provide the intelligence required to help the general achieve all ten-tenths of the tactics. The need for such experts has been clearly demonstrated by our experiences in crisis and conflict since the early 1980s. In developing these experts, increased attention is being given to guarding against the notion, convenient in a time of personnel and budget cuts, that an analyst can be assigned to any target anywhere and bring the expertise required—for example, that a ground order of battle analyst is fully capable of providing expert advice wherever the ground operation may occur—Africa, Asia, Europe, or the Americas.

In an excellent paper entitled "Thoughts on Irregular Warfare," Jeffrey White, an analyst and Senior Executive with DIA, discusses the professional investment that the government must continue to make in foreign country and regional experts. Any analyst is expected to know the enemy's numbers, order of battle, command and control, and doctrine. Yet more is demanded of any expert:

> For the intelligence analyst looking at a tribal conflict, all of these traditional factors must be seen in the context of the micro-climate of that conflict. The struggle's history, its specific geography, its leaders and their roles and relations, the nature and capabilities of its warriors, how they are developed and supported within the society, and the tradition of warfare; these become the essential elements of information for the intelligence analyst, policymaker, and commander.[13]

A NEW INTELLIGENCE AGENDA FOR MODERN TIMES

The pace of change is causing the Director of Central Intelligence to reassess U.S. covert actions and clandestine operations to determine whether expansion of such operations against new target sets is required. The focus of attention has shifted from Cold War actions against communist governments and countering subversion overseas, to actions aimed at countering the spread of nuclear weapons and other weapons of mass destruction and to actions against international drug smuggling, international terrorism, or international crime.[14]

The complex dynamic also includes the intelligence requirements of the information age. Lieutenant General Kenneth Minihan, USAF, a distinguished graduate of the Naval Postgraduate School, Class of '79, addresses the need to refocus on infrastructure analysis, modeling and simulation, and systems analysis. He emphasizes the need for defense intelligence to control the information realm

> so that we can exploit it while protecting our information, information-based processes, and information systems from enemy action; exploit control of the

information to employ information warfare against the enemy; and enhance overall force effectiveness by fully developing information operations. [He speaks of the need to maintain] a virtual intelligence presence any place that we need to be anytime.[15]

The new intelligence agenda and challenges, the new systems, and the systems yet to be conceived around the turn of the century by those who in their own time will be very modern, as well as the longstanding requirements for expertise in collection, collection management, and analysis, are all part of the MSSI course of study.

I have already mentioned Admirals Studeman, Sheafer, and Wilson. Other College graduates at the top of the profession today include Vice Admiral Mike McConnell, Director of NSA, and Lieutenant General Paul Menoher, Assistant Chief of Staff, Intelligence, U.S. Army. Others, the next generation on their way up, include Marine Captain Mike Decker, Class of '88, now in the Senior Executive Service as the Marine Corps Deputy Assistant Chief of Staff for Intelligence, and Navy Lieutenant Mark Hooper, Class of '93, the Strategic Command's 1994 company grade officer of the year.

As you move to your next assignments, as you move up in your careers, be on the lookout for these JMIC graduates. Be on the lookout for talented young officers who should be encouraged to enter this Master's program. When naval officers graduate from JMIC, the Navy formally designates them as Joint Intelligence Subspecialists and assigns them the career subspecialty code of 0016P. That code, assigned only to JMIC graduates, identifies joint intelligence assignments. They will serve with you in outstanding fashion and will serve you well.

Earlier this year, Secretary of Education Richard Riley said, "If we want this country to remain a world leader, we have to make sure that the next generation is ready to address the technological challenges that will be confronting all of us."[16] Fully effective intelligence for our armed forces is no small part of that technological challenge. I am presently working in close cooperation with the Department of Education and the Congress to expand the JMIC degree-granting authority to meet that challenge better.

INTELLIGENCE EDUCATION WITH A MODERN VISION

Within the Intelligence Community and within the armed forces, growing numbers of highly motivated, talented, dedicated noncommissioned officers and intelligence technicians have acquired a number of college credits but do not yet have their bachelor's degree. Since 1992, the College has been offering a nine-month undergraduate intelligence program, with competitive enrollment from the services and agencies growing from 35 to 46 in this academic year.

Over the course of the next eight months, at the request of the Department of Education, we are teaching a prototype, fourth-year, degree-completion, Bachelor of Science in Intelligence (BSI) Program. Next June we will submit the records and academic credits of each student who successfully completes the BSI prototype to the Regents College of the State University of New York for credit validation and award of the Regents College undergraduate degree. We will then look forward to a site visit and, hopefully, favorable findings by a senior Department of Education Advisory Committee. With a green light from the Department of Education, the Department of Defense will forward our request via the Office of Management and Budget to the Congress, seeking statutory authority to grant the BSI degree, just as we now have authority to grant the MSSI degree.

This BSI academic program will provide a formal intelligence education that cannot be duplicated by any private or public non-federal college or university in the nation. Like the master's program, it will be unique because it will be taught at the highest level of classification, drawing on all sources and methods of intelligence. It is a BS degree that is structured to be remarkably cost-effective to the student, to the government, and to the nation. It is, in the vernacular of our times, a "seamless" program—taking highly motivated professionals at the right moment in their careers, providing them with the year of degree-completion study they require, and then returning them immediately to their profession, better prepared for career advancement and more senior responsibilities. Beyond this, in terms of the graduates it will produce, the BSI degree program will contribute to the sustained growth of the very heartwood of the nation.

This past June, Naval Academy Superintendent Admiral Charles Larson spoke of the unique, value-added nature of the service academies' education, which produces the "core of strong young leaders of character who are dedicated to the principles on which this nation was founded." He pointed out that "the service academies give us a source of stability that is very important not only to the military but to our society as a whole."[17] The same can be said for those in the BSI program.

Who are some of the talented professionals who will receive the BSI degree? They are the intelligence technicians who will be able to climb the career ladder to expert analyst. They are the Army Staff Sergeant and Sergeant First Class who will become tactical intelligence NCOs-in-charge at the battalion and brigade levels. They include the Air Force Master Sergeant directing collection operations on an RC-135 mission; the Navy Chief Petty Officer deploying as intelligence chief with his SEAL team; the Marine Corps Gunnery Sergeant who will deploy as intelligence chief with a Marine Expeditionary Force Command in joint task force operations. All these noncommissioned officers, with the BSI degree, will be able to open the door to Officer Candidate School and other accession programs. Wish us well as we seek this degree-granting authority. The professionals who receive the BSI degree will serve you and serve with you in outstanding fashion.[18]

We know from history that the eight-inch cruiser, if you will, of today will soon give way to the ten-incher of tomorrow; that the ultimate 14,000-ton Big Ten cruiser will be rendered obsolete by the Dreadnought. Adding the BSI degree to the MSSI degree, which has proven itself so grandly, will allow us further to strengthen the partnership between intelligence and operations, a partnership essential to national security at this turn of the century. We will be providing for the professionals who will be serving beyond the limits of our vision, even though that vision is very modern.

CHAPTER 8
FA34 + MSSI/2000 ≥ JV 2010

In this 1999 inaugural address to the first class of U.S. Army Functional Area 34 (FA34) students at Fort Huachuca, Arizona, the author focuses on the importance of intelligence in today's world of rapid changes—intelligence both as a professional discipline and as a subject for academic study. He calls attention to the range of classified and unclassified Master's theses being produced by students at the Joint Military Intelligence College, some of the most cutting-edge research on intelligence being performed anywhere. He applauds the growing teaching and study of intelligence at colleges and universities across the United States, believing that it will inform an increasingly larger cross-section of Americans on the role and place of intelligence in the American democracy—and the importance and rewards of service to the nation—at a time when they are still weighing decisions on their careers. He says that the growing partnership between the Army and the Joint Military Intelligence College, reflected in the new course at Fort Huachuca, is ensuring that some of the finest talent in the land will be helping to meet the nation's complex intelligence requirements. That partnership is a positive step toward achieving the objectives of Joint Vision 2010 (JV2010) envisioned by former Chairman of the Joint Chiefs of Staff General John Shalikashvili.

Colonel Bob White, members of the first Functional Area 34 Strategic Intelligence Officers' Course, thank you for your invitation. I am honored to be present at the creation of this new program of such importance to the military capabilities and to the security of the nation.

This is my first visit to Fort Huachuca. I was a student at intelligence school just 40 years ago, but you will forgive me if I tell you that my classrooms overlooked San Francisco Bay at Naval Air Station Alameda.

In fact, I am here both to speak, and as a student. The U.S. Army Intelligence School, Fort Huachuca, has a national reputation as a leader in advanced technology and technological innovation. It is the right moment for us to learn more about your capabilities.

It is also the right moment to consider this new program and the educational programs of the Joint Military Intelligence College (JMIC) in the context of the growing need for intelligence in an international era where the ground rules are rapidly changing. Accordingly, I am very pleased that you have asked me to talk about the work of the College.

I was having lunch with one of China's attachés the other day, and the conversation turned to Y2K. He feigned calm, cool, and collectedness, said that China is not too worried, that large sectors of the country will not be affected. Raising a hand just slightly, he said that the head of their Civil Air Organization had sent a Y2K advisory to China's airline managers stating that he expects each manager to be on his airline's first flight after midnight on

A. Denis Clift

January 1, 2000. Y2K is a remarkable issue, unique, one that has us engaging around the world with our relative strength, "can do" spirit, and national self-interest involved.

ECHOES OF GLORY AND A LEGACY OF DUTY

"If we are to be a really great people, we must strive in good faith to play a great part in the world. We cannot avoid meeting great issues. All we can determine for ourselves is whether we shall meet them well or ill."[1] Good words—not Y2K but TR. New York's Governor Teddy Roosevelt spoke those words at the Hamilton Club of Chicago almost 100 years ago to the day—10 April 1899. The Philippines, Cuba, Puerto Rico, and Hawaii were the issues he saw before the American people. "The guns that thundered off Manila and Santiago left us echoes of glory," he said, "but they also left us a legacy of duty. If we drove out a medieval tyranny only to make room for savage anarchy, we had better not have begun the task at all."[2]

Addressing the great national and international security issues confronting us today, Professor Lawrence Freedman has done some succinct packaging. He told a conference in St. Petersburg, Russia, this February:

> The range of potential enemies covers everything from fanatical terrorists to disaffected superpowers, while the means they might employ takes in a spectrum of means from the improvised explosive device in a shopping mall, to guerrilla ambushes, to traditional battles, to nuclear exchanges. Terrorists might gain access to weapons of mass destruction, while renegade states might insert bombs into public places.[3]

Director of Central Intelligence George Tenet struck a similar theme in opening his testimony on threats to U.S. citizens and the nation before the Senate Armed Services Committee earlier this year. "What is noteworthy," he told the committee, "is the manner in which so many issues are now intertwined and so many dangers mutually reinforcing."[4]

Great Britain's General Sir Michael Rose, adjusting his focus to look at the world through a peacekeeping lens, further refines the tough issues and challenges: 26 major conflicts in the world in regions where nation-states have ceased to exist; the greatest mass movements of populations—those in the Great Lakes area of Africa—in the history of mankind; 36 million of the world's peoples either refugees or displaced; and a quarter-million people—half children—killed each year. Rose, who commanded the UN Protection Force Bosnia-Herzegovina in the mid-1990s, says: "As we come to the end of the 20th century, armies everywhere need to review their defense strategies if they are going to be able to respond appropriately to the changing nature of conflict." Recalling the words of Dag Hammarskjold on peacekeeping, he says, "it is not a job for soldiers, but only soldiers can do it."[5]

The former Chairman of the Joint Chiefs of Staff, General John Shalikashvili, had earlier translated these visions of the emerging challenges to U.S. and allied interests into his vision of the armed forces we will have by the year 2010. Building from the fundamental proposition that our forces will be organized, trained, and equipped to defeat any adversary, he stated that forces optimized for wartime success have proven to be the best forces for peacekeeping, for humanitarian assistance, for operations other than war. In this complex environment, he said that "future leaders at all levels of command must understand the interrelationships among military power, diplomacy, and economic pressure, as well as the role of various government agencies and non-governmental actors, in achieving our security objectives."[6] Enhanced command and control and much improved intelligence will be essential to the success of future operations.

JV2010 AND THE JMIC

Much improved intelligence is the educational business of the Joint Military Intelligence College. Now in its 37th year, the College has the distinction of being the nation's only accredited institution of higher learning awarding the Master of Science of Strategic Intelligence and Bachelor of Science in Intelligence degrees. In terms of positive outcomes assessment, the College's graduates speak for themselves. Rear Admiral (select) Kevin Cosgriff is Director of the White House Situation Room. He was at the College just a few weeks ago to participate in a video on the institution—including mention that he looks for our alumni when he is recruiting and that he currently has three alumni on his staff. Lieutenant General Mike Hayden (Class of '80) was sworn in as the new Director of the National Security Agency on 30 March 1999. Rear Admiral Tom Wilson, Director of Intelligence on the Joint Staff and 1975 JMIC graduate, has been nominated by the President for promotion to Director, Defense Intelligence Agency at the rank of Vice Admiral—not a bad cornering of the market.

This past March, a member of the staff of the Supreme Allied Commander Europe in Belgium contacted the College on a Friday afternoon to say that a thesis produced by one of our graduate students—Army Major Richard Paquette—in August 1998, a work entitled *Ethnic Conflict: Kosovo and the Next Balkan War,* had been recommended as an outstanding research work on an issue of top priority. Would it be possible to have a copy? The thesis was on disc—all of our Master's candidates are now required to submit their work both on disc and in hard copy. The College's Director of Applied Research had the work in SHAPE's hands within minutes.[7]

A few weeks prior to this request from SHAPE, I had asked the Director of the College's Writing Center to give me a sampling of theses over the past year or two, which in his opinion represented good master's research on the tough menu of issues being addressed by the likes of General Rose, Professor Freedman, Director Tenet, and General Shalikashvili. Not surprisingly, Major Paquette's work was on his list. What were some of the others? To list just a few of them is to see the building blocks of the structure of intelligence in the years ahead—probing, critically constructive research and analysis by future leaders on issues central to their evolving, growing responsibilities.

In *Intelligence, Dominant Battlespace Knowledge, and the Warfighter,* Air Force Captain David Foglesong addresses what I would call a "high church" issue—the doctrine, flatly

A. Denis Clift

outdated but still alive at too many levels in too many places, that formally separates intelligence officers and operations officers, with the former responsible for information on the enemy and the latter for information on one's own forces. Captain Foglesong writes:

> Military intelligence officers of the 21st century will be vested with the responsibility to provide Dominant Battlespace Knowledge to the commander, as well as serving the traditional role of analyzing the enemy. They will be required to possess enemy, friendly, and battlespace environmental information and to use that information to accurately assess enemy intentions and capabilities.[8]

In two other theses, the authors come to grips with the challenges posed by General Sir Michael Rose, the issues, the ways in which intelligence can improve its contributions to operations other than war. U.S. Army Captain Chris Carver, in his thesis *Square Peg: Round Hole,* writes:

> The crystalline clarity of the objective of warfare, "close with and destroy the enemy," is replaced in Operations Other than War with the ambiguities of diplomatic, political, and humanitarian objectives in which the application of combat power may actually be counterproductive. . . . While the Special Operations Forces intelligence model is not the panacea for all Operations Other Than War intelligence ills, it does provide a model for intelligence improvement. It illustrates the advantages of a trained, language-capable, regionally-experienced and requirements-aware collection element.[9]

In *The Awakening,* Army Captain Peter Don proceeds from the benchmark that special forces missions—including special reconnaissance, unconventional warfare, direct action, foreign internal defense, and counterterrorism—are intelligence-driven and intelligence-dependent. He assesses fresh approaches to meeting the very particular intelligence requirements of such missions.[10]

These works bring to mind an observation by Australia's General John Sanderson when we met in Washington following his command of the UNTAC peacekeeping forces in Cambodia. "We didn't need more artillery pieces or help of that sort," he said—and I am paraphrasing. "It was an entirely different situation. We needed pipeline and people who could lay that pipeline to bring potable water to the villages."

Four recent JMIC theses address major dimensions of intelligence collection challenges: urban warfare, narcotics interdiction, technology transfer, and growing reliance on commercial capabilities. In *Concrete Hamlet,* Marine Captain Christian Veeris examines the lessons from the Vietnam-era combined action pacification program, lessons to be learned by Marines serving in future urban-area expeditionary forces, including greater emphasis on human-source intelligence reporting and the individual Marine's responsibilities in such reporting.[11] Marine Captain Michael McCrane also revisits the Vietnam conflict in his work, *Time-Sensitive Document Exploitation,* to highlight document exploitation lessons that can contribute to greater effectiveness in present and future drug enforcement operations.[12]

In *The National Security Implications of the Commercial Space Launch Industry,* Army Staff Sergeant Robert Ives examines the tensions between commerce and national security in terms of U.S. delivery of satellites to foreign launch markets and the level of risk that is acceptable in terms of transfer of technology.[13] And, in *Emptying a Bucket with a Spoon,* Air Force Second Lieutenant Darin Hoenle examines the risks associated with current reliance on commercial satellites for high-volume, real-time unmanned aerial vehicle (UAV) video transmissions.[14]

In the research field of weapons of mass destruction, Army First Lieutenant Jean M. Lewis addresses intelligence strategies to deal with new biotechnology threats:

> Modern methods of biotechnology have the potential to produce sophisticated biological weapons capable of distinguishing between or targeting specific genetic characteristics such as skin color, eye color, or hair color. Biotechnology can also manipulate benign and virulent microorganisms, creating pathogens that are highly virulent and for which no known cure exists. Some of the technology that may be used to produce these "super germ warfare" agents takes the form of dual-use technology, such as pharmaceutical or other consumer products. The dual-use technology is constantly transferred to the worldwide scientific community and is available indiscriminately.[15]

Such research by the College's master's students—being produced at both the classified and unclassified levels and being selected for publication and dissemination at both levels—shapes the cutting edge of some of the most important research on intelligence being performed anywhere in the world. It is, at the same time, part of a far broader process.

THE RICHER LANDSCAPE OF INTELLIGENCE IN THE 21st CENTURY

Two years ago, I addressed the Patterson School at the University of Kentucky on the new chapter being turned in the literature of intelligence, how government review was carefully, selectively approving publication of works with far greater specificity and, accordingly, of far greater value to a much broader audience—the audience of the American people. I cited Dewey Clarridge's memoirs, *A Spy for all Seasons,* and the Joint Military Intelligence College's freshly published, 24-author volume *Intelligence for Multilateral Decision and Action* as examples.

This past February, I read a newer work marking the further expansion of publication boundaries: *TOP SECRET INTRANET: How U.S. Intelligence Built INTELINK-The World's Largest, Most Secure Network.* It is a 380-page work, with a self-explanatory title and a CD-ROM bound inside the back cover. Published by Prentice Hall, it was written by former NSA executive Frederick Thomas Martin. From pages 53-56, the reader finds the instantiations of Intelink service—from Intelink-SCI down to Intelink unclassified; page 144 mentions the multilevel information systems security initiative, Fortezza and Rosetta; and page 332 refers to the "Agile Intelligence Enterprise."[16]

A. Denis Clift

This increasing flow of works by researchers and authors either serving or who have formerly served in the U.S. Intelligence Community is being paralleled by an increase in works from the broader academic community both in the United States and overseas, part of the increasing teaching and study of intelligence at colleges and universities.

I praised this phenomenon in remarks delivered at the Georgia Institute of Technology last year, noting that, increasingly, numbers of young Americans will have an appreciation of the place and role of intelligence at a time when they are making decisions about their future careers. Following those remarks, the Joint Military Intelligence College announced 18 June 1999 as the date for a conference on the subject and issued a call for papers.

In considering what we are about here, one need go back no further than the mid-1980s to witness a very strained, very limited, often hostile relationship between intelligence and the academic community. In a 1984 work titled *Military Intelligence and the Universities: A Study of an Ambivalent Relationship,* Alvin Bernstein wrote, "While it is true that the political climate of the campuses is now less hostile to the government in general and to the Defense Department in particular, it is also true that the basic ingredients still exist for another conflagration should outside events provide the appropriate catalyst."[17]

In the same year, 1984, the National Intelligence Study Center conducted a survey of American academic institutions offering some component of intelligence course work. In her Foreword to the resulting monograph, Editor Marjorie Cline wrote:

> [T]here was until recently an almost complete void in our universities insofar as specific courses devoted to the subject of intelligence as part of our political process and international affairs. Initially, most of the research and instruction have been based on the personal initiatives of a number of individual teachers with special interest and experience.[18]

It is a far richer landscape these days. Our conference's principal speakers will be retired Lieutenant General Sam Wilson, President of Hampden-Sydney College, and Lloyd Salvetti, Director of CIA's Center for the Study of Intelligence. The Central Intelligence Agency, through its Center for the Study of Intelligence, has a very strong, productive relationship with Harvard University, for example, embracing the co-hosting of conferences, cooperation on case studies, and co-sponsorship of monographs. The Center also sponsors faculty in residence at a number of colleges and universities. As a college president, Sam Wilson teaches intelligence, and does so against a background of achievement in the field—with special forces in Burma in World War II, as Defense Attaché in Moscow, and as Director of the Defense Intelligence Agency—during earlier chapters of his career.

Our conference call for papers has seen the submission of more than two dozen abstracts, a selection by the faculty from among those abstracts, with the papers selected focusing on different aspects of the conference's central themes: educating for careers in intelligence; teaching intelligence—topics, methods, and techniques; studies on terrorism and weapons of mass destruction; and competitive intelligence instruction. Robert Burnette and Robert

Pringle of the Patterson School faculty are co-authoring one of the conference's papers, "Teaching Intelligence: Diagnosing the Threat of Weapons of Mass Destruction."

Some of the past great successes in U.S. intelligence have reflected the genius and have been the labors of citizen-soldiers—men and women from across the land who have answered the call to service during times of crisis and conflict. It is important that the upcoming generations continue to answer the call, to meet the nation's complex intelligence requirements. It is vital that we have the finest talent in the land.

JV2010, JMIC, AND ARMY INTELLIGENCE

The growing partnership between the Army and the Joint Military Intelligence College as we educate and deliver some of the finest talent in the land is what brings me to Fort Huachuca today. The creation of Functional Area 34—the strategic intelligence officer—and the inauguration of the Strategic Intelligence Officers' Course represent a forward-looking investment by the Army that bodes well for the Army's and the nation's intelligence capabilities this year, the year 2010, and the years beyond.

I congratulate Major Rick Hoehne and Major Saul Gomez on your design and structuring of the new course. Rick Hoehne, an alumnus of the Joint Military Intelligence College, has kept us closely posted in recent months. He has told us that some of our Joint Military Intelligence College textbooks—*The Style Guide, Writing With Intelligence,* and *Briefing With Intelligence*—will be used in your course. As he heads for his next assignment, two members of the College's current Master's class are looking forward, following the award of their degrees, to joining you at Huachuca later in the year.

It is in both our interests to build on these ties so that we have connectivity between this campus and our campus at Bolling Air Force Base in Washington that will benefit both student bodies, both faculties. As early steps we can draw on the synchronous capabilities of the Joint Worldwide Intelligence Communications System and the Secure Distance Learning Network. Working together within the framework of the Joint Intelligence Virtual Architecture, and acting on your vision of Classroom XXI, we will go far beyond.

The Joint Military Intelligence College looks forward to welcoming graduates of this course into the College's Master of Science of Strategic Intelligence (MSSI) program, knowing that your work will build on the essential professional research I have earlier described, and knowing that your contributions as strategic intelligence officers will meet the high standard set by General Shalikashvili in *Joint Vision 2010.*

I opened with Teddy Roosevelt's vision from a century ago. I will conclude with another quote—another message from the past guiding us to the future:

If there was one Department on which money could be spent with advantage it was the Intelligence Department. . . . We wanted an Army based on economy; it should be an Army of efficiency, and it should be an Army of elasticity, so that comparatively small regular units in time of peace might be expanded into

A. Denis Clift

a great and powerful Army in time of war. For that expansion nothing was more needed than an efficient and well-staffed Intelligence Department.[19]

The words are those of Winston Churchill, in his remarks to the House of Commons in 1902.

CHAPTER 9
THE COMMANDER'S KIT

Addressing the World Affairs Council in San Antonio, Texas in April 2000, the author cites the work of two Joint Military Intelligence College graduates—U.S. Air Force Lieutenant General Michael V. Hayden and U.S. Air Force Captain Sean Cantrell—in improving intelligence support to military operations and force protection. In this "911 era for America's armed forces," he points out the critical challenges faced by intelligence professionals in ensuring that the commander's kit of intelligence tools—sustained by continued investment of resources in intelligence—is maintained in the most modern fashion to fight tomorrow's wars and to meet the technological advances on the horizon.

We are in an era of challenges and opportunities for U.S. intelligence that brings to mind the image of the drunk who was looking under a street lamp for his lost keys. "Is this where you dropped them?" asked a passer-by. "No," replied the drunk, "I dropped them over there, but the light is better here."[1]

As we address the nation's intelligence needs of tomorrow and beyond, we know that the keys to our success will be found not so much in the glow of current practice as in the still-dark land-, sea-, sky- and space-scapes of new sources, new methods, new applications and capabilities.

KEEPING UP WITH THE TECHNOLOGY

What is this new age? Even the term *post-Cold War era* is obsolete. It is the information age, the knowledge age, a time when we as humans find ourselves fitted with a remarkable kit of new tools—tools that spawn tools newer still—and we are just beginning to learn how to use them to best advantage. Kelly Air Force Base here in San Antonio is the home of organizations that have abandoned the old in favor of the altogether new—the Air Intelligence Agency, the Joint Information Operations Center, and the predecessor Electronic Security Command in the Joint Electronic Warfare Center. More than 20 years ago, when Major General Doyle Larson was tasked by the Air Force Chief of Staff with establishing the Electronic Security Command to bring fresh applications of science and technology to modern warfare, he invited the British scientist R.V. "Reg" Jones to San Antonio to lecture and to tutor.[2]

In his memoirs *Their Finest Hour*, Winston Churchill had described the painful shock he received in June 1940 when told that the Germans appeared to have developed a radio beam device that would guide their bombers like an invisible searchlight, allowing them to bomb targets in Great Britain day or night, whatever the weather. He had been told that a young scientist in the Air Ministry, Dr. R.V. Jones, had made the discovery, and he summoned Jones to the Cabinet Room to brief.[3]

A. Denis Clift

Intelligence, the decoding of German Enigma traffic, had played an important role in Jones' work. In a 20-minute extemporaneous review for the Prime Minister and his senior military and civilian advisers, Jones described the evidence, how intelligence had led to the discovery of the beam transmissions, and their strategic military applications. He then went on to say how the German system could be foiled, how the beams could be countered, how the radio guide paths could be bent sending the bombers and their payloads wide of target.[4]

After the war, Churchill, doing business as he so often did from bed, invited Reg Jones by for a chat. He told Jones that when he had heard those words in the Cabinet Room—that the Germans could bomb just as accurately by night when British nightfighters would still be almost powerless—it was for him one of the blackest moments of the war. But, as Jones had continued, Churchill told him "the load was again lifted because [Jones had] said there could be ways of countering the beams and so preventing our most important targets being destroyed."[5]

Jones' subsequent tutorials at the Electronic Security Command at Kelly Air Force Base would offer fresh ideas and insights that would help to shape Air Force strategy for command and control warfare pointing toward today's joint information operations— operations embracing, in Jones' words, the commander's kit of tools, lethal weapons, operational security, deception, jamming, and psychological warfare.[6]

There is another story about Reg Jones and Churchill. During the war, Jones had a mischievous secretary named Daisy Mowat. One day Churchill's secretary called and Daisy told him that Dr. Jones was not available. By the time Jones was able to get to the telephone, he heard a grieved voice saying, "This is Peck, the Prime Minister's Secretary—is that really Dr. Jones? I have just been talking to a most extraordinary lady who asserted that you had just jumped out the window!" With some presence of mind Jones replied, "Please don't worry, it's the only exercise that we can get."[7]

INTELLIGENCE FOR FORCE PROTECTION

As we meet today, important contributions are being made to the commander's kit of intelligence and national security tools. Permit me to cite the work of a young Air Force officer on the rise and another officer already at the top, both graduates of the Joint Military Intelligence College.

Captain Sean Cantrell is an outstanding young Air Force officer who holds a 1998 Master of Science of Strategic Intelligence degree from the Joint Military Intelligence College. He is currently serving at Goodfellow Air Force Base in San Angelo, Texas. In June 1996, he was deployed to King Abdul Aziz Air Base in Dhahran, Saudi Arabia, where he was serving as intelligence officer for the 58th Fighter Squadron, an F-16 squadron flying sorties in the Southern No-Fly Zone of Iraq as part of Operation SOUTHERN WATCH. On 25 June 1996 at 9:53 p.m., in his words: "a life-defining maelstrom of glass, concrete and blast overpressure erupted from a 5000- to 6000-pound truck bomb parked in a field adjacent to that corner of Khobar Towers" where he was meeting with the squadron's flight surgeon.[8]

Captain Cantrell survived; 19 of his fellow airmen did not. Since the time of the blast he has examined, as part of his service to the nation, how intelligence can play a more agile, effective, proactive role in force protection—in providing for the physical security of Air Force units deployed, often with little advance notice, to foreign bases overseas. He has engaged a number of very senior officials in this work, including General Wayne Downing, the former Commander-in-Chief of U.S. Special Operations Command, as his mentor and his editor.

Cantrell's work begins with an examination of the Air Force's organizational lines of responsibility for force protection at the time of Khobar Towers, when the special agents of the Air Force's Office of Special Investigations—special agents trained primarily for law enforcement counterintelligence—had primary responsibility for the intelligence flowing to force protection operations. He finds that it is imperative, both now and in the future, that the operational commander receive one integrated intelligence picture that appraises the entire battlespace. He looks at the way the Navy has melded its combat intelligence relating to foreign entities and counterintelligence in the work of its Naval Antiterrorist Alert Center. He finds that such integration of Air Force combat intelligence and counterintelligence is essential for future force protection work.

But, he says, such merging alone cannot do the job. He recommends an integrated intelligence organization that combines combat intelligence and counterintelligence

- with aviators on the team to evaluate force protection from the vantage point of the flying mission;
- with security forces personnel to gauge whether proposed defenses can be accomplished given Air Force capabilities; and
- with Air Force special operations personnel to evaluate whether proposed defenses can be breached by hostile terrorist, covert or special forces.[9]

Through his professional commitment, through his research and writing, Captain Cantrell is shaping new tools for the commander's kit.

INTELLIGENCE TOOLS FOR THE 911 ERA

If this is the knowledge age and the information age, it is also the 911 era for America's armed forces. The Army, Navy, Air Force, Marines, and Coast Guard are deployed around the world, often on very short notice, in crisis management, coalition operations, peacekeeping, and military operations other than war. These are incredibly demanding assignments and missions. Take peacekeeping; the late UN Secretary General Dag Hammarskjold said it well: "It is not a job for soldiers, but only soldiers can do it."[10] The operations tempo is fast; the role of intelligence is central to the success of such operations.

Lieutenant General Michael V. Hayden, U.S. Air Force, another graduate of the Joint Military Intelligence College, is an intelligence leader of prominence in this 911 era. As a Brigadier General in the mid-1990s he was Director of Intelligence at the U.S. European Command, with missions ranging from Kilgali, Rwanda, to Incirlik, Turkey and Dahuk,

A. Denis Clift

Iraq, to Sarajevo in Bosnia, and Zagreb in Croatia. "The nature of the intelligence required was...frequently out of the normal mold," he has written. Citing one of many examples: "Several days into the Rwanda crisis, we asked our theater intelligence center to take the template they had developed for tracking artillery tubes in Bosnia—site number, location, date located, equipment, etc.—and replace the artillery entry with an entry on displaced human beings."[11]

General George Joulwan, former Supreme Allied Commander Europe, has discussed this Great Lakes African refugee crisis in meetings with our students. He has emphasized the lead role of intelligence for him in his decisionmaking process. Based on intelligence from this distant reach of the world, General Joulwan would give priority on the first heavy-lift cargo flights into the region not to weapon systems but to potable water trucks able to bring relief to the thousands upon thousands in distress and on the verge of dying.

Following his tour in European Command, General Hayden took command of the Air Intelligence Agency and the Joint Command and Control Warfare Center. He would then move on to become Deputy Chief of Staff, United Nations Command and U.S. Forces Korea, before being nominated by the President and confirmed by the Senate in 1999 as the current director of the National Security Agency, Fort Meade, Maryland.

The National Security Agency, NSA, was established in 1952 as a national-level intelligence agency to provide for the signals intelligence mission of the United States and to ensure secure communications systems for the departments and agencies of the U.S. Government. Through its remarkable signals intelligence work, NSA helped to win the Cold War. Today it is an agency in change, an agency addressing a world in the midst of technological change, with such changes occurring exponentially. Forty years ago, General Hayden has noted, there were 5,000 stand-alone computers, no fax machines, and not one cellular phone. Today, there are more than 180 million computers, most networked, 14 million fax machines, and 40 million cell phones.[12]

Director of Central Intelligence George Tenet has described NSA's challenges in terms more vivid still: "The telecommunications industry," he has said, "is making a $1 trillion investment to encircle the world in millions of miles of high bandwidth fiber optic cable. What does that mean?" he asks. "It means that the challenge for signals intelligence has grown, and that our targets are harder than ever to cover."[13]

For NSA to continue operations in the lamplight of current practice would be for U.S. intelligence the equivalent of assuring security with the Maginot Line. General Hayden is questioning every aspect of NSA's current practices. He has completed a major review of the agency, identified areas for improvement, and empowered a leadership team charged with 100 days of change. He has begun the preparation of a detailed statement for consideration by the executive and legislative branches of government of the substantial, sustained investments in intelligence—new tools for the commander's kit—that will be required in coming years if the nation is not to be outflanked in a blitzkrieg of technology.

CHALLENGES FOR THE FUTURE

To speak of Captain Cantrell and General Hayden, two graduates of the College, is to give you the very slightest sampling of the contributions our graduates are making across the armed services, across the intelligence and law enforcement communities. They are men and women in positions of leadership; full partners with their policy, planning, and operations counterparts; leaders anticipating and tailoring intelligence required at the national, theater, and tactical levels; leaders who constitute a unique asset to the nation.

The intelligence such graduates collect, analyze, and disseminate addresses issues with implications for the very survival of this nation, for example: the capabilities and future trends of strategic and tactical nuclear forces and advanced conventional forces of other nations; the proliferation of materials contributing to the development of nuclear weapons capabilities; the status of chemical and biological warfare research and development; the character, disposition, and intentions of terrorist organizations overseas.

In the context of this broad range of threats, intelligence must deal with both asynchronous challenges and asymmetric challenges. In his testimony before the Senate Select Committee on Intelligence earlier this year, Vice Admiral Tom Wilson, Director of the Defense Intelligence Agency and another alumnus of the College, described the asymmetric military dimension as follows:

> The superiority of U.S. military concepts, technology, and capabilities has been a key theme in foreign military assessments since Operation DESERT STORM...Potential U.S. opponents...do not want to engage the U.S. military on its terms. They are more likely to...develop asymmetric means—operational and technological—to reduce U.S. military superiority, render it irrelevant, or exploit our perceived weaknesses.[14]

For those of you here today who are in school, who are weighing career decisions, I would first commend to you a career of service to the nation. Secondly, I would commend the field of intelligence, a central component of the nation's national security structure and operations, together with defense and foreign policy, since the signing of the National Security Act in 1947. And thirdly, to those of you who do enter intelligence, either on active duty or in a civilian capacity, I would commend to you the degree programs at the Joint Military Intelligence College.

CHAPTER 10
SEMPER PROTEUS

In 2002, the United States Coast Guard formally entered the United States Intelligence Community, building on a long and distinguished career in law enforcement, defense, and myriad other maritime operations. In this October 2000 speech, the author told the cadets at the Coast Guard Academy in New London, Connecticut, of the challenges they would face in their service. The ever-changing, evolving role of the Coast Guard evoked the image of the Greek god Proteus, with powers to change into any shape he pleased. So must the Coast Guard continue to face its challenges with the same spirit it has shown for hundreds of years. Those challenges require the best possible intelligence, and the Coast Guard is steadily improving its capabilities in that regard, as well as its interaction with the Intelligence Community. In closing, he cites some of the outstanding research conducted by United States Coast Guard officers in the master's degree program at the Joint Military Intelligence College.

When Lieutenant John F. Kennedy sailed for the Pacific aboard the Navy transport USS *Rochambeau* in March 1943, he found himself sharing a stateroom with Ensign James A. Reed. They debated politics and became friends during the long westward passage. They fought the war from PT boats. When Kennedy was elected President, he named Reed in 1961 to be Assistant Secretary of the Treasury for Law Enforcement, the secretariat position in that senior Department then overseeing the United States Coast Guard. In just a few months, the President would be aboard the Cutter *Eagle*, accompanied by Reed, to address the importance of the Coast Guard mission.

In 1965, during Reed's tenure at Treasury, the Coast Guard marked its 175th anniversary. I was editor of the United States Naval Institute *Proceedings* at the time. I invited the Assistant Secretary to write the lead essay for the August 1965 anniversary issue, which he did, an essay titled "Renaissance of the Coast Guard."

COAST GUARD RENAISSANCE

As his title suggested, those were exciting times for your distinguished service. The first two units of the new *Hamilton*-Class cutters were on the building ways. *Reliance, Diligence*, and *Vigilant*, the first three of the new medium-endurance-class cutters, had just entered service. New aircraft and new shore installations were in the works. "What we are aiming at," Assistant Secretary Reed wrote, underscoring the privilege he felt at playing a part, "is nothing less than a total modernization of this service which has been obliged for too long to conduct its highly important functions with obsolete facilities."[1]

Invoking the image of the Greek god Proteus, who had the powers to instantly change himself into any shape he pleased—be it lion, serpent, or tongue of fire—Reed wrote that the Coast Guard must be capable of assuming many different shapes on short notice. He reviewed the quickening tempo of operations in the missions of law enforcement, merchant marine safety, recreational boating, search and rescue, aids to navigation, the International Ice Patrol, oceanographic research, the Cuban Patrol, and military operations ranging from the surveillance of the nation's coastlines to the deployment of 82-footers to southeast Asia for operations in Vietnam.

"In this renaissance of the Coast Guard," he wrote, "all previously held concepts are being carefully examined in light of changing times and technology. Nothing is being taken for granted solely because it has been honored by custom."[2] Today, 35 years later—a ship-life generation later—these same words capture the forces at work shaping the Coast Guard of the 21st century.

CONTINUING CHALLENGES

While the pace of change is quickening in terms both of on-rushing technologies and the scope and substance of national security challenges, certain factors remain constant. Among them, people—people everywhere break laws, people generate crises and engage in conflict—human beings do it with great and continuing regularity.

In July 2000, Norwegian fisherman Olaf Iversen was trawling for shrimp some 15 miles off Stavern, Norway, and took a great strain on his gear when his nets snagged 1,650 gallons of liquor in 31 submerged oil drums waiting pick-up beneath the surface. The rum runners are still at it in the 21st century. Being an honest man, Iversen did what any good citizen should do. He summoned the Norwegian Coast Guard.[3]

In the same month of July, one of this nation's outstanding military leaders, Marine General Anthony Zinni, Commander in Chief, U.S. Central Command, published his reflections on critical challenges facing the U.S. armed services. In his view, the military action involved in kicking Iraq out of Kuwait—Operation DESERT STORM—was the exception rather than the rule in terms, in his words, "of the terrible mess that awaits us abroad. ...In the high- and top-level war colleges, we still fight the Saddam Hussein type of adversary, an adversary stupid enough to confront us symmetrically with less of everything so that we always win." That is not going to be the case, General Zinni says, as "more and more U.S. military men and women are going to be involved in vague, confusing military actions, heavily overlaid with political, humanitarian, and economic considerations."[4]

As you weigh his words, you might agree that of the nation's five armed services the Coast Guard more than any other, day-in, day-out, is in the thick of this asynchronous, asymmetric mess—as you deal with enforcement of embargoes, drug smuggling, illegal migration, oceanic over-fishing and pollution—as you guard against international terrorism and weapons of mass destruction in defense of the homeland in an era when annually 165 million containers are moving in and out of U.S. ports predominantly under foreign flag.

COAST GUARD ON THE FRONT LINES

I developed my first deep appreciation for the front-line role you play with a telephone call at about 3:00 a.m. on a 1971 spring morning. I had just joined the National Security Council staff in the administration of President Richard Nixon. While the Cold War was still frigid in the early 1970s, the President had opened a diplomatic dialogue with the Soviet leadership that would lead to the 1972-1974 summits of détente. The superpower relationship was complex.

When the telephone rang at my home in Annapolis, the senior watch officer, Coast Guard Operations Center, was on the line. I can still hear that very distinctive, periodic beep coming in over his voice reminding that the conversation was being recorded. One of your cutters had spotted and intercepted a Soviet trawler fishing in U.S. waters off Alaska. The Soviet was making a run for it, ignoring orders to heave to for boarding and inspection. The skipper of your cutter was requesting permission to fire a warning shot across the trawler's bows. Your watch officer was asking me to grant that permission.

Standing there in my full majesty in the kitchen at 3:00 a.m., I may have lightly scratched my chest while contemplating this first opportunity to ignite U.S.-Soviet crisis and war. In fact, as I remember, and I am sure there is a tape in some archive capturing the event, I thanked the watch for bringing the request to the NSC and told him that my boss, Major General Al Haig, the Deputy National Security Adviser, would be the one to grant authority. I gave him Haig's White House switchboard number and recommended that he relay the request directly, rather than going through me, given the need for fast action. Permission would be granted, and the trawler would receive the Coast Guard inspection party.

The senior watch officer was sharp; the Coast Guard was sharp in that fast-breaking action. I see that same, sharp professionalism today in your charting of the strategy, the new capabilities, and the new ships, aircraft, and facilities—to include the command, control, communications, computer, intelligence, surveillance, and reconnaissance capabilities—required for the Coast Guard of the 21st century.

INTELLIGENCE AND THE COAST GUARD

Intelligence—together with defense and foreign policy—has been a central, formal part of the national security work of this nation since the time of the National Security Act of 1947, an act born of Pearl Harbor and the coming of the nuclear era. Presidential Executive Order 12333 of December 1981, which spells out the duties and responsibilities of those engaged in U.S. intelligence work, sets the tone for the nation's approach to such work in its opening lines:

> Timely and accurate information about the activities, capabilities, plans, and intentions of foreign powers, organizations, and persons, and their agents, is essential to the national security of the United States. All reasonable and lawful

A. Denis Clift

means must be used to ensure that the United States will receive the best intelligence available.[5]

The Coast Guard today—as the nation's maritime law enforcement agency and as a military service—is stating the priority it places on being a full-fledged participant in the intelligence work of the nation. In March 1999, the Coast Guard's Intelligence Coordination Center and the Navy's Office of Naval Intelligence co-authored the report *Threats and Challenges to Maritime Security 2020,* projecting the range of legal and illegal maritime activities to be expected in the years ahead.[6]

The December 1999 interagency report on Coast Guard roles and missions states in remarkable clarity and detail the new intelligence capabilities required to accomplish the 2020 mission. Like the Greek god, the Coast Guard is again about to change shape, this time to be able to see from space, to be able to listen around the world, to be able increasingly to divine the intentions of those who would do this nation harm. If the Coast Guard is *Semper Paratus,* truly as Secretary Reed suggested 35 years ago, you are also *semper proteus* as you once again adapt to be of most effective service to the nation.

In identifying the role that intelligence can play, to cite one example, against illegal immigration operations, the interagency report states that

> law enforcement agencies must operate within the "decision cycle" of smugglers. It will require focused operational intelligence to cue interdiction efforts; accurate and agile surveillance of immigration avenues; and effective apprehension "end games." The result will be improved interdiction effectiveness which will bolster deterrence. DoD and other federal agencies in the intelligence community have considerable information gathering capability that can and should be employed to improve the execution of this mission. Specifically, national intelligence systems and wide area surveillance capabilities (both national and commercial) can offset the need for some Coast Guard resources to counter illegal migrant activity, if made available for this purpose.[7]

Recognizing that most Coast Guard Deepwater missions involve a search problem, your planners state that an effective intelligence, surveillance, and reconnaissance system must collect multi-source information, using the information received from one source to cue other collection sources. Your planners identify how existing Coast Guard intelligence capabilities should be joined with current national-level intelligence capabilities, those of low- and high-altitude satellites, aircraft, and unmanned aerial vehicles, and surface-based systems such as over-the-horizon radars. They identify the cooperation required with organizations of the national intelligence community, if future intelligence capabilities—from remote sensors to agents on the ground—are to contribute even more effectively to the surveillance, detection, classification, and identification steps leading to the prosecution and engagement phase of the mission.[8]

IMPROVING INTELLIGENCE

The Coast Guard is moving to strengthen its intelligence capabilities in this, the cyber-era, the information age, a time when the U.S. Intelligence Community is developing remarkable new techniques for collection, analysis, and dissemination of intelligence at the national, theater, and tactical levels. The Intelligence Community has had a tremendous learning curve since the delivery of intelligence in Operation DESERT STORM, now a decade ago.

The Director of Intelligence on the Joint Staff, Rear Admiral Lowell E. "Jake" Jacoby, United States Navy, recently assessed the effectiveness of intelligence in Operation ALLIED FORCE, the operations in Kosovo in 1999. First, he found improvements since the early 1990s. Secondly, he found the modernization initiatives now underway are on the right path from the perspective of the Chairman of the Joint Chiefs of Staff's goals as set forth in *Joint Vision 2010*. Third, he found that today's military commander wants and expects *Joint Vision 2010's* intelligence capabilities today.

> The commanders in Operation ALLIED FORCE expected integrated intelligence support that delivers unqualified information superiority, continuously and seamlessly, throughout all phases of mission planning and execution. Translated into intelligence terminology, information superiority entails a capability to obtain and maintain a coherent, real-time view of the operating environment, in all its dimensions. It entails a capability to seek, locate and *watch* target objectives wherever they reside, transit, or hide.[9]

If these expectations are to be met, Admiral Jacoby writes, the Intelligence Community must continue its drive to create "a partnership of highly skilled people—I repeat of highly skilled people—and leading edge technologies providing warfighters, policymakers, and planners with assured access to required intelligence."[10]

The need for highly skilled people, highlighted by Rear Admiral Jacoby, is underlined and reinforced by the Director of Military Intelligence Vice Admiral Tom Wilson and the Director of Central Intelligence George Tenet. In my position as President of the Joint Military Intelligence College, the nation's only accredited College awarding the Master of Science of Strategic Intelligence degree and Bachelor of Science in Intelligence degree, I have the privilege and trust of educating the next generation of the nation's intelligence leaders. This generation includes young and rising stars from the Army, Navy, Air Force, Marine Corps. It includes their civilian counterparts from the Central Intelligence Agency, National Security Agency, Defense Intelligence Agency, State Department, National Imagery and Mapping Agency, Drug Enforcement Administration, Bureau of Alcohol, Tobacco, and Firearms, Federal Bureau of Investigation, and Immigration and Naturalization Service. Year after year, it includes extremely talented and motivated Coast Guard officers who are contributing to the work of intelligence and to the Coast Guard's intelligence expertise through their Master's thesis research at the same time that they are receiving their degrees.

A. Denis Clift

RESEARCH AT THE COLLEGE

To give you a flavor for this work, in 1998, Coast Guard Lieutenant Eric Ensign won the Joint Chiefs of Staff's Fleet Admiral Chester W. Nimitz Archival Research Award for his Master's thesis *Intelligence in the Rum War at Sea, 1920-1933*. In 1924, four years into the prohibition era, it had become clear that Americans had no intention of abiding by a self-imposed ban on alcohol. Buyer boats were doing a brisk business with seller ships lying along rum row three miles off the Atlantic coast. Gin and whiskey were running freely. In Treasury, lead agency responsibility for suppressing the illegal flow of liquor from the sea was transferred from the Prohibition Bureau to the Coast Guard. In his Master's thesis, drawing on primary research of declassified Coast Guard Intelligence Division records, Lieutenant Ensign examines the intelligence capabilities the Coast Guard developed to carry out the new mission.[11]

In 1924, at the outset of the campaign, the Coast Guard Intelligence Section was a one-man operation. Lieutenant Commander Charles S. Root reported directly to Commandant Billard, tracking the name, nationality, and homeports of the ships on rum row, plotting the positions of suspected rum runners—a precursor to today's suspect vessel look-out lists—and disseminating the information to the Coast Guard Fleet via intelligence circulars.

By 1927, Root had been promoted to Commander. He now had a staff of five. With the arrival of the Coast Guard's first seaplane the year before, he had a limited capability to scout sea areas off Long Island and New England. He and his staff developed a working intelligence relationship—national-level interagency intelligence sharing—with the Departments of State, War, Navy, Justice, Post Office, Interior, Commerce, and Labor. Commander Root was shaping an all-source intelligence capability—human source reporting, open-source reporting, communications intercepts, and imagery. Root's small team of cryptanalysts began breaking the smugglers' codes. Agents' reports were fed by Root and his colleagues to the cutter crews, telling them where to look beneath the false bottoms, the double bottoms, beneath the cargoes of lumber, sand, coal, where to probe with long iron rods beneath the cargoes of fish.[12]

There are striking parallels between this pioneering intelligence work in the early 1920s and the intelligence challenges today in drug interdiction and illegal alien migration. There is splendid research being conducted at the College in the fields of camouflage, concealment, and deception theory. This is research at the classified level aimed at tactical deception and psychological operations. It is research aimed at improved intelligence cueing, refined intelligence collection on concealment modification practices aboard suspect vessels, the use of new scientific and technical intelligence methods to assist boarding parties in locating hidden compartments and the contraband they conceal. Excellent work has been done on improving intelligence and law enforcement cooperation in countering maritime alien smuggling. Research has examined the Commandant of the Coast Guard's international engagement strategy, the benefits to be realized from the Coast Guard's networking with different nations in different regions of the world to gain better cooperation in future operations, to strengthen other nations' capabilities to catch smugglers in their waters before they reach our own.

In recent years, your officers at the Joint Military Intelligence College have examined Caribbean and Western Hemispheric issues and operations—the lessons to be learned from the Mariel boatlift and Haitian migration in the 1990s, the different dimensions of the drug war, ranging from the different cultures of the region, to the dynamics of international drug movement and interdiction, to the role of intelligence and the operational security challenges.

In an era of increasingly close operational ties between the Coast Guard and the Navy, Navy students studying at the College are conducting research on the challenges of improving maritime intelligence capabilities in counter-drug operations, and on the enhancement of intelligence cooperation with law enforcement in our maritime economic zones, in our maritime defense against asymmetric threats to the homeland, in our ability to detect, watch, and intercept high-interest cargo movements.

Master's theses have examined different dimensions of the challenges posed by oceanic over-fishing, the ramifications of the Pacific salmon conflict, for example, and challenges of enforcing the high seas driftnet moratorium. In 1997, Coast Guard Lieutenant Commander William Quigley's research entitled *Driftnet Fishery Enforcement: A New Intelligence Problem,* was published by the College as a chapter in the book *Intelligence for Multilateral Decision and Action,* a text now being used both on our campus and at other colleges and universities across the country.[13]

Lieutenant Commander Joe Hester came to the Master's program at the Joint Military Intelligence College in the Class of 1999 following three years as the Commanding Officer of the Cutter *Attu*. His research would contribute to the interagency study on Coast Guard roles and missions published last December. Now, following in the footsteps of the rum war's Lieutenant Commander Root, he is the pioneering first Chief of the new Maritime Intelligence Support Team attached to the Atlantic Area Command, providing a surge intelligence capability to Coast Guard operations here and abroad.

CONTINUING COAST GUARD CONTRIBUTIONS

The contributions to the nation's security made through research such as that cited will continue to expand and increase in value as the role of intelligence in the Coast Guard evolves into its new, more prominent form. The partnership between the Coast Guard and the Joint Military Intelligence College is expanding and increasing in value as part of this process. We have welcomed your Commandant Admiral James Loy as a distinguished speaker at the College as well as your new Vice Commandant for Operations Rear Admiral Terry Cross. Former Commandant Admiral Robert Kramek serves with distinction as a member of the College's Board of Visitors. Of even greater importance, in September 2000 we welcomed four Coast Guard officers as members of the incoming academic year 2001 Master's program—double the Coast Guard enrollment of the year before.

A. Denis Clift

When President Kennedy addressed ship's company and the nation from the decks of the *Eagle* in August 1962, he said of the Coast Guard: "This is the oldest continuous seagoing service in the United States, stretching back to the beginning of our country, so I want all of you who are cadets to know how proud we are of you. I hope" the President said, "you and your fellow Americans realize how vital this service is."[14] I salute these words. I commend you as you embark on your service to this nation. In the years ahead, I will look forward to welcoming at least some of you to your graduate studies at the Joint Military Intelligence College.

CHAPTER 11
TWO IF BY SEA ... THREE IF BY CYBERSPACE

In this 30 November 1999 address to the U.S. Merchant Marine Academy at Kings Point, New York, the author observes that "the wealth of the world is moving by sea." Sealift has been vital to our nation's well-being, in peacetime and in war. Merchant marines represent the globalization of commerce. He recounts some of his own experiences as a young naval officer and later in key national security posts where he participated in important negotiations and conferences relating to maritime security, on-site inspections, and pollution of the seas. Now the high-technology environment of cyberspace—the Internet, information technology, and instantaneous worldwide communications—offers a new challenge to seafarers and the intelligence professionals who support them. Paul Revere's 1775 contribution to early warning, "one if by land and two if by sea," must now be updated to include "three if by cyberspace."

In the early 1990s, I was presented with a bronze sheathing nail from the oak hull of the ship of the line USS *New Hampshire,* one of the nation's first training ships. This artifact, wrought in the foundry of Paul Revere, has a place of honor. It serves to remind first of the intelligence provided by Revere to his compatriots, a warning that readied the Minutemen for the following morning's battle on Lexington green; and, second, it reminds of the role of the schoolship, the importance of seafarer training from the earliest days of the nation.

My late father was the first to tell me of seafarer training. I have his 1926 Sea Service Bureau card confirming his Rating as Deck Boy, his Nationality as Pennsylvanian and his ship as the SS *American Shipper.* On his maiden voyage, he was ordered to stand night bow watch and instructed to be on the lookout for other shipping, hazards, and, to his mind, demons of the night. He was also responsible for checking that his own ship's running lights were in good order and for singing out "Lights Bright!" at regular intervals.

Alone, he peered into the night, turned as he had been instructed, checked port and starboard lights, sang out "Lights OK!", then turned back to again peer into the night. A tremendous kick to the seat of his pants knocked him flat on the deck. The Mate's voice barked, "It's lights bright, not lights OK. It's lights bright!" Alone again, he resumed his watch.

As you prepare for your futures as seafarers and as experts in the business of shipping in both civilian and military careers, I welcome this invitation to meet with you. We should consider Paul Revere's warning in a more contemporary context: one if by land, two if by sea, and three if by cyberspace—the changing face of maritime affairs, intelligence, and national security.

A. Denis Clift

INTELLIGENCE IN THE 21st CENTURY:
A THREAT FROM CYBERSPACE

In his commencement address at the Naval Academy in May 1998, President Clinton framed the new challenges facing the nation:

> As we approach the 21st century, our foes have extended the fields of battle from physical space to cyberspace, from the world's vast bodies of water to the complex workings of our own human bodies. Rather than invading our beaches or launching bombers, these adversaries may attempt cyber-attacks against our critical military systems and our economic base, or they may deploy compact and relatively cheap weapons of mass destruction, not just nuclear but also chemical and biological, to use disease as a weapon of war.[1]

The President then announced that he would appoint a National Coordinator for Security, Infrastructure Protection, and Counter-Terrorism, and on the same day he signed Presidential Decision Directive 63 implementing his plan. Presidential Decision Directive 63 has established a U.S. national goal of protecting critical infrastructures including telecommunications, energy, banking and finance, transportation, water systems, and emergency services within five years. Lead Federal Agencies are identified for each of these sectors, to include Justice and FBI for law enforcement, Department of Defense for National Defense, the Central Intelligence Agency for foreign intelligence, and the Department of Transportation for waterborne commerce. Partnerships to meet the goals are encouraged between the government and the private sector.[2]

Technology, the information age, the Internet are increasing our global reach, shaping our global interdependence, highlighting our strengths and exposing our vulnerabilities. The merchant marine is the assumption on which globalization is based. More than 90 percent of our commerce is moving in ships. The wealth of the world is moving by sea. Such commerce is vital to U.S. political-economic health. Such commerce forms connective tissue of the nation's security. Such commerce must receive fresh, far-reaching attention if the goals of Presidential Decision Directive 63 are fully to be met.

MARITIME SECURITY IN THE 21st CENTURY

Earlier this year, the Coast Guard Intelligence Coordination Center and the Office of Naval Intelligence published a study entitled *Threats and Challenges to Maritime Security 2020*. It is a forecast of the maritime security environment over the next two decades aimed at contributing to strategic planning on force structure and the development of command, control, communications, computers, intelligence, surveillance, and reconnaissance requirements.[3] The report moves from an examination of the implications of climate change for the maritime environment, to a review of current maritime challenges, to an estimate of future maritime operations. It addresses future operations first in terms of legal maritime trade and activities and then illegal trade and activities. Over seven pages it touches on the projected growth of container shipping, the cruise line and high-speed ferry industries, as well as continuing growth in tanker traffic, movement of nuclear waste, undersea cable laying, and the mounting pressures on port infrastructure. It projects that bulk and break-bulk cargo shipping will remain relatively stable.

The report projects that the illegal seaborne trafficking in narcotics, arms, and people will continue to increase as a challenge, stating: "The corrupting influence of the organized crime groups controlling these activities will threaten the safety of peoples and the security of governments. The ability of these organized crime groups to form alliances and easily permeate international borders in 2020 will intensify their threat to the state."[4] This is a good report. I commend it to you. But it does not touch on all of the maritime challenges that are with us now and that can only grow between now and 2020.

To look at the future is essential. To deal with the present is breathtaking. Operations ranging from port security, to the interdiction of international drug-running, to the arrest of international terrorists, pirates, and other criminals, to the evacuation of U.S. citizens overseas, to the engagement of U.S. forces in international crises, peacemaking, peacekeeping, and regional conflict are on the rise. The intelligence flowing to these operations from the national, theater, and tactical levels is making a central contribution to their success in ways never before imagined.

To outrun law enforcement detection and law enforcement cutters, international drug runners have modified speedboats as "Go-Fast" boats to carry a metric ton of narcotics on trans-Caribbean runs at speeds of more that 40 knots. The Coast Guard has responded this year by putting sharpshooters aboard its helicopters to knock out the Go-Fast engines. The early results include four Go-Fast boat seizures with more than three tons of cocaine and marijuana. Assessing these new operations, Coast Guard Commandant Admiral James Loy has said, "We made significant investments in intelligence assets that improved our ability to detect where smugglers are departing from, the way points they use and their destinations."[5]

On 11 August 1999, Immigration and Naturalization Service Agents, acting on a tip, boarded the Cyprus-flagged ship *Prince Nicholas* when she arrived in Savannah, Georgia, cut through a sheet of steel and a hatch that had been welded into place, and discovered 132 Chinese illegal immigrants in a secret hold compartment.[6] That same day, another 150 Chinese illegal immigrants were arrested by the Royal Canadian Mounted Police after they were dropped from a ship and had waded ashore at Sandspit, British Columbia.[7] The story is being repeated up and down the 12,000 miles of U.S. coastlines month after month, and reflects just one dimension of the increased tempo of operations in the INS Intelligence Division.

DEALING WITH THE THREAT

In dealing with acts of terrorism and terrorist threats, as with drug running and illegal immigration, the nation's intelligence agencies and law enforcement agencies are designing new strategies of cooperation that respect the rights and freedoms provided by our Constitution while allowing more effective identification, pursuit, and prosecution of foreign enemies. The Federal Bureau of Investigation, for example, is working with the

A. Denis Clift

Department of Defense on the mounting challenges of counterproliferation. Quoting from FBI Director Louis Freeh's testimony to the Congress this past February:

> The goals of this program are to train and equip foreign law enforcement personnel to detect, prevent, investigate, and prosecute incidents involving the illegal trafficking in weapons of mass destruction and to deter the possible proliferation and acquisition of weapons of mass destruction in Eastern Europe, the Baltic States, and the former Soviet Union. ... Reducing the opportunity for terrorists to obtain radiological and similar materials at the source is the first step toward preventing their use against the United States.[8]

Such innovative approaches are becoming the norm in both the intelligence and the law enforcement communities. The Director of Central Intelligence George Tenet told the members of my College's graduating class this September that his highest priority is preparing the Intelligence Community to ready for an uncertain future. "U.S. intelligence must be smart, bold and agile," he said, "willing to think big and think different and take risks. There is no single-point solution to any of our most difficult challenges."[9]

Graduate students at the Joint Military Intelligence College have been taking the DCI's message to heart in their Master's research. Air Force Captain Steve Magnan's thesis, *Information Operations: Are We Our Own Worst Enemy?* for example, looks at the nation's vulnerability to cyberspace and computer attack as a self-created problem. We are not practicing good operations security.[10] Navy Lieutenant Jay Wylie, a surface operations officer, looks at the new long-range cruise-missile attack missions being assigned to destroyer squadrons, a dramatic change from their carrier battle group screening missions in the Cold War era. He says intelligence must catch up with this change in missions, and he recommends solutions to the problem.[11] Marine Captain Jim Lose came to the Master's program after having served on a National Intelligence Support Team in Bosnia. He looks at the extremely valuable, innovative intelligence teams that deploy on quick notice from the national-level intelligence agencies to serve with forward-deployed joint task force commanders around the world, and he develops a checklist of improvements that would make the teams' intelligence more valuable still.[12]

THE EVOLUTION OF CHALLENGES

When we consider the evolving merchant marine, the changing world of shipping, and the implications for our national security, the need for innovative thought and action is paramount. I first heard from the merchant marine about 60 years ago. When I was just starting off in the west Village of lower Manhattan, there was scarcely a day when the windows of my room were not shaking to vibrations of the deep-throated steam horns of merchantmen and liners arriving and departing on the Hudson.

Those were the days of impending war and the days of World War II. An ocean and a sea away, German Military Intelligence was sabotaging allied shipping on the Black Sea by putting explosives in barrels of Bulgarian fruit juice to be rolled aboard British freighters, timed to the sailing date, timed to blow just beyond the three-mile limit. Abwehr Section II also fashioned explosives as lumps of coal destined for merchantmen's stokeholds and furnaces.[13] In New York, 40 blocks to the north of my childhood home, foreign intelligence, the British under the leadership of William Stephenson—the man called Intrepid—were running operations that included the monitoring of hemispheric port security and the flow of people, mail, and cargoes between the United States and Europe.[14] Shipping was the strategic lifeline. The intelligence services of allies and foes worked both to safeguard and to sever.

In the years that have followed, from my vantage points as a naval officer, Editor of the Naval Institute *Proceedings*, and government official, I have followed and occasionally played a part in both the headlines and the footnotes of the merchant marine and its place in world affairs and the nation's security. In the 1960s, I sailed on the SS *United States* and the nuclear ship *Savannah*, and I walked the decks and reported on the liner *QE 2* while she was still abuilding on the Clydebank in Scotland.

The SS *United States* had troop transport as her Cold War mobilization mission. The *QE 2* would transport troops to the Falklands in the early 1980s. The NS *Savannah* was a graceful ship to behold with her white-hulled clipper bow and long foredeck running to stackless, streamlined superstructure and cruiser stern. The *Savannah* was an experiment in the nation's vision of atoms-for-peace, an American-flagged merchantman demonstrating the potential of nuclear power to shipping industries around the world. The *Savannah* fell victim to labor disputes; the demonstration was short-lived, stultified.

In those years, there were other, far more powerful and enduring forces at work in the merchant marine. In 1963, George Sanders, a Kings Point graduate, would write in the *Proceedings* about the future mobilization potential of a new addition to the U.S. merchant fleet—a ship type being labeled the containership. He wrote that there were not sufficient numbers yet to make a significant contribution, with an average of only two or three entering active service each year, but for future planning they should not be ignored.[15]

The early 1960s also marked the dawning of the supertanker era. In the month and year that Sanders was publishing on the containership, there were only four tankers in the world with deadweight displacement in excess of 100,000 tons: the *Manhattan*, 108,000 tons; the *Universe Apollo*, 114,000 tons; the *Universe Daphne*, 115,000 tons; and the *Nissho Maru*, 131,000 tons.[16] With the coming of the 1970s, ships of this tonnage were being relegated to feeder service from the terminals of the 300,000 tonners to the ports the newer, much bigger tankers could not enter.

Readers marveled at Noel Mostert's description in his book *Supership* of life and operations aboard these crude carriers, the experience of conning a ship from a bridge nearly a quarter-mile aft of the bows, 150 feet from wing to wing, 100 feet above the waterline. In one deadpan understatement he wrote of the ships: "They cannot respond to split second timing. It takes at least three miles and 21 to 22 minutes to stop a 250,000 tonner doing 16 knots."[17]

A. Denis Clift

The seas were being fouled by these new ships. In 1970 I was Secretary of the U.S. Delegation to a NATO Conference on Pollution of the Seas by Oil Spills. The U.S. Delegation Chairman, Secretary of Transportation John Volpe, told the Conference:

> My government proposes that NATO nations resolve to achieve by mid-decade a complete halt to all intentional discharge of oil and oily wastes into the oceans by tankers and other vessels. This is a fundamental and major goal; it may involve steps such as improved ship design aimed at clean ballast operations and the development of adequate port facilities to receive waste, oily bilge and ballast waters.[18]

The conference adopted these recommendations, and they moved next to the Intergovernmental Maritime Consultative Organization—IMCO—en route to becoming accepted international standard and practice.

In the 1960s, the nation had relearned some of the fine points of maritime intelligence. At the height of the 1962 Cuban Missile Crisis, when it had been confirmed that Soviet SS-4 and SS-5 nuclear-tipped ballistic missiles were in Cuba and on the verge of becoming operational, photo interpreters reexamined earlier photography to try to figure out when and how these weapons systems had arrived. In September and October, Navy surveillance aircraft had photographed the Soviet freighters *Poltava* and *Omsk* en route to Cuba. Reexamination showed that the ships had been riding high in the water; they had long cargo hatches. They had been carrying a relatively light, high-volume cargo—missiles—that had been offloaded at night.[19]

By the early 1970s, relations with the Soviets had moved from the depths of Cold War confrontation to the first U.S.-Soviet Summits of Détente. The merchant marine would play a role. I worked as a member of the National Security Council staff with U.S. Maritime Administrator Bob Blackwell as he negotiated the U.S.-USSR Agreement on Maritime Relations, signed in October 1972. Of particular commercial importance, the Soviets wanted to buy a substantial tonnage of U.S. grains. The maritime agreement eased port security procedures for access to specified U.S. and Soviet ports. It established the procedures for setting cargo rates, and, as agreed by the U.S. side with the American unions, it provided that U.S.-flag and Soviet-flag ships would carry equal shares of this new ocean-borne commerce.[20]

On 8 December 1987, U.S.-Soviet relations turned another major, new chapter when President Ronald Reagan and General Secretary Mikhail Gorbachev signed the Intermediate-Range Nuclear Forces Treaty—the INF Treaty. The agreement provided for teams of inspectors from each country to be on the ground in each country monitoring and reporting on the elimination of the missile systems to be destroyed. The new arms control era of on-site inspections had begun. Provisions of the treaty called for portal monitoring, inspectors at missile production plants in the United States and the Soviet Union whose job it would be to make sure that missile systems banned by the treaty were no longer being produced.

To solve the technical challenges of monitoring the missiles in canisters in railcars emerging from the Votkinsk Missile Production Plant in the USSR, the U.S. Government borrowed from the world of shipping to modify an off-the-shelf CargoScan X-ray system used to scan containers in major ports. When the system was up and running, U.S. inspectors could determine with certainty that no SS-20 missiles banned by the treaty were exiting the plant.[21] The world bridging maritime affairs and national security had produced a pragmatic solution essential to the success of this new, historic on-site inspection agreement.

21st CENTURY CHALLENGES

The headlines and the footnotes just mentioned—the nuclear-power experiment, the advent of the containership and supertanker types, clean ballast operations, and the Cold War superpower relationship—are part of a merchant marine voyage that has been subjected to forces far greater still. Those forces have produced a shipping world that is as new as the coming millennium.

"The scope and scale of our maritime trade is mind boggling," Chief of Naval Operations Admiral Jay Johnson recently observed. "It is a testament," he said, to how far we have come in securing the world's commerce. Yet it is also a warning of how far we can fall and how great the impact would be if we fail to protect the ports and sea lanes which keep that trade flowing."[22] We need to know what it is that we are protecting and what we are protecting it from, if we are to weigh Admiral Johnson's statement fully.

America's shipping interests and the role of Americans as bankers, insurers, investors, in the global shipping world are enormous. To cite an example, China today leads the list of foreign nations as the United States' largest liner cargo trading partner, container trade that in 1997 amounted to more than 1,800,000 20-foot container equivalent units. China's shipping company-COSCO-the COSCO Group has a fleet of almost 600 ships, including 130 containerships. U.S. banking and U.S. investors do considerable business with COSCO and its off-shoot companies.[23]

Our nation's peacetime maritime trade today moves to and from our shores in ships predominantly under foreign flag. In our most recent, significant experience of partial mobilization for conflict-Operations DESERT SHIELD and DESERT STORM, the expulsion of Iraq from Kuwait in l991-385 ships met the nation's sealift requirements: 32 from the Military Sealift Command's fast sealift and afloat pre-position ships; 71 from the Ready Reserve Force; 72 chartered from U.S.-flagged or U.S.-controlled cargo and tankers; and the majority-210-from foreign-flagged cargo and tankers.[24]

In its April 1992 report to the Congress, *Conduct of the Persian Gulf War,* the Department of Defense stressed the value of sealift in the campaign. At the same time, the report offered a broader observation on the status of the U.S. Merchant Marine, the fact that with the Cold War over, planners could no longer assume a NATO theater of operations with 400 NATO merchantmen available for sealift requirements. "[I]n a non-NATO environment," the report

A. Denis Clift

stated, "the United States found itself depending on the merchant fleet (which had dwindled from 578 ships in 1978 to 367 in 1990), coalition shipping, and the world market. Foreign-flagged shipping provided more than 20 percent of the dry cargo lifted."[25]

To ensure that sufficient sealift is available for future crises and conflicts, the Maritime Administration provides subsidies through the Maritime Security Program and the Voluntary Intermodal Sealift Agreement so as to have ready when needed a privately owned, U.S.-flagged and U.S.-crewed liner fleet, to include access to the carriers' total sealift, infrastructure, and intermodal systems.[26] What we must bear in mind is that, while neither good nor bad, for a ship to be U.S.-flagged does not mean that ship must be U.S.-owned.

American President Lines offers a case in point. From its beginnings as the Pacific Mail Steamship Company, through its renaming as the Dollar Lines in 1925 and the American President Lines in 1938, APL has more than 150 years of service in the U.S. merchant fleet. APL is a participant in MARAD's Voluntary Intermodal Sealift Agreement. APL is 100 percent foreign-owned, 12 U.S.-flagged, U.S.-crewed ships owned by Singapore. Lykes Lines, another VISTA participant, is owned by Canadian Pacific. Sea-Land Services, in both VISTA and the Maritime Security Program, was purchased earlier this year by Maersk of Denmark.

When we look at the anatomy and functioning of the global commercial maritime environment we find it is an environment in which:

- four of the five top country flags by deadweight tonnage are flags of convenience nations-Panama, Liberia, Cyprus and the Bahamas;
- the shift is to globalization, away from U.S. flags;
- economic power flows from mobile, not fixed, assets;
- multinational corporations are contributing two-thirds of total world trade by value;
- ocean carriers are becoming total logistics providers with the goal of one-stop, global-reach Internet customer service;
- there is a near-universal containerization of commodities, with oil, iron ore and coal among the few future holdouts, with some eight-to-ten million containers involved in more than 165 million moves each year.
- container cargo flows through a hub and spoke network, with 15 mega-hub ports—Long Beach, Halifax, Rotterdam, Singapore, Hong Kong, for example—increasingly essential to smooth and efficient world trade;
- Rotterdam, Europe's mega-port, is three times larger than the second largest port in Europe;
- Singapore is the largest container port by volume and the largest bunkering port by volume in the world;
- such mega-ports become non-substitutable focal points and as such, potential weak links in the global maritime commerce chain. The threats to such focal points are both "electronic" and physical.[27]

The Internet increasingly is the medium of the global commercial maritime world. American President Lines speaks of its championing of information technology, how its award-winning website enables its customers to track and trace their shipments. COSCO, China's Shipping Company, speaks of itself as a computer-based company with access via Internet, with paperless offices and a global communications network.

The big shipping companies today are information technology companies. They are logistics services companies with shipping just a part of their overall intermodal operations. Service to customer is their mission, and that service moves and depends on the net—from inland pick-up, to the loading ports, to high-seas transit, to the mega-hubs, to off-loading at feeder ports and inland delivery.

What are the security implications of this new, paperless, Internet global maritime environment? Clearly, they go beyond the ageless concerns over cargo theft, piracy, and smuggling. Clearly they include the new transnational threats of illegal drugs, terrorism, and weapons of mass destruction. When viewed in the context of Admiral Johnson's warning of how far we can fall and how great the impact would be if we fail to protect the ports and sea lanes which keep our maritime trade flowing, the threats include the entire open-access global cyberspace environment which orders the very existence of global shipping. The threats open a new order of questions about the challenges of infiltration, disruption and sabotage, ashore and afloat, in peacetime, crisis, and conflict. The threats open fundamental questions in the context of Presidential Decision Directive 63 about America's security and critical infrastructure protection that must be answered.

The U.S. Intelligence Community is pressing ahead on a number of fronts to ensure that the most current information technology is available to the government and the nation to meet the mounting cyberspace challenges. The Central Intelligence Agency has established a new venture capital company with U.S. high-technology companies—a company named "In-Q-Tel," after the master technologist Q in James Bond. In-Q-Tel will be a source of venture capital. It will contract and work with industry to bring the latest cyberspace technology into the Agency's work, modernizing computer systems, improving database development, maintenance, and exploitation, as well as improving cyberspace security and privacy.[28]

U.S. Customs recognizes that information technology and associated telecommunications infrastructures will be the driving force of intermodalism. Customs' Intelligence Division has joined forces with partners in Canada, Australia, and New Zealand to assess the threat and to discover new ways of exploiting information to identify where among the 165 million containers moving annually the law enforcement targets lie.[29]

In any important work of the nation such as this, it is essential to bring together Americans from across the nation from government and private life, Americans with the knowledge and the mixes of skills able to surface the problems and chart the solutions. As you prepare for your futures as seafarers and experts in the business of shipping, you have the opportunity to engage in these problems and their solutions.

A. Denis Clift

As you move ahead in your careers, I look forward to welcoming some of you to graduate studies at the Joint Military Intelligence College, as we have welcomed distinguished Kings Point graduates such as Rear Admiral Kevin Cosgriff, United States Navy, in years past. In whatever course each of you sets, I wish you well in your contributions to the maritime health, strength, and heritage of this nation.

CLIFT NOTES

INTELLIGENCE AND THE NATION'S SECURITY

PART THREE

INTELLIGENCE, NATIONAL SECURITY, AND POLICY

CHAPTER 12
THE EMERGING BUTTERFLY:
CIVILIAN CONTROL OVER INTELLIGENCE IN THE
UNITED STATES

In 1996, at a time when Romania was beginning earnest work to shape a new democracy, the author addressed the National Defense College of Romania on the importance of civilian control over the Intelligence Community in the United States, tracing the roots of such control to the establishment of the Republic. He compares the changing post-Cold-War Intelligence Community to a butterfly emerging from its 50-year-old cocoon. He underscores the continuing importance of the National Security Act of 1947, and of subsequent Presidential Executive Orders, in providing both mission and direction to the different organizations of the Intelligence Community; and he highlights the important oversight role of the Congress. His perspective is based in part on his own experience of Executive Office of the President and White House service in the Johnson, Nixon, Ford, and Carter administrations.

The year 1997 marks the 50th anniversary of the National Security Act of 1947; 1997 will also be the 50th anniversary of the establishment of the Central Intelligence Agency and of the national security structure in which the agencies and offices of the U.S. Intelligence Community operate.

In the United States on the eve of this 50th anniversary, we are engaged at the highest levels of government in study and debate on the future mission and structure of the Intelligence Community. The Cold War has ended. On 28 February, Secretary of Defense William Perry told the Corps of Foreign Defense Attachés in Washington, "Our challenge is to begin the world over again."[1] New national security challenges confront us and confront our friends and allies around the world. Like a butterfly, the U.S. Intelligence Community is emerging from 50 years of development in the rigid cocoon of the Cold War era, emerging in a changing form with wings that will loft it into the 21st century. *Lepidoptera Intelligens* is on the verge of taking flight.

March 1996 is a month in which a Presidential Commission—the Aspin-Brown Commission—has just presented its findings and recommendations on the future of the Intelligence Community. It is a month in which the important work of the Senate Select Committee on Intelligence and the House Permanent Select Committee on Intelligence of the U.S. Congress is looming larger in the debate on the future of the Community. The Presidential Commission and the Congressional Committees are, of course, civilian bodies.

A. Denis Clift

THE ROOTS OF CIVILIAN CONTROL

The precedents, the requirement for civilian control over U.S. intelligence activities, trace back to the 18th century, to the very beginnings of the United States of America. They trace back to the abhorrence of dictatorship, of totalitarian rule, that our founding fathers brought to the drafting of the Constitution. Professor Stanley Falk and Dr. Theodore Bauer discuss this bedrock American principle in their enduring work, *The National Security Structure:*

> Sensitive to the dangers of militarism, the makers of the Constitution established an elaborate system of "checks and balances" to safeguard the Nation and the liberty of its citizens. They designated the highest elected civilian official, the President, as Commander in Chief of the Armed Forces, including the State militia when called into national service. They endowed the Congress with the power to impose and collect taxes for defense, to declare war, and to raise, support, maintain, and regulate military and naval forces. Most importantly, they implanted a strong national philosophy of civil control over the military, of civilian direction and administration of the means and men of war.[2]

Within this system of check and balances—which I would underscore included from the outset the Judicial Branch to interpret the laws as well as the Executive and Legislative Branches—there was in the most important circles, from the beginning of the Republic, a recognition of the importance of good intelligence to the new nation's interests. I have on the wall of my offices in Washington a copy of a 26 July 1777 letter from General George Washington to Colonel Elias Dayton, addressing tactical developments in the Revolutionary War. The letter's concluding paragraph is as follows:

> The necessity of procuring good intelligence is apparent and need not be further urged—All that remains for us to add is, that you keep the whole matter as secret as possible. For upon Secrecy, Success depends in most Enterprises of the kind, and for want of it, they are generally defeated, however well planned and promising a favorable issue.[3]

As the nation's first President, Washington requested and received authority from the Congress for a Contingency Fund for the Conduct of Foreign Intercourse, placed in the budget of the Department of State, to be available for intelligence purposes. In the years that followed, U.S. Presidents would reject requests from the Congress for an accounting of expenditures from the fund. In the 1840s, President James Polk turned down such a request, responding in part to the Congress:

> The experience of every nation on earth has demonstrated that emergencies may arise in which it becomes absolutely necessary for the public safety or the public good to make expenditures, the very subject of which would be defeated by publicity. In no nation is the application of such funds to be made public.[4]

Intelligence operations of the separate U.S. military departments and civilian organizations would continue and would evolve through the 19th and the first half of the 20th century. The nation would turn a new chapter with the passage of the National Security Act of 1947, an act born of Pearl Harbor and the coming of the nuclear era, an act reshaping the nation's defense organization, an act creating the National Security Council—with the President, Vice President, Secretary of State, and Secretary of Defense as statutory members—an act creating a Central Intelligence Agency responsible to the National Security Council, a Central Intelligence Agency to be headed by a Director of Central Intelligence to be appointed by the President with the advice and consent of the Senate. Section 102 of the Act expanded on these organizational arrangements and responsibilities:

(d) For the purpose of coordinating the intelligence activities of the several Government departments and agencies in the interest of national security, it shall be the duty of the Agency, under the direction of the National Security Council—

(1) to advise the National Security Council in matters concerning such intelligence activities of the Government departments and agencies as relate to national security;

(2) to make recommendations to the National Security Council for the coordination of such intelligence activities of the departments and agencies of the Government as relate to the national security;

(3) to correlate and evaluate intelligence relating to the national security, and provide for the appropriate dissemination of such intelligence within the Government using where appropriate existing agencies and facilities: *Provided*, That the Agency shall have no police, subpena [sic], law-enforcement powers, or internal security functions: *Provided further*, That the departments and other agencies of the Government shall continue to collect, evaluate, correlate, and disseminate departmental intelligence: *And provided further*, That the Director of Central Intelligence shall be responsible for protecting intelligence sources and methods from unauthorized disclosure;

(4) to perform, for the benefit of the existing intelligence agencies, such additional services of common concern as the National Security Council determines can be more efficiently accomplished centrally;

(5) to perform such other functions and duties related to intelligence affecting the national security as the National Security Council may from time to time direct.[5]

The Act provided for the intelligence work and responsibilities of the separate military departments and other governmental organizations in addition to the Central Intelligence Agency. Within the framework of the Act, new intelligence organizations—the National Security Agency in 1952 and the Defense Intelligence Agency in 1961—would join the U.S. Intelligence Community. Successive U.S. Presidents would interpret and implement the authority vested in them by the Act through the formal issuance of Presidential Executive Orders.

THE EXECUTIVE AND LEGISLATIVE BASIS
FOR INTELLIGENCE

In the plaza of DIA's Defense Intelligence Analysis Center, the home of the Joint Military Intelligence College, which I am privileged to lead, there is a handsome, polished, six-sided chunk of granite bearing the seals of each of the Armed Services, the Joint Chiefs of Staff, and the Secretary of Defense. Atop the granite there is a plaque with the words, "Let us never forget that good intelligence saves American lives and protects our freedom," words chosen by President Ronald Reagan in December 1981 when he issued Presidential Executive Order 12333, the executive order that governs U.S. intelligence operations as we meet in March 1996.

The Executive Order spells out in remarkable clarity and detail the Intelligence Community's responsibilities to the President and the National Security Council, including those of the Director of Central Intelligence, other senior officials of the Community, the CIA, the Department of State, the Department of Treasury, the Department of Defense, the Defense Intelligence Agency, the National Security Agency, the intelligence arms of the Army, Navy, Air Force, and Marine Corps, the Department of Energy, and the Federal Bureau of Investigation.

The Executive Order provides the President's guidelines for the conduct of intelligence activities, including collection techniques, activities where approval of the Attorney General is required, and authorized assistance to law enforcement agencies. With regard to approval by the Attorney General of certain U.S. intelligence operations, the Executive Order states that "Electronic surveillance as defined in the Foreign Intelligence Surveillance Act of 1978, shall be conducted in accordance with that Act, as well as this Order."[6] Here it is important to reemphasize that civilian control over U.S. intelligence extends to the checks and balances of the three branches of government—in this case, the Judicial Branch. The Foreign Intelligence Surveillance Act created the Foreign Intelligence Surveillance Court "made up of seven U.S. district justices from around the country who hear *in camera* ex parte requests for surveillance orders from the Justice Department, acting on behalf of the NSA, the FBI and, occasionally, other intelligence agencies."[7] The introduction of the requirement for a judicial warrant was designed to provide one more check, one more safeguard against improper practices.

In the 1970s, newspaper revelations of Intelligence Community covert actions and alleged wrongdoings, coming at the time of national and international turmoil over the conflict in Vietnam and the Watergate scandal at home, caused the Congress to impose itself far more directly on the workings of U.S. intelligence.

The first legislative response was enactment in 1974 of the Hughes-Ryan Amendment to the Foreign Assistance Act of 1961. This amendment addressed the question of CIA covert actions and prohibited the use of appropriated funds for their conduct unless and until the President "finds" that each such operation is important to the National Security of the U.S. and submits this "finding" to the appropriate congressional committees-a total of six committees.[8]

In 1975, both the House and the Senate established committees to investigate the Intelligence Community. Known by the names of their respective chairmen—Representative Otis Pike and Senator Frank Church—the Pike and Church Committees cut a broad swath through the community. This was a period of pronounced confrontation between the Executive and Legislative Branches of Government. The recommendations of each committee would lead to the establishment of the Senate Select Committee on Intelligence in 1975 and the House Permanent Select Committee on Intelligence in 1977. In 1978, the oversight committees enacted the first Intelligence Authorization Act, giving them the control they sought of the Intelligence Community's budget.[9] As we meet, these committees are on the threshold of their third decade of service.

I would witness this transformation in the mid-1970s, first from my vantage point in the administration of President Ford and then from the administration of President Carter. As the head of President Ford's European staff on the National Security Council, I had the singularly unpleasant experience, as did many of my colleagues, of dealing with the abrasiveness and the rudeness of demands from members of the Pike Committee staff. In less than two years I would see the two branches of government begin the swing back from raw confrontation to more civil dealings. Senator Walter Mondale had served as a member of the Church Committee. As President Carter's Vice President, very early in the new administration, he would recommend steps aimed at a more constructive approach. As the Vice President's Assistant for National Security Affairs, I would participate in the first meeting between the President, the Vice President, and the Members of the Senate Select Committee in the Cabinet Room of the White House in 1977.

CIVILIAN CONTROL OF INTELLIGENCE: NOW AND IN THE FUTURE

In the United States, effective intelligence is viewed as an extremely important dimension of national security. The checks and balances shaped by the founding fathers have ensured that the entire workings of a democracy—of a government of the people, by the people, for the people—extend to and include the U.S. intelligence structure and operations. Civilian control of such structure and operations lies first with the President and the members of his National Security Council. Independent civilian oversight and funding for such structure and operations lie with members of the Senate and the House of Representatives of the Congress. The third dimension of civilian control—that of interpreting relevant laws—lies with judges of the Judicial Branch. The President, the Director of Central Intelligence, and the Heads of Agencies of the Community have advisory boards to assist with oversight. Last but not least, totally independent from government, there is the Fourth Estate, the nation's free press and electronic media, both

A. Denis Clift

reporting on the Community and its operations and volunteering very powerful opinions through editorials and commentary.

The United States has the most remarkable, most capable intelligence structure and operations of any nation in the world. We show remarkable candor, remarkable openness in the management of our intelligence affairs, at the same time that we exercise sensitivity, discretion, and silence on certain aspects of such work. As a nation, we are perpetually discontent with the Intelligence Community's status quo. For anyone working within the Community, this discontent can translate on any given day into a life of high stress, friction, and impossible demands. For the citizens of the United States, this constant attention to intelligence structure and operations is one more reflection of the government's commitment to providing for the security of our democracy.

CHAPTER 13
THE ROLE OF DEFENSE INTELLIGENCE

The author delivered "The Role of Defense Intelligence" as a speech at Princeton University, Oklahoma Baptist University, and the Foreign Service Institute in 1987, when he was serving as the Defense Intelligence Agency's Deputy Director for External Relations. The speech provides an excellent perspective for subsequent chapters in this book of readings. He "slits open the very full envelope" of defense intelligence to examine the creation of the Defense Intelligence Agency in 1961 as a principal member of the United States Intelligence Community. He examines its role in the 1960s, '70s, and '80s; the defined direction given by Presidential Executive Order 12333 in 1981; and the role played by Congressional oversight in the shaping of defense intelligence policy. He reviews the major pillars of DIA's contributions, including the provision of timely intelligence to U.S. warfighters around the world, the shaping of National Intelligence Estimates, management of the Defense Attaché System, and cooperation with allies in coalition operations.

For many years, perhaps more so than ever in the wake of this summer's televised Iran/Contra hearings, the mere mention of intelligence agencies evokes the image of secrecy and clandestine operations. Shortly after his confirmation, the new Director of Central Intelligence Judge William H. Webster was given a lapel button reading, "My job is so secret that even I don't know what I'm doing."

When I served on the National Security Council (NSC) staff, we handled a tremendous volume of intelligence as consumers of the Intelligence Community's products. I remember during one meeting with General Brent Scowcroft, who was then Assistant to the President for National Security Affairs, one of my colleagues saying that he understood the need for compartmentation, for need-to-know, for precise handling of information involving sensitive sources and methods. But, he said, the NSC was going too far. The day before he had received a hand-delivered, sealed envelope, stamped Top Secret / Sensitive / Eyes Only, with a red "Expedite" tag on it, from the West Wing of the White House. He had carefully slit it open and found it completely empty.

What I propose to do today is to slit open the very full envelope containing the world of defense intelligence and to examine the origins of the Defense Intelligence Agency (DIA), the role of defense intelligence, and the important position held by DIA in the U.S. Intelligence Community.

On 1 October 1986, Secretary of Defense Caspar Weinberger awarded the Defense Intelligence Agency the Joint Meritorious Unit Award for exceptionally meritorious service during 1985-1986. The words chosen for his citation provide a useful point of departure. During this period, he wrote,

> DIA provided unparalleled intelligence support encompassing the broadest range of intelligence analysis, technical services, photographic processing, and

reconnaissance imagery to meet the real-time requirements of national decisionmakers. Responding directly to immediate requirements, the Agency provided vital intelligence to policymakers during the tense periods of the TWA 847 hijacking incident, to on-site operational units during the *Achille Lauro* hijacking, to the White House staff during the Philippine crisis, and to Naval and Air Force component commanders during the Libyan counterterrorist operations. Never faltering in its commitment, the Agency provided the critical information demanded by the tactical commanders, without which success could not have been achieved, and national objectives would not have been realized.[1]

Implicit in that citation is the fact that the Defense Intelligence Agency is a leading authority, expert on the composition and the capabilities of the armed forces of other nations, as well as technically expert on foreign weapons systems. DIA is expert on the political and military environment in which those forces operate, expert on projecting through intelligence estimates the character of those forces in years ahead, and expert on the political and military character of the nations and the regions in which they operate.

The flow of intelligence from DIA—indications and warning, current intelligence, estimates, arms control monitoring, and targeting intelligence—is on the one hand directed to the Secretary of Defense, the Chairman of the Joint Chiefs of Staff, and other policy-level officials within the national security community in Washington. At the same time, the flow is to the Commanders in Chief of the Unified and Specified Commands, to their component commands in the Atlantic and Pacific theaters, for example, and to their operational units at the tactical level. DIA is also the expert on shaping intelligence information systems, networks of computerized intelligence information systems and their communications links permitting this two-way flow from national to tactical levels around the world.

This said, the Defense Intelligence Agency is only in its 26th year, and as such a member of a still very young U.S. Intelligence Community.

ORIGINS OF DIA

It was in the summer of 1941 that President Franklin D. Roosevelt was persuaded to create a formal U.S. foreign intelligence organization—the Office of the Coordinator of Information—to better enable the United States to deal with the storm of war already raging in Europe. Within the military services, there was quite literally almost no real intelligence capability.

In early February 1942, with the nation newly at war, Dwight David Eisenhower was promoted to the temporary rank of Major General and named by General George Marshall to become Chief of the nascent Operations Division of the War Department General Staff. His assignment was to help General Marshall reorganize the War Department for its wartime mission. Years later, in *Crusade in Europe,* Eisenhower would write:

Within the War Department, a shocking deficiency that impeded all constructive planning existed in the field of intelligence. The fault was partly within and partly without the Army. The American public has always viewed with repugnance everything that smacks of the spy; during the years between the two world wars no funds were provided with which to establish the basic requirement of an intelligence system—a far-flung organization of fact finders.[2]

A wartime military intelligence structure was built and continued to expand after the war ended. By 1947, the civilian Office of Strategic Services (OSS), which had emerged from the original Coordinator of Information, was transformed into the Central Intelligence Agency (CIA). In 1952, the National Security Agency (NSA) was established with prime responsibility for the nation's SIGINT, or signals intelligence. And, throughout the post-war period, the intelligence components of the Army, Navy, and Air Force grew as well.

In his book *The Real CIA,* Lyman Kirkpatrick, former Executive Director of CIA, examined this military intelligence growth within the services and how the evolutionary process led to the establishment of the Defense Intelligence Agency. Again, Eisenhower, now in the next-to-last year of his two-term presidency, had an important role to play. Although a habitual user of intelligence, Eisenhower had not realized how large the intelligence effort had grown since World War II. It took a dramatic incident to call it to his attention: the denunciation of U.S. intelligence activities in Berlin by Soviet Foreign Minister Andrei Gromyko in 1959. His allegations that U.S. intelligence work created a dangerous environment in Berlin prompted Ike to once again take a more direct interest in intelligence activities.

The result was a spate of studies in 1959 and 1960. A Joint Study Group, headed by Kirkpatrick, was given a vast subject to cover: "Foreign Intelligence Activities of the United States." But it was specifically asked to pay considerable attention to military intelligence and to probe at depth into the organization and procedures of the various Pentagon agencies. What the Joint Study Group found in the military intelligence system was a duplicatory and cumbersome method for issuing requirements for intelligence collection, with each of the three services often sending out identical requests for information both to their own collectors and to others. The Joint Study Group was also concerned about the fact that with each service and command publishing its own intelligence periodicals, the policy and command level was getting a multiplicity of views and interpretations.

It should also be recalled that these were years of intense inter-service rivalry for procurement funds—when plans for the Air Force's new strategic bombers were clashing with plans for the Navy's new generation of carriers. These were the years of the missile gap, and years of differing estimates by the Services' intelligence components on the nature and the severity of the Soviet Union's strategic and conventional challenge. There was thus the matter of participation in the production of national intelligence estimates. At that time there was no unified military view presented to the United States Intelligence Board (USIB), the governing board of the intelligence system in Washington. Then, six different military members from various organizations sat on the board. The Joint Study Group strongly recommended that there should be one presentation of the Defense estimate and not a possible six.

Late in 1960, the Group submitted its recommendations. The Eisenhower administration concluded that a consolidation of the Services' general intelligence activities (defined as all non-SIGINT, non-overhead, non-organic intelligence activities) was needed. The study group's most important proposals were to establish a Defense Intelligence Agency, remove the armed services' separate intelligence agencies from the USIB, charge DIA with resolving the conflicting service estimates, and, as the final judgment of the Department of Defense, report the findings to the USIB.

In February 1961, with the coming of the Kennedy administration, Secretary of Defense Robert S. McNamara advised the JCS of his decision to establish a Defense Intelligence Agency and tasked them with developing a plan that would integrate the military intelligence efforts of all DoD elements. In the fall of 1961, the Defense Intelligence Agency was established by Directive of the Secretary of Defense.

Two footnotes are in order about the dawning of this new era in the history of the U.S. Intelligence Community. First, Lyman Kirkpatrick and his Study Group members had taken it upon themselves in the summer of 1960 to visit a number of U.S. and Allied installations in the field and foreign capitals in Europe. And as they concluded this on-site work, Kirkpatrick put his finishing touches to a proposed first draft of their report. Rather than immediately winging their way back to Washington, they boarded the SS *United States* in Southampton and installed themselves in a suite of cabins including one reserved for drafting and conferences. They persuaded themselves that the ship's crew had mistaken them for a conference of beer salesmen. They met twice a day, and during the course of eight working sessions dissected the initial draft, defined their areas of agreement and disagreement, and settled on the additional information required before they tackled their final report. Those shapers of America's intelligence future were not victims of airliner red-eye; they knew how to travel. They had the good sense to set aside enough time for serious deliberations.

Secondly, the Services—as I was to witness in person—were not uniformly gracious in their acceptance of the new DIA. I was on active duty as a naval officer at the time, thousands of miles to the south on the second of two Antarctic expeditions. With the Berlin crisis of December 1961, I received orders to the Office of Naval Intelligence—high up, on the fifth floor, in the most remote regions of the Pentagon. During the day, officials of the new DIA would install the Agency's title and office symbols on Navy offices that had been earmarked for transfer. By night those signs came down and the old navy names and numbers were restored. There was everything but the crack of sniper gunfire as the young Defense agency labored to take its place alongside the separate services.

DIA's EARLY YEARS

It is not my intention to provide a detailed history of the Defense Intelligence Agency's first 25 years. The Agency would play military intelligence roles of central importance in the Cuban Missile Crisis of 1962[3] and throughout the years of U.S. forces fighting in Vietnam. In the mid- to late-1970s, defense intelligence weathered reductions in manpower following the U.S. withdrawal from Vietnam. It also survived the hearings and the findings of the Church Committee and the Pike Committee in the Congress. I will return to congressional oversight later.

DIA IN THE 1980s

The 1980s marked more than a half decade of very significant growth for the Defense Intelligence Agency—growth in manpower, in funding, and in professional responsibilities. The document undergirding that growth is the President's Executive Order 12333 of 4 December 1981. I had served in the preceding administration, the Carter administration, as Assistant to the Vice President for National Security Affairs. Working for Vice President Mondale, who had been a member of the Church Committee as a senator, I had tracked the crafting of the Carter administration's intelligence executive order 12036. That executive order came into being while the Executive and Legislative branches were working to heal the wounds of the mid-1970s and to restore a greater degree of trust between the two branches on intelligence activities. It was restrictive in tone, with primary attention given to the limited powers and the carefully defined limited scope of operations entrusted to the Intelligence Community.

Executive Order 12333, signed by President Ronald Reagan, was of an entirely different character. It looked to broaden the authority of the members of the Intelligence Community, and it recognized the importance of a strong intelligence capability to the foreign policy and national security interests of the United States. Indeed, one sentence from the President's statement introducing the Executive Order has been preserved and displayed on a granite stone in the plaza of DIA's Defense Intelligence Analysis Center: "Let us never forget, good intelligence saves American lives and protects our freedom."

Executive Order 12333, which guides DIA's role in the Intelligence Community today, opens with these words:

> Timely and accurate information about the activities, capabilities, plans, and intentions of foreign powers, organizations, and persons, and their agents, is essential to the national security of the United States. All reasonable and lawful means must be used to ensure that the United States will receive the best intelligence available.[4]

The Executive Order charges the community with providing the President and the National Security Council the information necessary for decisions required to safeguard the nation and to advance U.S. national interests. It places maximum emphasis on analytical competition within the community. Quoting the document again: "All means, consistent with applicable United States law and this Order, and with full consideration of the rights of United States persons, shall be used to develop intelligence information for the President and the National Security Council."[5] Detection and countering of espionage against the United States are given specific emphasis.

A. Denis Clift

Within this policy context, the Executive Order sets forth the mission of the Defense Intelligence Agency as follows: collection and production of military and military-related intelligence for defense consumers and for national foreign intelligence and counterintelligence products; coordination of intelligence collection requirements within the Department of Defense; management of the Defense Attaché System; and provision of foreign intelligence and counterintelligence staff support to the Chairman and the Joint Chiefs of Staff.[6]

CONGRESSIONAL OVERSIGHT OF DEFENSE INTELLIGENCE

Given this strong Executive Branch mandate, it is important as well to note the subject of congressional oversight. Earlier this year [1987], at the outset of the confirmation hearings of Judge William Webster to be the Director of Central Intelligence (DCI), Senator David Boren, Chairman of the Senate Select Committee on Intelligence, said:

> This Committee and the Senate have a duty to the American people to ensure that the new Director of Central Intelligence will conduct a program of effective intelligence gathering within the framework of our laws and our democratic institutions. It is imperative that the Director of Central Intelligence be a person of exceptional ability and integrity, capable of exercising the independence necessary to protect against any possible misuse of the Agency and its resources.[7]

Two weeks ago [September 1987], Congressman Louis Stokes, Chairman of the House Permanent Select Committee on Intelligence, addressed a graduating class of the Defense Intelligence College [now the Joint Military Intelligence College]. As we know from having followed the Iran/Contra Hearings this summer, Mr. Stokes is also a member of the Select Committee. At the Defense Intelligence College, he asked, rhetorically, if the Iran/Contra hearings were worth it. He answered:

> I think so. I think we are a stronger nation today because we are able to critically examine our nation under the world's microscope. Other nations around the world marveled at our ability to hang our dirty linen on the line. That to me is the strength of a free, open, democratic society. And that to me is how you ensure the continuation of such a society.[8]

Just as the members of the House and Senate attached importance to those specific hearings, so the members of the House Permanent Select Committee and the Senate Select Committee on Intelligence attach importance to their broader, continuing intelligence oversight responsibilities. In his commencement address, Chairman Stokes went on to say:

> Virtually every member of Congress supports a strong intelligence community. From that point of agreement, we get into arguments about how much, about how it should operate, and about how far secret, and more particularly covert actions shall go in a free and democratic society. These are legitimate and diffi-

cult issues and sometimes they are divisive, but don't let those disputes hide from you the fact that the Congress supports strong intelligence. There are budget problems. The intelligence world is evermore complex. There are simply more areas of the world that are of concern to us today than 10 or 20 years ago. There are more people, more governments, more communications, more radars, more military units which we need to know about. It costs a lot of money, and the intelligence budget has increased dramatically in recent years. But we all know that the last couple of years have been tough. Government deficits are too high, and the tendency is to take cuts pretty much across the board. The intelligence committees and those elements of the appropriations committees which handle your budgets are your advocates.[9]

I have drawn so liberally from Chairman Stokes' words because they serve to confirm, from his important position, some key points:

- The House and Senate Select Committees on Intelligence have taken root; they have large professional staffs, and they work hard at their responsibilities for oversight of the Intelligence Community, year round. Given my responsibilities for management of DIA's legislative liaison with the Congress, I can say that the committees are heavy consumers of our defense intelligence; they are demanding consumers; and they are informed consumers.

- Second, and flowing from the first, there is, indeed, a healthy tension between the Executive and Legislative branches as to the limits of this oversight role and its management. Many of you have no doubt read or heard of the calls from various quarters for a single joint House-Senate Intelligence Oversight Committee, with a single, more modestly sized staff.

- Third, we must appreciate the fact that these Committees are the Intelligence Community's budget advocates, not adversaries. Good intelligence costs money, and in an era of fiscal restraint, a healthy respect between Congress and the Intelligence Community is critical to the realization of national security goals.

In the final analysis, in the framework of all the checks and balances we impose upon ourselves as a government and a society, we have today a state of relations that is more positive than negative between the Executive and Legislative branches.

DIA IN 1987

Having sketched in the origins of the Defense Intelligence Agency and the policy setting in which DIA operates, we should take a few minutes to focus more closely on DIA today: how it is structured, and the manner in which it is meeting its responsibilities. DIA today, with its headquarters in the Pentagon, is an organization of some 5,000 military and civilian personnel. Its leadership includes a military Director and a civilian Deputy Director. Its internal directorates are headed by military and civilian Deputy Directors. The vast majority of DIA employees, along with the Defense Intelligence College, are located in the new

A. Denis Clift

Defense Intelligence Analysis Center on Bolling Air Force Base, in southeast Washington, DC. Various supporting activities located throughout the world complete the DIA mosaic.

The Director of DIA serves in several major capacities: He is the senior substantive intelligence advisor to the Secretary of Defense; he is the senior intelligence officer, or J-2, on the Joint Chiefs of Staff; he is the Director of the Defense Intelligence Agency; he manages the Defense Special Security System; he is manager of the General Defense Intelligence Program (GDIP), which oversees intelligence budgets for the Army, Air Force, Navy, Marine Corps, and DIA; he is the manager of Human Intelligence (HUMINT) assets; he is a member of the National Foreign Intelligence Council; and he is the principal Department of Defense member of the National Foreign Intelligence Board (NFIB) for all substantive matters.

The NFIB, chaired by the Director of Central Intelligence (DCI), is the successor to the United States Intelligence Board and the forum in which National Intelligence Estimates (NIEs) are formally considered and adopted by the U.S. Intelligence Community. To coordinate the views of the separate military services and to bring a coordinated defense intelligence position to the board—one of the principal reasons Lyman Kirkpatrick and his team had in 1960 recommended the creation of a DIA—the Director of DIA chairs a Military Intelligence Board, with the Intelligence Chiefs of each of the Services as members.

A year ago, in a speech honoring DIA, the late Director of Central Intelligence William Casey, commenting on the national intelligence estimates process, said:

> There can be no question that DIA is a full and valued partner in the Intelligence Community as you celebrate your 25th year. Rather, the critical question before us is how each of us as partners can best harness and blend our professional contributions to accomplish the vitally important missions this nation expects of us. If we are to accomplish these missions, we must continue to work together to enhance intelligence collection, analysis, production, and dissemination. To this end, I have revamped the national intelligence estimates process—intelligence analysis which is vital to the decisionmaker—with the goal of ensuring the integrity and objectivity of each estimate, together with its accuracy and timeliness. I have emphasized the importance I place on having all members of the Intelligence Community participate in the estimates process, and the Defense Intelligence Agency continues to play an increasingly larger role, particularly on those estimates requiring your expert military knowledge.[10]

DIA AND NATIONAL ESTIMATES

DIA plays a principal role in the NIE process. The Agency's Directorate for Foreign Intelligence produces the defense intelligence estimates and the DIA contributions to the NIEs. In addition to estimates, as the producer of finished military intelligence this directorate develops and maintains intelligence databases. These include military ground, naval, air, missile, and space forces around the world; military and paramilitary organizations; foreign national terrorism and counterterrorism capabilities and activities; war resource material production; military-related political and economic development; biographies of foreign military officials; and details on foreign military installations. The Directorate's work involves intensive analysis and production relating to the military forces of the [former] Soviet Union.

Last month, the Soviets permitted a congressional delegation to visit the Large Phased Array Radar under construction at Krasnoyarsk, prompting considerable debate here and abroad on their motives. There is a story making the rounds in Europe these days which poses the question: What would happen if you were on a train with one of the Soviet leaders from Moscow to Smolensk, and you found the train had stopped because it had run out of tracks? Actually there are four answers:

- If you had been traveling with Lenin, he would have ordered everybody out of the train, had them tear up the tracks behind the train, carry them to the front, and then repeat this process until the train reached Smolensk.
- If you had been traveling with Stalin, he would have had the engineers and conductors shot and marched the passengers to their destination.
- If you had been traveling with Brezhnev, he would have ordered all the train's curtains closed and had the peasants in the neighboring fields come over to shake the cars to give the sensation of motion.
- And if you had been traveling with Gorbachev, he would have smiled, opened all the train's windows and cried out for all to hear, "We have run out of tracks, we have to change the system."

The jury is still out on Mr. Gorbachev and his policies. The fact is that the USSR still exercises extreme secrecy in regard to its military forces, and the role of defense intelligence in monitoring those forces and analyzing their composition and capabilities is of tremendous importance to this nation's defense and those of our allies. To cite just one example, the USSR has recently announced that its new rail-mobile SS-24 ICBM is entering operations. We see this push for greater strategic mobility across Soviet forces—mobility for survivability and increased operational flexibility. Mobility multiplies the intelligence challenge geometrically. Defense intelligence necessarily is an extremely dynamic business.

DIA AND STRATEGIC WARNING

As part of its mission, the Defense Intelligence Agency monitors signs of crisis throughout the world on an around-the-clock basis, managing a worldwide indications and warning network; it operates the nation's 24-hour-a-day national military intelligence center; manages and operates the Defense Intelligence Collection Coordination Facility, which tasks various collection systems and coordinates with national reconnaissance authorities; manages and operates the Defense Attaché System; manages all Department of Defense Human Intelligence assets; and provides intelligence support to the Commanders in Chief of the Unified and Specified Commands, the "war-fighting CINCS," as they are known.

A. Denis Clift

To cite one area of increasingly important support for these operational commanders, DIA is placing priority on rapid preparation of various intelligence products involving terrorism and low intensity conflict. Such products can be used to assist planners and operators faced with short-fused requirements. DIA can prepare and disseminate large volumes of very detailed area of operations information within 48 hours of notification.

In order to be in a position to anticipate, rather than react to a crisis, DIA has established two permanent crisis support groups—one that addresses terrorism and another that addresses low intensity conflict. All terrorism analysis—and the policy, planning, and operational support that results—is accomplished by a 40-man DIA team, an element manning a 24-hour watch in the National Military Intelligence Center, publishing daily summaries of worldwide terrorist activity and developing the detailed databases needed to support the implementation of U.S. counterterrorist strategy. This organizational concept allows rapid shifting of analytical emphasis in response to international terrorist activity.

This means that if a hijacking or other act of terrorism suddenly occurs, the branch can shift immediately to its crisis mode and be responding to rapidly developing requirements in a matter of minutes. Similarly, DIA is organizing a dedicated analytical staff to provide the full range of defense intelligence support relating to counterinsurgencies, narcotics interdiction, and low intensity conflict issues, support that extends today to our forces operating in the Persian Gulf and neighboring regions.

DIA manages the Defense Attaché System, with Army, Navy, Air Force, and Defense Attachés in capitals throughout the world. It manages the Department of Defense's human source intelligence collection operations. And, again as called for by the Kirkpatrick study group in 1960, DIA manages, levies, and evaluates all Department of Defense intelligence collection, imagery, SIGINT, and collection from other technical sensors.

DIA: DEFENSE INTELLIGENCE FOR THE NATION'S SECURITY

As a nation, as Congressman Stokes has said, we do tend to look at our Government, including the Intelligence Community, under a microscope. We focus on the problems and the flaws—as part of the business of checks and balances, as part of the process of contributing to the nation's revitalizing powers and long-term strengths. If we want to be reminded of these strengths, and of the way that others look to the strengths and role of the U.S. Intelligence Community, it is instructive to reflect upon the words of British masters of intelligence literature for another perspective:

John LeCarre, in *Tinker, Tailor, Soldier, Spy,* has an inebriated Roddy Martindale of the Foreign Office telling George Smiley, recently retired Dean of Intelligence at MI-6: "And don't tell me the Americans have started trusting us again, either."[11]

Frederick Forsyth, in *The Fourth Protocol,* has John Preston of MI-5 speaking to the Director General Sir Bernard Hemmings, and I quote:

Preston explained briefly and concisely what had happened at the Ministry of Defence that morning, and the view of Capstick regarding the feasibility of the documents' departure from the Ministry's being anything other than a deliberate act.

"Oh my God, not another," murmured Sir Bernard. The memory of Vassall and Prime still rankled, as did the acid reaction of the Americans when they had been apprised.[12]

And finally, Graham Greene, in *The Human Factor,* has Colonel Daintry investigating a leak to the Soviets from somewhere in MI-6. Sir John Hargraves asks him:

"Suppose we did prove Davis to be the culprit-or Castle or Watson. What should we do then?"

"Surely that would be up to the courts," Daintry said. "Headlines in the papers. Another trial in camera. No one outside who would know how small and unimportant the leaks were. Whoever he is won't rate forty years like Blake. Perhaps he'll serve ten if the prison's secure."

"That's not our concern surely."

"No, Daintry, but I don't enjoy the thought of that trial one little bit. What cooperation can we expect from the Americans afterwards?"[13]

Suffice it to say that there is cooperation with friends and allies as part of the work of the U.S. defense intelligence community. It is in so many ways an extremely capable community, with the Defense Intelligence Agency working primarily to unify the intelligence efforts of the entire Department of Defense, strengthen Department of Defense capabilities for the collection, production, and dissemination of intelligence, and provide for the most efficient allocation and management of defense intelligence resources.

CHAPTER 14
NATIONAL SECURITY AND NATIONAL
COMPETITIVENESS: OPEN SOURCE SOLUTIONS

Freedom of expression, freedom of publication, freedom of the press—open access to information that other nations might safeguard as sensitive or classified—are at the core of American democracy. In a 1992 speech delivered to the Symposium on National Security and National Competitiveness and subsequently published in the American Intelligence Journal, *the author emphasizes the importance of greater use of authoritative, unclassified information by the Intelligence Community, especially in a future marked by shrinking budgets and reduced intelligence resources. Drawing on his experiences as Editor of* United States Naval Institute Proceedings, *he cites the thoroughness and intensity with which other nations exploit U.S. unclassified information. He highlights some excellent unclassified databases and points to the expanding access to information offered by the electronic era.*

When I came to defense intelligence in 1981, my first major assignment was to serve as editor in chief of a new publication that would become one of the better-read official open source documents in the world. That publication—*Soviet Military Power*—over 10 successive editions would provide annual unclassified, indeed officially declassified, updates on the strategic and conventional forces of the Soviet Union, from their buildup in the early and mid-1980s to their transition in the late 1980s and early 1990s, first with the collapse of the Warsaw Pact and then the impending dissolution of the USSR. NATO Allies, friends and allies around the world used the document. When Secretary of Defense Dick Cheney dropped in on a committee of the Supreme Soviet in session in 1990, one of the committee members was waving a copy of the 1990 edition in support of his argument.

Earlier in my career, from 1963 to 1966, I had been the editor of an even more enduring, extremely valuable open-source publication, the *United States Naval Institute Proceedings.* Thinking about my meeting with you today, I randomly selected one of the issues from that time, the September 1964 *Proceedings.* I was not disappointed. Its contents by article title included: "The East European Alliance System," written by a Naval War College Professor; "Protection of Merchant Shipping," by an active-duty Lieutenant Commander; "An Approach to ASW," by a Lieutenant Commander; "Data Processing in Personnel Management," by a Navy Captain; "The Chinese Communist Navy," by another active-duty Captain; "Cost Effectiveness: Fact and Fancy," by a Commander; "Rocket Development" (a history), by a Navy Captain; and a pictorial essay on the Indian Head, Maryland Naval Propellant Plant with brilliant, detailed photography examining the plant's internal and external layout and the processes involved for the propellants used in ZUNI rockets, antisubmarine rockets (ASROC), and the Polaris missile.

This was an issue, as are most issues of the *Proceedings,* that would be read and referenced by good friends and adversaries in many countries.

A. Denis Clift

THE CONSTITUTIONAL CORE OF OUR DEMOCRACY

Freedom of the press is at the core of our democracy. The free flow of ideas is central to our resilience, evolution, and strength as a people and nation. We are better informed, better served as a military profession and as a democracy because of our open discussion of issues that would be considered too sensitive or classified in *other* nations. One other result, as we all appreciate, is that the United States for decade after decade has been an unprecedented source of open source information for other nations, and they have *attempted* to use that information to maximum advantage. I say "attempted" because, given the incredible volume of open source information available, the challenge for them has been to narrow the field, to understand their sources, and to exercise professional care in the information selected for further reading, reference, and analysis.

A few years ago, one of Canada's attachés assigned to Washington said: "You get so much information you don't know what to do with it. Starting with the paper in the morning, you get *choked*." And this is the challenge for us today, in defense intelligence as elsewhere in the national community: to appreciate fully the critical changes in the world transforming closed societies into more open societies where information of interest, of importance to us, is now openly available—*if* we are aware of its existence; to train ourselves to discover and use emerging open sources; to train ourselves to rework our professional fields with the keen awareness that there have been and continue to be invaluable sources of open information that we have either been ignorant of or have discarded in favor of seemingly more exotic classified sources of information; to learn to avoid tangential excursions; to avoid choking on this new wealth of open source information; and to engage government, the academic and research communities, and the private sector to maximize our talents, our capabilities, our successes in using open source information.

OPEN SOURCES AND DEFENSE INTELLIGENCE

In fact, within defense intelligence today, open source intelligence plays a significant role in finished intelligence production both in its own right and in conjunction with information from other sources. It has proven essential to intelligence analysis and operations. It provides unique information; it provides complementary and confirming information in support of the defense intelligence mission.

In our business it is fun, truly a pleasure, to see our professionals "twig" to this marvelous "INT." One of our analysts was working a critical problem using other sources, and had reached a juncture in his analysis at which he had two alternative paths to pursue. He was looking at a photograph of some buildings and could not determine what one of them was. The building had an unusual architectural feature that made it stand out. He showed the photo to a colleague, asked if he had ever seen anything that looked like it. The other analyst looked at the photo and said, "You know, I believe I have seen that somewhere." He went back to his office and dug through some open source journals he had been looking at-and there it was! Not only was there a clear picture, but the picture had a caption that identified the purpose of the building. EUREKA!!

A principal open source strength of defense intelligence is the scientific and technical intelligence information services program, which had its genesis in an early 1960s program at the Air Force's Foreign Technology Division—today the National Air Intelligence Center. Major components of the program include Central Information Reference and Control (CIRC), the automated, predominantly open source database of foreign scientific and technical information references and abstracts; *The Foreign Languages Program,* a major component of which is the machine translation program; and the information services activities at each of the Defense Scientific and Technical Intelligence Centers. Taken together, this program provides a very professional repository, a source of considerable experience and expertise in dealing with open source information which will serve defense intelligence and the Intelligence Community at large in good stead. This is the case for future development of community open source functional support centers for scientific and technical intelligence at the National Air Intelligence Center. It is the case for general military intelligence at DIA.

As an illustration of the growth of the CIRC database—in 1968, the database contained 1.2 million records; it now contains over 10 million, about 6 million of which are open source records. There were seven user organizations initially, and now there are over a hundred, including Intelligence Community components, other government agencies, and government contractors.

Another defense intelligence open source strength resides in the broad, worldwide defense intelligence collection infrastructure. Both Service and DIA capabilities include activities that can and do acquire open source information such as foreign S&T publications and materials, publications containing information about foreign weapons systems, training and doctrine manuals, military organization and planning documents, maps and town plans, and other materials useful for contingency planning or otherwise responsive to defense information requirements.

Still another defense intelligence capability is DODIIS—the Department of Defense Intelligence Information System—which is the foundation for the infrastructure that will provide our capability to place open source data where needed and in formats that are usable by analysts and warfighters. Fortunately, much of this foundation, which will be integral to the community's broader architecture and open source information exchange, has already been built or is underway.

I mentioned being a *producer* of open source information. At another point, in the 1970s, I was a *consumer* on the NSC and White House staffs. Bulletins, fast-breaking news, can be of critical importance to Presidents, the policy level of government. In those days, before CNN, the wire service reports flowing through the White House Situation Room—AP, UPI, Reuters, Agence France Press—were monitored as closely as the classified intelligence traffic. They were the cutting edge, the tip-off, the current information. Today, of course, we are well into the electronic, video era—an era in which CNN cameras capture cruise missiles in combat, en route to their targets.

In defense intelligence we are part of this era. We are pioneering in the community with our classified Defense Intelligence Network (DIN), a television broadcast system. We are pioneering with video flow of intelligence in JWICS—the Joint Worldwide Intelligence Communications System. We are working hand-in-hand with the Foreign Broadcast Information Service, FBIS, drawing on its television collection capabilities at the same time that we continue to draw on its voice and print capabilities. In the video field, we are developing a global capability for I&W, current intelligence, the sharing of data at the national, theater, and component levels. This is a growth area for defense intelligence; open source is central to our capabilities.

A NEW AGE OF OPEN SOURCE INFORMATION

Returning to the changes around the world, indeed, returning to the reason for this first symposium, new world realities—the recent collapse of authoritarian regimes in the former Soviet Union and Eastern Europe, political liberalization elsewhere in the world, advances in media production and dissemination technologies, and the increasing commercialization of information—have resulted in more available and accessible open source information than ever before. We stand, in essence, at the beginning of the open source information age. The availability and value of open source information to defense intelligence will continue to grow, as will its contribution in comparison to higher cost collection systems and methodologies. As budgets shrink and defense intelligence resources are adjusted, open source data will be invaluable for continued monitoring of military forces, military facilities, and military developments around the world, as well as the analysis and flow of intelligence required by the operator for effective and timely responses to them.

In 1992 the Director of Central Intelligence (DCI) established the position of Intelligence Community Open Source Coordinator. Paul Wallner, one of DIA's senior executives, was selected for that new position, and defense intelligence is playing an important role in the development and implementation of the DCI's open source strategic plan. To this end, and to ensure that all defense intelligence efforts follow a common path, we have developed a strategy for open source as a unique entity within the General Defense Intelligence Program (GDIP). This strategy is intended to build on existing strengths, address critical shortfalls, and, in general, to support and leverage the community plan in meeting defense intelligence requirements.

Defense intelligence has a significant number of strengths on which we and the larger Intelligence Community can build for the future. We have significant challenges still to be met. Taking stock of our capabilities, most open source material remains in hardcopy, and there does not exist a widely available on-line index and catalogue of available open source information. Current capabilities remain predominantly aimed at the production and dissemination of hardcopy products. To make the huge amount of open source information available to users, we must foster the use of electronic media by the producers of open source information, convert paper products to electronic ones, and disseminate the information electronically to national and tactical users.

Our automated tools do not provide sufficient capabilities for data retrieval and extraction to cope with either the current or the future "infoglut" which plagues defense intelligence analysts. A related problem is the need for higher volume, more reliable scanning and optical character recognition systems to aid in the capture of open source information. And finally, current machine translation capabilities are not adequate for the diversity of foreign language material of interest to General Defense Intelligence Program users and customers.

WHITHER OPEN SOURCE?

To build on our strengths and to address our shortfalls, we have established the following GDIP priorities for the open source program over the remainder of this decade:

- First, maintain current capabilities as a baseline for the GDIP open source program.
- Second, make careful investments to redress fundamental shortfalls in the infrastructure and automated tools.
- Third, establish a coherent management structure. As a first step, we are forming a GDIP open source steering group that will be chaired by a representative of the functional manager for scientific and technical intelligence, who will also serve as the GDIP Open Source Program Manager. Standing members of the steering group will be representatives from the other functional managers, the Services, and DIA.
- Fourth, improve acquisition and collection capabilities.
- Finally, under the auspices of the Community's Strategic Plan, fully implement functional support centers, or "storefronts," for science and technology and for general military intelligence.

In summary, defense intelligence involvement in and commitment to open source information have had a long and productive history. Improvements to increase our access to and use of this valuable resource should provide not only the defense establishment but also the government at large with a significantly improved return on its investment in open source. We look forward to meeting these exciting new challenges and to the role of defense intelligence as an integral component of the overall Intelligence Community effort.

CHAPTER 15
THE FIVE-LEGGED CALF: BRINGING INTELLIGENCE
TO THE NATIONAL SECURITY DEBATE

In this essay, which originally appeared in the American Intelligence Journal *in 1989, the author examines the relationship of classified intelligence and public policy, and the contributions of intelligence to policy debate. He looks at the increasing use of formally declassified intelligence information in Government White Papers on major issues, focusing on the Department of Defense's annual report* Soviet Military Power *as his principal case study. The essay provides a fascinating perspective on global intelligence issues. It draws on experiences from the Cuban Missile Crisis, when intelligence materials formerly considered sensitive—such as U-2 reconnaissance photos—were released for the greater good of keeping the American public informed of a developing threat to national security. Significant, continuing contributions by the Intelligence Community to public dialogue and to informed policy decisionmaking, he notes, have caused the public to begin regarding government-provided information as something less of a marvel than a five-legged calf.*

On 13 June 1989, *The Washington Post* illustrated a story on the resumption of the Strategic Arms Reduction Talks with a photograph of the U.S. MX intercontinental missile and an artist's rendering of the USSR's SS-24 rail-mobile ICBM launcher. The rendering, which had originally appeared in the 1985 edition of the Department of Defense's annual report *Soviet Military Power,* remains the most detailed unclassified picture of the Soviets' fifth-generation rail-mobile ICBM system. Its appearance in the *Post* served as a reminder of the role of intelligence in the greater availability of authorized information on Soviet weapons systems.

CRACKING THE GREEN DOOR

The U.S. Intelligence Community has entered an era in which Presidents and the policy level of government are attaching increasing importance to formal public release of declassified intelligence studies to assist in the structuring of public debate on critical international issues. Such releases, in effect, have become government White Papers on key issues of our time.

The reason for this growing practice is clear. Declassified intelligence analyses, often supported by photography and graphics, offer hard, persuasive facts not otherwise available. The challenge for the Intelligence Community and the government is to ensure first that sources of the information and the methods of its collection are protected as necessary, and second that the work of the community is presented objectively and the intelligence is not slanted to accommodate a policy objective. With these safeguards in place, the Intelligence

---

A. Denis Clift

Community is emerging with increasing frequency from behind its "green door" to assume a visibly relevant role in national and international debate.

On 19 February 1989, A.M. Rosenthal began his column "Profiles in Terrorism," in *The New York Times,* on the destruction of Pan Am Flight 103, with the following:

> Name: Popular Front for the Liberation of Palestine — General Command (P.F.L.P.-G.C.)
> Date Formed: 1968
> Estimated Membership: 500
> Headquarters: Syria
> Area of Operations: Middle East, especially Lebanon, Jordan and Israel
> Leadership: Ahmed Jabril
> Other Names: None
> Sponsors: Syria, Libya
> That is an entry in a United States Government publication profiling all known terrorist groups.[1]

The publication Mr. Rosenthal referred to was *Terrorist Group Profiles,* published by the Department of Defense a few weeks before with an introductory letter by then-Vice President George Bush. The fact that it was referenced so quickly in the press attested to its relevance and value to the public debate on terrorism. The fact that it could be produced in a timely, authoritative manner attested to the capabilities of the Intelligence Community.

In releasing the publication at the Pentagon on 19 January 1989, the Assistant Secretary of Defense for Special Operations and Low Intensity Conflict, Ambassador Charles Whitehouse, made reference to the 1986 Vice President's Task Force on Combating Terrorism report and its call for an effort to make the public aware of the realities of the terrorist threat, and through the dissemination of factual information the removal of the mystique often surrounding such groups. Toward that end, the *Terrorist Group Profiles* have been published "not as an intelligence document," Ambassador Whitehouse said, "but rather a compilation of open-source material that has been verified by classified sources. The Terrorist Analysis Branch of the Defense Intelligence Agency did a splendid job of preparing and editing the text."[2]

UNCLASSIFIED INTELLIGENCE REPORTING

It comes as no surprise that the Intelligence Community produces unclassified research publications and presentations as part of its normal business. These have ranged from CIA's *The World Factbook* to more detailed studies in such fields as agriculture and energy; to excellent atlases highlighting regional geographic, sociological, and economic perspectives; to annual testimony before the Joint Economic Committee of the Congress in open session by CIA and DIA on the Soviet economy.

From time to time, there has also been other, candid, far-reaching unclassified testimony on major international military issues, such as the statement on Soviet Strategic Force

Developments given 16 June 1985 by CIA's Deputy Director for Intelligence and the National Intelligence Officer for Strategic Programs before a joint session of subcommittees of the Senate Armed Services and Appropriations Committees. *The Washington Post* of 17 June 1985 reported that certain Senators present questioned whether the testimony had a political, partisan purpose, to which the *Post* quoted the senior CIA witness Robert Gates as

> saying he would not "address motives of the White House," . . . that profes-
> sional intelligence officers "face somewhat of a dilemma." . . . "We're fully
> aware of the dangers of a public presentation to the integrity and objectivity of
> our assessments." . . . "We also recognize the value of making available on a
> broad basis a commonly agreed set of facts for discussion of Soviet strategic
> force development."[3]

Getting the facts before the American public on Soviet political and military developments—and the correct role of intelligence in that process—has been a multifaceted challenge confronting policymakers for decades. Following the 1962 Cuban Missile Crisis, there were strong doubts in certain quarters that the USSR had, in fact, withdrawn its offensive nuclear weaponry. To eliminate such doubts, Secretary of Defense Robert S. McNamara presided over a nationally televised briefing on 6 February 1963—a briefing drawing on previously classified reconnaissance photography—to document the USSR's withdrawal. At the conclusion of the briefing, a reporter asked: "Mr. Secretary, in as much as you had to reshow, in effect, the photographs to re-establish what is taking place in Cuba, what is your rationale for at first refusing to release photographs taken in Cuba and since then restricting how many photographs you release for publication?" Secretary McNamara responded:

> We are dealing with very sensitive matters this afternoon. A number of ques-
> tions have been raised regarding the type of Soviet equipment currently in
> Cuba. A number of doubts have been expressed as to whether the offensive
> systems which were introduced into Cuba by the Soviet Union have been
> removed. We considered it so important to expose you to the extent of our
> knowledge that we have done so, even at the risk of degrading our intelligence
> capability. It is always a fine line to draw between the release of the informa-
> tion that is in the public interest on the one hand, and the maintenance of secu-
> rity of our intelligence collection efforts on the other.[4]

When decisions have been taken on an ad hoc basis by those in authority to cross the fine line, to release intelligence in the national interest, controversy has been repeatedly rekindled on the rules and ethics governing such release. As in the case of Secretary McNamara in 1963, those lawfully charged with responsibility for the government are in positions to make decisions releasing previously classified information to the public if the national interest so warrants. Those opposed to official policies have argued through the years that they have as much a right and a responsibility to make information publicly available as do those who are in authority. In defense of their argument they have observed cynically that the U.S. Ship of State is "the only vessel that leaks upward from the top." The result is that disclosure of information, both authorized and unauthorized, is a fact of the current era.

Clearly, release of information cannot be delegated to the cynics and the disenchanted. The laws and executive orders governing classification and the distribution and declassification of classified information have been drafted, debated, and enacted by the government throughout the life of the Intelligence Community. They must be strictly enforced in the best interests of the nation. The challenge for the policymaker has been and continues to be how best to systemize declassification of important information in a manner best serving the public interest. From this process has emerged the growing use of the White Paper. The publication of eight successive editions of the government's report *Soviet Military Power* provides an instructive case study.

SOVIET MILITARY POWER: A CASE STUDY

In May 1981, NATO drew a line for the Soviet Union when the NATO Foreign Ministers' Communique included the following statement:

> The more constructive East-West relationship which the Allies seek requires tangible signs that the Soviet Union is prepared to abandon the disturbing buildup of its military strength, to desist from resorting to force and intimidation, and to cease creating or exploiting situations of crisis and instability in the Third World.[5]

As part of his participation in the NATO Defense Ministers' meeting in that spring of 1981, Secretary of Defense Caspar Weinberger had presented classified briefings on the breadth and rapidity of the USSR's military buildup. Several NATO colleagues asked if he could help them find a way to present the substance of these briefings to wider publics in their countries. He undertook to do so. To reveal the magnitude of the disturbing buildup of military strength on the Soviet side of that line, the Department of Defense, in coordination with other Executive Branch departments and agencies, published the first edition of *Soviet Military Power* that following September.

The Soviets had begun the 1980s with strategic nuclear, intermediate nuclear, and conventional armed forces that, in both absolute and relative terms, were substantially more capable than Soviet Forces of a decade before. The first edition of *Soviet Military Power* was released by the Secretary of Defense in a press conference at the Pentagon on 29 September 1981, a press conference transmitted simultaneously via satellite to some 200 European journalists gathered at NATO Headquarters.

IMPACT ON FOREIGN AUDIENCES

Largely as a result of the original NATO Ministers' request, the first edition of *Soviet Military Power* was prepared mainly for U.S. and Western European audiences, with its primary focus on Soviet force capabilities in the Western Theater of Operations, and with related information on the military-industrial base and the USSR's research and development aimed at modern military technology. The publication received wide publicity in terms of media coverage both in the United States and overseas. The first printing of 30,000 copies went quickly, and a second printing was ordered. The publication had instant champions and instant critics. *Izvestia's* Washington correspondent's review of 7 October 1981 was headlined "99 Pages of Lies." *The New York Times* of 4 October 1981 opened a story datelined London: "The European allies of the United States have generally welcomed the publication this week of the Defense Department's comprehensive study of Soviet Military Power. . . . '[I]t will be very useful in countering the unilateralists,' a British diplomat said, reflecting a common view."[6]

"Countering the unilateralists" is in the role of the White Paper to influence a broad segment of the population. Edward R. Murrow, testifying before a Senate Subcommittee as Director of the U.S. Information Agency (USIA) in 1962, almost 20 years before, reflected on the links between foreign governments, media, and public opinion, and on the role of official U.S. information directed at influencing minds abroad.

> Governments are susceptible to what appears in print, what is on the radio, what is on television. All three exercises have some degree of influence. The degree varies from country to country. Certainly governments are responsive to the general climate of opinion and the will of the electorate, and to the extent that we can persuade these media to tell our story . . . it is part of our function to provide to the mass media the background and the information upon which our policy is based in order that they may give that a more sympathetic treatment.[7]

The first edition of *Soviet Military Power* charted new waters with its official presentation on Soviet force developments at a level of detail never before available to the public. Of equal importance, the first edition inspired a bold, parallel undertaking by the NATO Alliance. In October 1981, at the conclusion of a NATO Nuclear Planning Group meeting at Gleneagles, Scotland, NATO Secretary General Joseph Luns held a press conference summarizing the discussions. He said that the Defense Ministers had emphasized the importance of keeping the public informed and added that NATO, as a first step, had begun compiling a study comparing the military power of the Soviet Union and its allies with that of the United States and its allies. He noted that it would be similar to the assessment of Soviet Forces just published by the U.S. Department of Defense.

When the North Atlantic Treaty Organization's report, *NATO and the Warsaw Pact: Force Comparisons,* was published in April 1982, Secretary General Luns, in his foreword, reaffirmed the Atlantic Alliance's commitment to improving East-West relations and to achieving verifiable results from arms control negotiations. At the same time, he pointed to the shift in favor of the Warsaw Pact. He stressed the need for the citizens of each NATO member nation to be informed, and he wrote:

> [T]his is why this publication comparing NATO and the Warsaw Pact Forces has been prepared. It carries the conviction and authority of all the NATO nations which participate in the integrated military structure of the Alliance; as

such its presentation is factual, objective, and unbiased. I commend it not only within NATO but to the much wider publics outside the Alliance for whom the maintenance of peace and security in the West is of fundamental importance.[8]

The first edition of *Soviet Military Power* triggered an official Soviet response, a publication entitled *Whence the Threat to Peace* that was distributed in early 1982. *The Economist,* in its 6 February 1982 issue, offered a critique that underscores the requirement to stick to objective presentation of the facts if a White Paper is to retain its credibility:

> Had the Russians stuck to documenting recent American advances, they could have made a powerful statement. But they also wanted to contest the American pamphlet's points. This meant talking about Soviet forces too; and this in turn meant setting out official Soviet statements about those forces, some of which are such obvious distortions of the facts that the booklet's whole message is undermined.[9]

In March 1983, a second edition of *Soviet Military Power* was published. It was released from the Oval Office of the White House by President Reagan. The President reaffirmed the defensive character of U.S. strategy, explaining that we design our defense programs to counter threats, not to further ambitions. "Today, and for the foreseeable future," he said, "the greatest of these threats comes from the Soviet Union, the only nation with the military power to inflict mortal damage on the United States. This also means," he said, "that if the American people are asked to support our defense program, they must get the straight facts about this threat." [10] The Department of Defense News Release of 9 March 1983 stated that *Soviet Military Power* 1983 contained much newly declassified information, that it had been produced by the Defense Intelligence Agency, and that it had been reviewed by the Joint Chiefs of Staff, the Military Services, the Department of State, the National Security Council staff, and other U.S. Government agencies.

In May 1983, a West German publishing house produced a 50,000 press-run German-language edition of *Soviet Military Power 1983* and included the 1982 official NATO Study under the same cover. In his preface to this edition Federal Defense Minister Manfred Wörner wrote:

> The Federal Government stands for communication and understanding. It undertakes great efforts to participate in the lessening of potential for a nuclear conflagration. This should, however, not shift our attention as to what is happening in the Warsaw Pact Nations. Only he who is informed of the extent and substance of Soviet rearmament and Soviet military-political goals will be spared surprises and illusions. Therefore I welcome the initiative of the publishing group Monch on the publication of this study. It will enhance political decision-making capability as well as continued military awareness.[11]

SOVIET MILITARY POWER AS AN ANNUAL INSTITUTION

Successive editions of *Soviet Military Power* followed annually. In 1984, NATO published its second official *NATO and the Warsaw Pact: Force Comparisons,* reflecting the decision of the member nations in the words of NATO's Secretary General Joseph Luns to provide more recent and up-to-date authoritative, factual, and objective information "from which the public could assess the relative strengths of the two alliances and hence the existing balance of power."[12]

Increased comparative data on U.S. and NATO forces appeared. The preface to the 1987 edition of *Soviet Military Power* reported, for example:

> To appreciate the commitment that the USSR makes to its armed forces, it is useful to start with a look at the weapon systems the Soviets are procuring for those forces and to place those figures alongside similar U.S. procurement. For the decade 1977-1986, the USSR built 3,000 ICBMs and SLBMs, the U.S. 850; the USSR 140,000 surface-to-air missiles, the U.S. 16,200; the USSR 24,400 tanks, the U.S. 7,100; the USSR 90 submarines, the U.S. 43; the USSR 28,200 artillery pieces, the U.S. 2,750.[13]

The 1987 edition reported that the USSR's 180 Ground Force Divisions as of 1981 had grown to 211 Divisions; the SS-20 deployed missile launchers had grown from 250 to 441; four additional TYPHOON ballistic missile submarines had now been launched, each to carry 160 nuclear warheads; and instead of the research and development program it had been when General Secretary Gorbachev came to power, the USSR's fifth-generation road-mobile intercontinental ballistic missile was now an operational component of the Strategic Rocket Forces with 100 SS-25s in the field.

The evolution of the USSR's armed forces was methodically documented in successive editions not only in text but also through graphs, tables, paintings, and photography. The paintings in the early editions had been the subject of criticism—they were not authoritative, hard evidence. As newly acquired photography that could be declassified became available, the paintings were replaced: The TYPHOON and DELTA IV ballistic missile submarines, the T-80 main battle tank, the CONDOR heavy-lift air transport, the FLANKER and FULCRUM fighter-interceptors, and the Pushkino Antiballistic Missile Radar complex all initially appeared as paintings that would for the most part bear striking resemblance to the later declassified photographs. And this new photography would quickly be carried in the media, contributing to fuller awareness and debate. The 1985 photograph of the TYPHOON SSBN with an accompanying graphic from *Soviet Military Power* placing its enormous hull size in perspective would appear for example on the front page of the 13 June 1985 edition of *The Christian Science Monitor* in an article on "The Contest for Undersea Supremacy."

Each new edition of *Soviet Military Power* represented a fresh, official U.S. statement on the status of the USSR's armed forces, a statement of facts to be read, weighted, challenged, and tested. Its role continued to grow in the debate on U.S. and allied defense requirements. Successive editions showed a responsiveness to demands from the public and the media for a more sophisticated analysis going beyond growing Soviet force numbers and capabilities to an assessment of the relative capabilities of those forces against the forces of the West. An editorial in the 30 April 1987 edition of *The New York Times* couched this demand with the following complaint: "It's true that over a period of steady military investment the Soviet

A. Denis Clift

Union has purchased a formidable arsenal. But counting beans is absurd as the main measure of military strength."[14]

The 1988 edition of *Soviet Military Power* responded to the need for greater perspective by devoting three chapters to the balance between U.S. and Soviet strategic forces, to an assessment of the principal regional military balances, and to a comparative assessment of emerging technologies with military applications. That edition also reported on Soviet foreign policy under General Secretary Gorbachev's impact on military doctrine, and the implications of the INF Treaty in terms of Soviet theater nuclear force capabilities. The 1989 edition, released by Secretary of Defense Dick Cheney on 27 September 1989, carried this process further. Entitled *Soviet Military Power: Prospects for Change 1989,* with a cover photograph of the last Soviet troops withdrawing from Afghanistan in February 1989, this latest edition documented General Secretary Gorbachev's growing, evolving agenda for change against the background of the USSR's continuing conventional, theater nuclear, strategic nuclear, and strategic defensive military capabilities.

TOWARD A BETTER-INFORMED PUBLIC

The official government reports, or White Papers, to which the Intelligence Community contributes also deal separately with specific aspects of Soviet policies and practices. While the editions of *Soviet Military Power* have touched on legal and illegal acquisition of advanced technology, in September 1985 the U.S. Government released a 34-page report, "Soviet Acquisition of Military Significant Western Technology: An Update," detailing the USSR's well-organized campaign to acquire Western technology for Soviet weapons development and military projects. It also covered the role of the KGB, GRU, and surrogate Warsaw Pact intelligence services in this process and the management of the entire process by the Military Industrial Commission of the Presidium of the Council of Ministers.

The issuance of reports such as the technology transfer report and publications like *Terrorist Group Profiles* and *Soviet Military Power* permits the government to highlight for public attention national security issues of particular significance. It is a process, in an era of instantaneous global communications and unprecedented volumes of often-contradictory information, that is contributing to the sorting of fact from fiction. The White Paper carries the imprimatur of government authority. It is a source, to be tested against other sources, that is generally treated as authoritative by the media. Indeed, it is likely that the steady flow of new facts on Soviet force developments from U.S. and allied unclassified publications has influenced, at least to a degree, Soviet decisions to treat its programs with greater openness and regard for the facts. *The Economist's* critique of 1982 had held true; there was little likelihood of acceptance of old-line Soviet distortions by the well-informed Western media and public.

The production of each White Paper, with the checks and balances of interagency reviews, provides an organized, authorized, and systematic method of declassifying information for public release. Facts developed by the sources, methods, and analysis of the Intelligence Community when so declassified are extremely relevant to the requirements of the policymaker, permitting the flow of important information to better inform the public when national policies are being debated and national decisions are required.

The White Papers' contributions to public education and better informed debate reflect an understanding of the skepticism and suspicions that citizens naturally bring to official policy pronouncements. H.L. Mencken captured the essence of such suspicions in his *Supplement 1* to *The American Language:*

> Ever since the first great battle between the Federalists and the anti-Federalists the American people have viewed politicians with suspicion, and the word itself has a derogatory significance in the United States which it lacks in England. . . . In this country it means only a party manipulator, a member of a professionally dishonest and dishonorable class. An honest politician is regarded as a sort of marvel, comparable to a calf with five legs, and the news that one has arrived is commonly received with derision.[15]

While public and media skepticism of government will remain a healthy, enduring part of the American scene, government facts, when presented objectively and authoritatively, are accepted and regarded as less a marvel than the five-legged calf. The Intelligence Community is playing a valuable, highly relevant role in contributing such facts, analyses, and assessments to the public dialogue on the nation's security.

CHAPTER 16
THE STRATEGIC BALANCE IN VERY ODD TIMES

Addressing the United States Congress in 1990, President Vaclav Havel of Czechoslovakia spoke to the rapid pace of change in the world, calling the new era "very odd times." In this speech, delivered in 1991 at the University of Virginia's National Security Law Institute, the author looks at the impact on intelligence challenges and opportunities posed by the end of the Cold War and the dawning of the new era: the residual might of Soviet strategic forces; the reductions, restructuring, and modernization of Soviet conventional forces; the meaning of DESERT SHIELD and DESERT STORM; and the continuing proliferation of arms, including weapons of mass destruction. "The competing demands," he writes, "between the needs of nations to export so as to contribute to their economic wellbeing on the one hand and to control the sale of products and technologies that could work against our security interests on the other are shaping a colossal international challenge."

Reflecting on the pace and breadth of global change in his address to the U.S. Congress in February 1990, President Vaclav Havel of Czechoslovakia observed: "We are living in very odd times. The human face of the world is changing so rapidly that none of the familiar political speedometers are adequate. We playwrights," he said, "who have to cram a whole human life or an entire historical era into a two-hour play, can scarcely understand this rapidity ourselves."[1]

When we assess the forces bearing on our strategic interests today, we look through the whirlwind of current events to the reality of the nuclear powers and of strategic deterrence; to the emergence of a diminished conventional warfare threat in Europe; to the trauma of regional instabilities—violence, crisis and conflict in Africa, the Middle East, Asia, and Latin America—to the cancer of advanced weapons proliferation threatening increased crisis and conflict.

THE DECLINE AND FALL OF THE SOVIET UNION

Events in and of themselves incredible must compete for our attention and are often crowded from the front-page headlines. When the final 1,220 Soviet tanks stationed in Czechoslovakia departed for the USSR, the story rated an inch on page 10 of *The Wall Street Journal*.[2] The Warsaw Pact has ceased to exist as a military alliance. Soviet ground and air forces are pulling back from all former Pact nations. The Berlin Wall has gone; the German Democratic Republic has gone. A united Germany has emerged, a most valued NATO ally, a nation straightened by the economic pains of its rebirth, a nation struggling to define its future global responsibilities. The NATO Defense Ministers, having just surveyed the geopolitical horizon, the changes in the East, and the blurring of lines between East and West, have proposed dramatic cuts in Allied ground forces to begin in 1994.

A. Denis Clift

In the Soviet Union, the genies of perestroika and glasnost released from President Mikhail Gorbachev's lamp are shaping nothing less than the second "Russian revolution" of this century. Gorbachev's initial shining goal of the 1980s, reforms that would quickly turn the Baltic Republics of Latvia, Lithuania, and Estonia into economic showcases for the Soviet Union, unleashed unintended forces of nationalism and independence that have led to the collapse of the Pact, the military withdrawal—a virtual retreat—from Eastern Europe, and the current struggle between the central government in Moscow and Soviet Republics insisting on independence.

The dimensions of the struggle are framed by tortured language of the All-Union Referendum proposition put to the Soviet voters on 17 March: "Do you consider necessary the preservation of the Union of Soviet Socialist Republics as a renewed federation of equal sovereign republics, in which the rights and freedoms of an individual of any nationality will be guaranteed?" Only 9 of the 15 Republics produced a majority in favor of the proposition. The contest continues with the center and the republics maneuvering politically on the collapsing field of contest that is the Soviet economy.

The increasing depths of the crisis were plumbed in the text of a letter from two of Gorbachev's economic advisers to the Group of Seven, the world's leading industrial democracies, a letter reported in the 30 May *New York Times* that began:

> The USSR has entered into a stage of deep social crisis. Three developments are taking place simultaneously: transition from totalitarianism to a democratic society, transformation of the economic system, and worsening of the national-ities problem, the solution of which has been postponed for too long.[4]

Think of the Soviet worker, who after hours in line, reaches the counter of his state liquor store only to see that the familiar sign VODKA-ONE RUBLE has now been changed to VODKA-TWO RUBLES.

"Why the increase?" he growls to the clerk. "It's outrageous!"

"Yes," the impassive comrade on the other side of the counter explains, "the price has changed-two rubles per bottle: one ruble for the vodka and one for perestroika."

The worker fishes two crumpled rubles out of his pocket and tosses them on the counter. The clerk takes one, pushes the other back: "Only one ruble today, comrade . . . we're out of vodka."

In May 1991, representatives of the Central Intelligence Agency and Defense Intelligence Agency testified before a subcommittee of the Joint Economic Committee of the Congress. The CIA witness stated: "[T]he Soviet economy is disintegrating and could be on the way to a disaster of historic proportions. . . . [O]utput is falling at an accelerating rate, inflation is increasing rapidly, interregional trade is breaking down, and economic relations with the rest of the world are suffering."[5] Not surprisingly, the witnesses testified, the heralded conversion of military industries to civilian production has thus far achieved inconsequential results.

THE CONTINUED THREAT OF RUSSIAN MILITARY POWER

Indeed, against the background of near-crisis, the USSR's defense industry is the one component of the economy that is relatively healthy, and these industries continue to produce intercontinental ballistic missiles, submarine-launched ballistic missiles, cruise missiles, tanks, submarines, bombers, fighter bombers, fighters, artillery, aircraft carriers, surface combatants, tanker aircraft, short-range ballistic missiles, and antiballistic missiles as part of military production. Indeed, against the background of near-crisis, the USSR continues to outproduce the United States in every category of major weapons system.

In August 1990, addressing the Aspen Institute on the defense capabilities required to meet the changing strategic requirements, President George Bush referred to the Camp David talks he had held with President Gorbachev during the June 1990 summit. "I was candid with him," the President said, "and I told him that for all the positive changes we have seen, the Soviet Union remains a world-class military power. Even after the conventional arms reductions that we're now negotiating, the Soviets will continue to maintain 2 to 3 million men under arms. And, of course, our number one concern," the President said, "the Soviets continue to maintain and modernize their arsenal of strategic weapons."[6]

A key item on the agenda of the next U.S.-Soviet Summit scheduled for Moscow this summer will be the Strategic Arms reduction negotiations—the START talks—aimed at significant reductions in both strategic launch systems and nuclear warheads on both sides.

In October 1990, General Colin Powell, Chairman of the Joint Chiefs of Staff, referred to the tasking that Secretary of Defense Dick Cheney and he had received from the President to shape a military strategy that would be at once responsive to fundamental change and at the same time to enduring realities. At the top of his list of enduring realities, he placed the Soviet Union. "Now and in the future," he said, "the Soviet Union will remain a military superpower-a superpower that can destroy the United States in thirty minutes."[7]

While the strategic balance is no longer shaped by the set piece of the Cold War, the strategic reality of Soviet military capabilities remains. What are these capabilities? What makes up the strategic balance?

The Soviets are conducting a comprehensive modernization of their strategic nuclear forces that will result in forces more accurate, survivable, and reliable. The Soviet strategic nuclear forces include intercontinental ballistic missiles, submarine-launched ballistic missiles, and cruise-missile-armed strategic intercontinental bombers. Soviet ICBM modernization has two major aspects: the deployment of two new missiles-the SS-24, in both a rail-mobile and silo version, and the road-mobile SS-25; and second, the modernization of the SS-18 heavy ICBM with improvements both to accuracy and yield in its fifth modification—accuracy that will permit the Soviets to reduce to smaller numbers of missiles in a new strategic arms agreement and still be able to cover all strategic targets.

A. Denis Clift

The SS-24 and SS-25 ICBMs represent the fifth generation of Soviet ICBMs. They are mobile, and mobility means greater survivability. While the United States has debated mobile ICBMs since the 1970s and presently has research and development money for such systems in the defense program, the Soviets have built and deployed more than 300 of the road- and rail-mobile ICBMs, and that deployment continues.

Recent strategic ballistic missile submarine force developments contribute to the more streamlined, highly capable strategic nuclear force. With 63 submarines, the sea-based force accounts for about 30 percent of the USSR's strategic nuclear warheads. Thirteen of the most modern, capable submarines—DELTA IVs and TYPHOONs—carry MIRVed long-range SLBMs. Production of the DELTA IVs continues.

New BEAR H and BLACKJACK manned strategic bombers equipped with long-range Air-Launched Cruise Missiles (ALCMs) continue to be produced and to enter the Soviet bomber forces. The Soviet Union has two nuclear-capable, long-range cruise missile systems—the air-launched AS-15 and the sea-launched S-N-21. These continue in production.

The USSR treats active and passive strategic defense as critical components of a nuclear strategy dedicated to limiting damage to the Soviet Union. The Soviets have extensive strategic air defenses, including multi-engagement surface-to-air missile units, advanced fighter-interceptors, computer-assisted command and control systems, and three-dimensional radars. They also have upgraded Moscow's antiballistic missile (ABM) system into a dual-layered system. Research and development continues on ABM technologies.[8]

UNITED STATES STRATEGIC NUCLEAR POLICY: THE TRIAD

As stated in Defense Secretary Dick Cheney's Annual Report to the Congress for 1991, U.S. policy has been based on deterring attacks—particularly nuclear attacks—against U.S. territory, deployed U.S. forces, or U.S. allies. Three fundamental objectives underpin U.S. strategic nuclear policy:

- Maintaining effective deterrence so that a potential aggressor would conclude that the cost of an attack against the United States or its allies would far exceed any expected gain;
- Fostering nuclear stability, a condition whereby no nation is pressured to use nuclear weapons preemptively; and,
- Maintaining the capability, if deterrence fails, to respond flexibly and effectively to an aggressor's attack.

Although the Soviet Union possesses significantly greater numbers of strategic nuclear delivery systems—launchers—than does the United States, an essential parity exists between the U.S. and the Soviet Union with regard to the number of strategic offensive weapons. The United States maintains a strategic triad of ICBMs, SLBMs, and bombers. Each component of the triad has unique capabilities that complement the others.

The U.S. ICBM force consists of 50 silo-based Peacekeeper missiles, 500 Minutemen IIIs, and 450 Minuteman II missiles. Current planning calls for the continued operation of these systems, with the gradual retirement of the older Minuteman II missiles.

The addition of mobility to the U.S. ICBM force would improve survivability without significantly reducing responsiveness and reliability. Therefore, the five-year defense program for fiscal years 1992-1997 continues development of the small ICBM.[9]

The current status of the mobile ICBM program was succinctly captured in an exchange between Senator Carl Levin of Michigan and General Lee Butler of the Strategic Air Command in a Senate Armed Services Committee hearing this spring:

> SEN LEVIN: Deterrence doesn't necessarily mean a symmetric force posture-we don't necessarily need a mobile ICBM force. Will our deterrent be adequate without a mobile ICBM?

> GEN BUTLER: Yes, with three caveats: 1) START continues on track; 2) there are no surprises on the part of the Soviets; and 3) there are no surprises in the sustainability of our force.

> SEN LEVIN: You are looking at one test of the rail-mobile MX and some sort of test for Small ICBM. Is this enough?

> GEN BUTLER: Yes. We basically want to protect our mobile missile option.

> SEN LEVIN: By keeping it in R&D.

> GEN BUTLER: Yes. We will revisit that decision for the '97 timeframe in a year when we go through the next budget cycle.[10]

The sea-based component of the U.S. strategic triad—the ballistic missile submarine force with its submarine-launched ballistic missiles—is also in the midst of significant modernization. A new missile, the TRIDENT II (D-5)—with greater accuracy and reliability—is going aboard the new Ohio-Class SSBNs. When this modernization is completed during the 1990s, there will be 18 Ohio-Class SSBNs, each carrying 24 missiles, each missile fitted with eight nuclear warheads.

Bombers are an extremely flexible element of the U.S. strategic triad, capable of being recalled or redirected while en route to their targets. They carry a variety of nuclear weapons-air-launched cruise missiles, short-range attack missile (SRAMs), and gravity bombs. The U.S. bomber force currently consists of B-52, FB-111 and B-1 aircraft. Plans for the next stage of modernization include the B-2 stealth bomber and the advanced cruise missile. In sum, these are the basic components of the U.S. and Soviet forces in the strategic balance, the forces under negotiation in START.

A. Denis Clift

THE STRATEGIC BALANCE: CONVENTIONAL FORCES

Turning to the conventional balance, last month, when the Chief of the Soviet General Staff General Mikhail Moiseyev was in Washington for arms control talks, I was introduced to him by the Soviet Defense Attaché as the author of the Department of Defense's annual report *Soviet Military Power.* With our Chairman of the Joint Chiefs of Staff General Colin Powell looking on, Moiseyev threw his arms out, his face lighting in a sarcastic smile, and said, "Ah, my favorite book. I can't wait to receive it each year, to learn how really important I am, how strong my forces really are."

As DIA has recently testified to the Congress, there are in fact significant changes to the USSR's armed forces, changes characterized by reduction, restructuring, and modernization.

The Soviet Navy is in the process of scrapping hundreds of 1950s- and 1960s-vintage surface warships and submarines and in their place introducing nuclear-powered cruise missile submarines, guided missile destroyers, guided missile cruisers, and a new generation of aircraft carriers. The first of these carriers, the 65,000-ton *Admiral Kuznetsov* has been commissioned and is on sea trials in the Black Sea; the second has been launched and is fitting out; the third, which will probably be larger and of a still more advanced design, is on the building ways.

Soviet ground force—or Army—reductions in Eastern Europe, coupled with the collapse of the Warsaw Pact, have eliminated the threat of a short-warning Soviet offensive on NATO territory. Thousands of pieces of combat equipment—tanks, artillery, and armored personnel carriers, for example—have either been moved east of the Ural Mountains or will be destroyed. If the Conventional Forces in Europe (CFE) Agreement is ratified and enters into force, the treaty-mandated reductions will further reduce Soviet capabilities to initiate offensive operations in Europe and will provide the Western Alliance a much longer warning period of changes in Soviet intentions. The Soviets will retain a more modern, still large, but less ready ground force structure of some 60 to 70 divisions and up to 30 mobilization divisions in the Atlantic-to-the-Urals zone.

Soviet Air Forces in the Atlantic-to-the-Urals zone have been restructured and modernized, and despite significant reductions remain the largest tactical air arm in Europe.

As Norway's Defense Minister Johan Holst stated earlier this year, "The CFE treaty does not eliminate the ability of the Soviet Union to initiate large-scale offensive action in Europe. However, it seriously constrains that capacity." Of importance to Norway, he said, "The CFE Treaty does not eliminate the threat of surprise attack on NATO's flanks. From the viewpoint of Norway the security order of Europe does not extend only from the Atlantic to the Urals, but also from the Barents Sea to the Mediterranean. . . . In Europe," he said, "NATO will remain the essential component in the security order." [11]

NATO's Secretary General Manfred Wörner, also underlining the fact that NATO is the only organization capable of balancing the considerable military power of the Soviet Union, has underscored the need for the Alliance to adapt to evolving security requirements. And the changes in the East have marked the beginning of a period of transition for the Western Alliance, with the first major proposals for change unveiled by the NATO Defense Ministers at the conclusion of their spring meeting in Brussels on 28 May 1991. The plan, which will require approval by NATO's heads of government at a summit later this year, would reduce and reshape the forces that had earlier been in position against the Warsaw Pact: cutting by 50 percent the more than 300,000 U.S. forces in Europe, creating a brigade of some 15,000 ready for action within 72 hours, creating a multinational Rapid Reaction Corps ready for action within a week, seven defense corps of 50,000 to 70,000 troops, and a U.S. reinforcement force to be called into action in the event of imminent war.

If these decisions by the NATO Defense Ministers are ratified by the Heads of Government, we can assume that the United States will remain in Europe as part of an Alliance that has succeeded brilliantly for more than four decades in deterring war between East and West. With the force reductions and the reduced threat of conventional war that will accompany ratification and implementation of the CFE Treaty, and with reduced levels of strategic arms, assuming U.S.-Soviet agreement in the START talks in the months ahead—a likelihood, but not an absolute certainty—there are the prospects for increased stability.

A NONETHELESS DANGEROUS WORLD

This said, there are other, destabilizing components, among them the reality of political and military tensions and crises in various regions of the world, and the potential for crises to erupt into regional conflicts impacting on U.S. strategic interests—tensions, for example, on the Korean Peninsula, in South Asia between India and Pakistan, in the Middle East. It has been less than a year since Iraq's invasion of Kuwait and Iraq's expulsion from Kuwait by U.S. forces and their coalition partners acting under United Nations mandate. Operations DESERT SHIELD and DESERT STORM brought into sharp focus the magnitude of Iraq's advanced weapons programs—nuclear facilities, chemical weapons, and ballistic missiles— and of the arms sales and international participation contributing to that program.

The proliferation of advanced weaponry poses a serious challenge to the prospects for peace. In his address to the Aspen Institute last August, President Bush said: "In spite of our best efforts to control the spread of chemical and nuclear weapons and ballistic missile technologies, more nations are acquiring weapons of mass destruction and the means to deliver them. Right now," the President said, "20 nations have the capacity to produce chemical weapons. And by the year 2000, as many as 15 developing nations could have their own ballistic missiles."[12] In February this year, Secretary of Defense Cheney estimated that some 30 nations will have chemical weapons and 10 a biological weapons capability.[13]

In the book *Trappings of Power*, on the spread of ballistic missiles in the Third World, Janne Nolan examines evolving complexities of proliferation control, writing:

> As the medium of exchange between industrial and industrializing countries has increasingly become technology rather than finished weapons systems, the importance of traditional instruments to control proliferation has progressively

diminished. The ready availability of commercial technologies that have potential military applications, along with maturing third world defense industries capable of exploiting these applications, has made distinguishing between civilian and military exports more difficult.[14]

The competing demands between the needs of nations to export so as to contribute to their economic wellbeing on the one hand and to control the sale of products and technologies that could work against our security interests on the other are shaping a colossal international challenge.

Earlier efforts to slow proliferation, such as the Missile Technology Control Regime (MTCR), have not achieved the required results. Late last month, President Bush focused the need for first priority attention to the volatile Middle East, proposing that the major arms suppliers—the USSR, China, France, the United Kingdom, and the United States—enter discussions on guidelines for the curb of weapons sales. Further, he proposed a freeze by nations in the region on the acquisition, production, and testing of surface-to-surface missiles; a ban on the production and importing of weapons-grade nuclear materials; adherence to the nuclear non-proliferation treaty; adherence by nations in the region to the proposed Chemical Weapons Convention; as well as enhancement of and adherence to the 1972 Biological Weapons Convention.

This is a tall order, but there is growing support. On 3 June, the Government of France announced its proposals for curbing both the international arms trade and the proliferation of weapons of mass destruction, and in so doing announced that France had now taken the decision to become a signatory to the 1968 Nuclear Nonproliferation Treaty, leaving only China among the nuclear powers as a non-signatory.

VERY ODD TIMES CONTINUE

And so the whirlwind of momentous events churns across the world at a pace often too rapid for familiar political speedometers. Whirling prominently in this time of change is Mikhail Gorbachev, who has both deliberately and unwittingly triggered the chain of events that is reshaping the face of Europe, the USSR, and indeed the role of international collective action under UN auspices—witness the USSR's constructive role in crisis and the conflict in the Gulf.

In concluding this scan of the challenges to our strategic interests, it is useful to consider Gorbachev's words in Oslo, Norway on 5 June 1991 in accepting the Nobel Peace Prize, words assessing the place of the U.S. and the USSR in the kaleidoscope of global change:

> The USSR and the USA, the two nuclear superpowers, have moved from confrontation to interaction and, in some important cases, partnership. This has had a decisive effect on the entire international climate. This should be preserved and filled with new substance. The climate of Soviet-U.S. trust should be protected, for it is a common asset of the world community. Any revision to

the direction and potential of the Soviet-U.S. relationship would have grave consequences for the entire global process.[15]

In these very odd times, the U.S.-Soviet strategic relationship stands prominently in the spotlight on the world stage, with the drama of the strategic balance in the 1990s shifting from scene to scene, with startling new twists in an unpredictable plot, with its global audience spellbound.

CLIFT NOTES

INTELLIGENCE AND THE NATION'S SECURITY

PART FOUR

INTELLIGENCE IN THE INTERNET ERA

CHAPTER 17
INTELLIGENCE IN PARTNERSHIP

In 1996 and 1997, the author would deliver two speeches on the subject of accountability and the intelligence profession. In the first, an address to the Romanian Institute for Higher Military Studies, delivered in Bucharest on 25 March 1996, he addressed national accountability, tracing the contributions of intelligence to the verification of arms control agreements—advances from the reliance on "national technical means" to on-site inspections. These advances have been paralleled in the 1990s by the need for and the challenges of international sharing between and among international coalition partners. He called in this speech for a conference the College would host in June 1997 on the challenges and opportunities to be addressed in international intelligence sharing.

Thirty-six years ago—1960—I was a front-line participant in the Cold War era's first successful treaty-based international on-site inspections. In 1958, during the International Geophysical Year, President Eisenhower had proposed to the 11 nations engaged with the United States in scientific research on the Antarctic Continent that they enter into a treaty preserving the continent for such research and other peaceful purposes.

The Antarctic Treaty was quickly negotiated and entered into force. Its 14 articles include the prohibition of all military measures there, including weapons testing, declaring that Antarctica is to be used only for peaceful purposes. For scientific purposes, however, military personnel and equipment are allowed. Also forbidden by the treaty are nuclear explosions and disposal of radioactive waste in Antarctica. Treaty-state observers are allowed free access—including aerial observation—to any area and may inspect all stations, installations, and equipment. Advance notice of all activities and of the introduction of military personnel must be given.

Under these treaty provisions, the United States invited and welcomed the other treaty signatories—including the Soviet Union—to visit our stations and inspect our scientific research firsthand. As a naval officer in Antarctic operations contributing to the support of this research in 1960 and 1961, one of my responsibilities was that of liaison officer looking after the foreign diplomatic, military, and academic visitors inspecting our far-flung Antarctic research operations.

I would ensure that they had the run of our stations at McMurdo, Byrd, and the South Pole. I would accompany Norwegian and British delegations to the South Pole to commemorate the 50th anniversary of the Amundsen and Scott expeditions—and would walk around the world in the process. I would embark on the icebreaker USS *Glacier*, accompanied by the icebreaker USS *Staten Island* with representatives from Chile, Argentina, South Africa, and Great Britain on the four-month 1961 Bellingshausen Sea expedition, an expedition that would include an inspection of a Chilean research station, an expedition in which our surveying would establish that the continent's Thurston Peninsula was, in fact, Thurston Island. Every aspect of our research and the support for that research was open for inspection. The United States attached importance to the confidence-building nature of the treaty's provisions. We took pride in our research. Other nations reciprocated. It was a splendid example of international cooperation.

With the lifting of the Iron Curtain from the post-Cold War stage, we view a drama in which many of the world's nation players—adversaries in yesteryears' productions—are embarked on cooperation modeled on the Antarctic Treaty example. The discourse and actions between and among these players extend beyond the stabilization and reduction of their forces to the confronting of new adversaries, both loud and surreptitious, appalling the world's audience in their turn-of-the-century plots.

We are learning new ways of cooperating, new ways of building confidence. What we have learned, and how we act, have had their effect on the role played by intelligence. In parallel, we have learned new ways of using intelligence, developed new doctrine, new sources and methods of collection, analysis, production, and dissemination. What we have learned and how we are applying this knowledge and capability, in turn, are influencing our cooperation as nations.

EXPERIENCE OF THE COLD WAR ERA

From the time of its signing through the mid-1980s, the Antarctic Treaty was virtually unique in such confidence-building cooperation. The Soviet Union and the nations of the Warsaw Pact were arrayed as adversaries against the United States and the nations of the North Atlantic Treaty Organization. For the NATO nations, more than one-sixth of the earth's land surface was denied territory, territory spawning and deploying armies, navies, air and strategic rocket forces, threatening the survival of the West.

The Cold War chill deepened throughout the 1950s. The 1960s opened with the Berlin Crisis of 1961 and the Cuban missile crisis of 1962—the latter followed by the introduction of the U.S.-Soviet Hot Line. While the Limited Test Ban Treaty would be signed in 1963 and the Nonproliferation Treaty in 1968, the U.S.-Soviet strategic arms race continued throughout the decade. In 1967, President Lyndon Johnson invited Chairman Aleksei Kosygin to meet with him in Glassboro, New Jersey. Johnson would write in his memoirs:

> We had known for some time that the Soviets were installing an antiballistic missile [ABM] system around Moscow. Pressure rose for us to follow suit to protect our major cities and ICBM emplacements with an ABM system. It was time, if not past time, for mature men to take stock together of how to achieve mutual security without the huge added costs of elaborate protective systems and the expanded offensive systems they would trigger into being.[1]

While the Glassboro talks would end in stalemate, a U.S.-Soviet ABM Treaty and the Interim SALT I Agreement would be realized in the first summit of détente, the 1972 Nixon-Brezhnev meeting in Moscow. These strategic arms agreements, the first steps toward limits on strategic nuclear arms, would be followed by the 1974 Vladivostok Accord signed by Brezhnev and Ford and the SALT II Agreement of 1979 signed by Brezhnev and Carter.

The need for monitoring of each side's compliance with these strategic arms accords was recognized in the documents of the 1970s. There could be no question of actual inspection. The rival superpowers would accept and acknowledge viewing each other from afar and specifically make allowance for such viewing in the treaties' language. The term "National Technical Means" was adopted to provide for the role played by orbiting, monitoring satellites. Article XV of the SALT II Agreement, for example, stated:

> 1. For the purpose of providing assurance of compliance with the provisions of this Treaty, each Party shall use national technical means of verification at its disposal in a manner consistent with generally recognized principles of international law.

> 2. Each Party undertakes not to interfere with the national technical means of verification of the other Party operating in accordance with paragraph 1 of this Article.

> 3. Each Party undertakes not to use deliberate concealment measures which impede verification by national technical means of compliance with the provisions of this Treaty. This obligation shall not require changes in current construction, assembly, conversion, or overhaul practices.[2]

Each side treated the issue of any impeding of verification by National Technical Means very seriously and was quick to challenge. I remember an occasion when I was with Secretary of State Henry Kissinger in the Kremlin for negotiations with Brezhnev in 1974. The Soviet General Secretary took the time to launch into a very specific complaint of alleged U.S. concealment and then, with a laugh, pointed across the table to one of my colleagues, asking if he personally was responsible. Secretary Kissinger assured the General Secretary that no deliberate concealment was intended and that my colleague was not involved.

Together with the modest progress toward limiting strategic arms, there was limited progress between East and West in the 1970s in the field of conventional arms. I traveled to Helsinki with President Gerald Ford in 1975 as a member of his Delegation to the Conference on Security and Cooperation in Europe (CSCE). In the splendor of Finlandia Hall, 35 chiefs of state and heads of government put their pens to the Final Act, a document which included agreement on confidence-building measures, including prior notification of certain military exercises, and which invited exchanges of observers at such exercises. The 1984-1986 Stockholm Conference on Disarmament in Europe, which flowed from Helsinki and the Madrid CSCE Review Conference, reached international agreement on provisions authorizing the first routine mandatory observations of military activities, exercises, and suspicious activities.

PROGRESS IN THE 1980s

More importantly, in terms of the ways in which the political world has changed and the impact of such changes on military intelligence, the mid-1980s marked the beginning of a new chapter in confidence-building, monitoring, and verification, with a dramatic new step by the U.S. and USSR to slow the nuclear arms race. The U.S.-USSR Treaty on the Elimination of Intermediate-Range and Shorter-Range Missiles, signed in December 1987 by Presidents Reagan and Gorbachev and ratified in May 1988, provided in Article XI for the conduct of on-site inspections. The treaty's depth of detail would have been unimaginable just a few years before, at the time of agreement on the three paragraphs on National Technical Means in SALT II. The INF Treaty's Inspections Protocol flowing from Article XI ran 18 single-spaced pages with a concluding Annex addressing the privileges and immunities of inspectors and aircraft crews.

The Protocol established pre-inspection requirements, notification procedures, specific points of entry for inspection teams in each country, as well as detailed rules for the conduct of inspections—rules which the two sides would continue to embellish long after the treaty had entered into force. While both sides would draw on intelligence to monitor remaining force levels as part of the monitoring of overall orders of battle, there was no longer any need to rely on the usual intelligence sources and methods in the inspections. Inspectors from the United States and Russia were on the ground in Russia and the United States. To carry out this work, the Secretary of Defense created a totally new military organization, the On-Site Inspection Agency.

The INF Treaty and its inspections protocol dealt with very specific classes of nuclear weapons systems. In contrast, the Treaty on Conventional Armed Forces in Europe signed in November 1990—a treaty in which Romania has played and continues to play so significant a part—addressed the drawdown of the vast Warsaw Pact and NATO conventional ground and air forces arrayed across Europe from the Atlantic to the Urals. The treaty provided for massive exchanges of detailed information on these forces by the 23 participants. Its Protocol on Inspections, not to be outdone by INF, ran 27 single-spaced pages. Under the Conventional Forces in Europe (CFE) Treaty, the United States and Romania readily and openly exchange conventional force data. We openly participate in the inspections of sites and objects of verification. I am sure a number of you here today have been or are a part of this process.

Confidence-building and cooperation in the field of arms—both conventional and strategic—have continued to unfold in the 1990s. For the nations of NATO, the nations of northern, southern and eastern Europe, and Russia, voluntary exchanges of detailed military data and voluntary compliance with on-site inspections are no longer startlingly new. They are expected international behavior. The Strategic Arms Reduction Treaty signed by the United States and Russia in 1991 provides not only for National Technical Means but also on-site inspections. The Vienna Document signed in 1990, following up on the Stockholm agreement, provides for an annual exchange of conventional force data. It is fair to say that analysts in both Bucharest and Washington routinely turn to such data, which has been voluntarily provided by other nations, as a fully authoritative source of information.

As this process continues to unfold, the rules of accepted, expected international behavior extend beyond Europe to appear, for example, in the form of sanctions such as those imposed by United Nations Resolutions 606 and 687 on Iraq until there is full and final disclosure that all capabilities for weapons of mass destruction have been eliminated and that disclosure has been verified. Sanctions imposed on the nations of the former Yugoslavia look to those nations to follow the CFE example.

MILITARY INTELLIGENCE IN PARALLEL

During this period, when national players have worked to modify and insist on improved norms of international behavior, contributing on the one hand to confidence-building and stability and on the other to addressing post-Cold War challenges, there have been important parallel changes in the ways we envision and practice the professional work of intelligence. In the United States, the National Security Act of 1947 provides the bedrock for the structure of our national security and intelligence communities. As we approach the 50th anniversary of that Act, a Presidential Commission, the intelligence oversight committees of the Congress, and departments and agencies of the Executive Branch are engaged in a marvelously mystifying way unique to the incredibly resilient U.S. Governmental process in arriving at findings, recommendations, and decisions on the Intelligence Community's future mission and structure. The time is right for such decisions.

The global confrontation between communism and democracy, the confrontation between NATO and the Warsaw Pact, and the superpowers' arms race combined to shape the Cold War Intelligence Community's structure. Beginning in the early 1980s, a number of international events and U.S. actions caused us to realize that fresh thinking, new ways of doing our work would be required if we were to anticipate and to meet the needs of both the operational commander and the most senior makers of policy.

The bombing of the Marine Barracks in Lebanon would teach us that the national-level systems that enabled us to monitor ICBM fields were virtually worthless in monitoring the intentions of a terrorist. We would learn that the pace and the method of the community's strategic arms intelligence production and dissemination were tragically inadequate in the face of an unidentified, unscheduled, unprogrammed truck bomb moving invisibly through urban alleys, along urban streets.

In turn, we would enter an era in the 1980s in which the U.S. Commander in Chief would decide on military operations involving the element of surprise, the delivery of high-technology, "smart" weapons precisely on the most finite of targets, with top priority given to zero U.S. casualties, zero civilian casualties, and minimum collateral damage. We would know that there is, in fact, no "smart" weapon, that the complex of data and expert analysis—the product of days, months, and years of work—would have to be available immediately for the preparation of precision targeting packages. We would learn that the demands of such operations more often than not would require the bringing together—the fusing—of our land, sea, and air intelligence capabilities, the harnessing and delivery of intelligence from national, theater, and tactical levels.

A. Denis Clift

LESSONS OF THE 1990s

With the coming of the 1990s, with Iraq's invasion of Kuwait, the United States would join with new coalition partners to resist and repel such aggression. I have a vivid mental image of the unspoken surprise during the DESERT SHIELD crisis, prior to DESERT STORM, when NATO defense attachés were joined in the Pentagon at our long National Military Intelligence Center briefing table by defense attachés from Egypt, from Senegal, and from Syria. In the words of the song: The times they were a-changing.

Following DESERT STORM, the United States Congress would pass legislation establishing in law the National Military Joint Intelligence Center, reflecting the Congress' favorable assessment of the progress in joint intelligence center operations both at the national level in Washington and at the Joint Intelligence Center — Forward in Riyadh. Annex C of the Department of Defense's *Final Report to Congress: Conduct of the Persian Gulf War* would review in considerable detail the performance of the joint intelligence centers, the performance of intelligence at the national, theater, and tactical levels, the role played by the 11 deployed National Military Intelligence Support Teams (NMIST), the strengths and deficiencies of battle damage assessment, the strengths and deficiencies of the intelligence performance overall, and the lessons to be learned. The NMIST had represented a very significant evolutionary advance for military intelligence—three- to four-member teams ready to deploy on a few hours notice with suitcase-sized equipment able in the computer era to provide the tactical commander in the field or aboard ship with satellite-relayed secure voice, data, and imagery links with the national community.

As we develop and deploy computer systems, more sophisticated communications, and advanced collection systems that form the nerve center in the global reach of intelligence, we must anticipate and be ready to receive the net wave of technological developments. Commercial high technology available on the world market will quickly outpace us should we turn our backs for a minute; should we do so, it would be at our national security peril.

We know as we run the technology race that the highly skilled collection manager, the regional expert, the gifted insightful analyst, bring the nerve system to life and are essential to its well-being. We know more than ever before in the history of the Intelligence Community that our best chances for success—given the complex spectrum of crisis management, peacemaking, peacekeeping, and combat operations before us—are found when we augment our own intelligence capabilities with those of our allies, our friends, and our coalition partners around the world.

INTELLIGENCE IN PARTNERSHIP

Following DESERT STORM, French Defense Minister Pierre Joxe said, "Without allied intelligence in the war we would have been almost blind."[3] The Final Report to Congress on the War included a section on coalition intelligence, finding that it had worked well. Such findings reflect the commitment made by the United States during both the crisis and the conflict to share our best intelligence as fully as possible with our coalition partners. This required a fresh appreciation by the analysts producing reports critical to the coalition effort. It required altering the mindset of those responsible for authorizing release or disclosure of intelligence to the partners. Large posters were created, much like security posters that still adorn walls at sensitive installations in the United States and Romania today, reminding our disclosure experts to clear as much essential intelligence as possible for release to the coalition while protecting sources and methods.

We have learned from DESERT STORM that with sharp minds and a few essential strokes of the pen or cursor it is indeed possible to protect sensitive sources and methods while providing information required by coalition partners. We know from post-Cold War operations that we must move this intelligence not only to senior staffs but also down to the tactical level—the airborne fighter pilots, the tank commanders, the naval vessels underway—move it in time to be of value to the warrior in action. In considering intelligence products for release, the issues are straightforward: Is it intelligence that forces participating in the coalition need? Has the U.S. commander requested release? Does the information, in fact, need to be declassified? How low a classification can be applied? Of central importance where sensitive sources and methods are involved, can the substantive information be provided without attributing it to either source or method? If the source or method is particularly sensitive, is there a plausible alternative source for the information?

To some, these considerations may not seem profound; but they are vitally important. When correctly exercised, they permit a far fuller flow of intelligence to a far broader range of authorized international recipients than could possibly have been contemplated just a few years ago. To cite just one example, today's Implementation Force (IFOR) for Bosnia includes a Russian Deputy under the Supreme Allied Commander Europe, and there are Russian recipients in IFOR authorized for releasable intelligence at SHAPE Headquarters, in Naples, and in the field in Bosnia. Romania, of course, is a recipient of our regular IFOR cable.

Romania is playing an expanding role on the world stage in ways that are of importance to the United States. You, too, are on the front-line, with your infantry battalion participating in Angola in the United Nations Angola Verification Mission III (UNAVEM III). You are a founding participant in NATO's Partnership for Peace begun in 1994, a partnership which as stated in the Framework Document aims at strengthening security within the Euro-Atlantic area, in part by pursuing "the development of cooperative military relations with NATO, for the purposes of joint planning, training, and exercises in order to strengthen their ability to undertake missions in the fields of peacekeeping, search and rescue, humanitarian operations, and others as may subsequently be agreed."[4]

Prior to becoming President of the Joint Military Intelligence College, it was my pleasure as Chief of Staff of the Defense Intelligence Agency to serve as host during a visit of the Chief of Staff of your Armed Forces and for visits by members of your Parliament exploring the legislative oversight process as it applies to the U.S. Intelligence Community. I also had the pleasure of hosting the first meeting with officers of your military intelligence service to learn from you the mission and the structure of that service. It is now a great pleasure for me to be in Bucharest once again and to have this opportunity to discuss with you the work of

A. Denis Clift

our College, the education of our intelligence professionals. I attach particular importance to exploring with you the possibilities for further cooperation between us in the field of education.

For years, we have welcomed participation by Romanian officers in the Combined Strategic Intelligence Training Program conducted at the Defense Intelligence Analysis Center in Washington—a good program. As I have told officers from all over the world attending past classes, we have taken professional interest and pride as we have watched many of their predecessors rise to become defense attachés, heads of their intelligence services, senior officers in their military services, and ranking members of their ministries of defense.

But clearly, there is more that we can be doing together. As President of the College, I have been paying very close attention to the quality of research being performed both by students and faculty. We have begun the publication of a new series of academic Occasional Papers—writings in the field of intelligence—and I am pleased to present to you the most recent of those papers, entitled *Getting Intelligence Right: The Power of Logical Procedure,* by Air Force Captain William Brei. This spring, one of my graduate students will be accepting the invitation of the Secretary of Defense of South Africa to carry out research in South Africa in the development of his Master's thesis. I would hope that there will be opportunities for others of my graduate students to come to Bucharest, to perform research in Romania.

I also believe that we are at a point in the work unfolding in the Partnership for Peace, we are at a point in the cooperation building between us in the post-Cold War world, where it might be useful to have a conference of intelligence officers from the United States, from other friends around the world, to take stock of the rapidly changing world, its impact on our professional work, our cooperation, the lessons we are learning, how to strengthen and deepen that cooperation in the years ahead. My thought would be to host a week-long conference at the Joint Military Intelligence College in the summer of 1997. I will very much value your reaction to these proposals.[5]

CHAPTER 18
THROUGH THE PRISM OF NATIONAL SECURITY: THE CHALLENGE OF INTELLIGENCE SHARING

Citing examples from history, the author reflects on both the challenges and the occasional perils of sharing intelligence with allies. Inherent in every exchange of intelligence is the innate skepticism of the intelligence profession as well as the danger of inadvertently revealing our own weaknesses and intelligence gaps. At the same time, we must be sure that we protect sensitive sources and methods from disclosure. Addressing the Kennedy School at Harvard University on 27 August 2001, he observes that intelligence sharing, done right, "is a uniquely important information and knowledge multiplier" that can go far in advancing U.S. interests in peace and in war. From the creation of the North Atlantic Treaty Organization to the allied coalition that drove Iraqi invaders out of Kuwait in Operation DESERT STORM, the need to share intelligence has been crucial, and it has never been more important than today.

D-DAY, OPERATIONS MARKET GARDEN AND NORTH POLE

Almost 60 years ago, Easy Company of the 506th Parachute Infantry Division, 101st Airborne was formed, and citizen soldiers from across the country trained for war. In his history *Band of Brothers*, Stephen Ambrose documents the World War II combat history of Easy Company, its jump and stunning D-Day success eliminating a battery of German 105mm cannon trained on Utah Beach, the company's furious campaigning in Holland, Bastogne, and the Battle of the Bulge en route to victory in Germany.[1] The planning and intelligence for Easy Company's D-Day mission had been excellent, in part because American and British intelligence staffs had been able to draw on valuable intelligence provided by the French Resistance.

The planning and intelligence for Easy Company's jump into Holland, Operation MARKET GARDEN, had been equally bad. The British did not tip the Dutch Resistance off to the planned jump because of concerns over penetration of the Resistance by the Germans. Thus the Dutch could not alert the allies to the presence of two enemy Panzer Divisions in the drop zone area.

British Intelligence had been burned badly earlier in the war. In Operation NORTH POLE, members of the Dutch Resistance, sent back into the Netherlands from the United Kingdom, had been turned by the Germans and had fed the UK extremely damaging false information. They did not want to risk being burned again. Such is the world of intelligence sharing.

A. Denis Clift

SHARING: THE BASIC PROPOSITION

In intelligence sharing, you have your choice of aphorisms: "It is a two-way street with dim lighting and few road signs." "There is no such thing as a free lunch." To translate: Every time you give away or exchange intelligence, there is an inherent cost. There is a cost, obvious or not, no matter how carefully you craft your work and your message.

Bear in mind, intelligence organizations are not trusting by nature. They are inherently doubtful about any sharing relationship, whether temporary or long-term. In some cases, whether the sharing is being encouraged from above or not, an inherently national attitude on the part of the intelligence players involved will block the chances for a good exchange. Indeed that attitude can be reflected in the offices responsible for releasability and foreign disclosures—the men and women known traditionally and collectively as "Dr. No." Additionally, there may be governmental or constitutional barriers—an issue that relates to the United States and sharing with the United Nations.

In intelligence sharing, you are telling someone else what you know, and inferentially—at least to the initiated—what you do not know. That is, you are revealing your strengths and your weaknesses. And, you are providing your interlocutor with the opportunity to probe further on both the positive and negative sides of the subject matter.

If sharing is working the way you want it to work, it is a uniquely important information and knowledge multiplier. You are taking appropriate steps to safeguard those sources of information that must be protected. You are safeguarding those methods of intelligence collection that you wish to remain yours alone. At the same time, you are acquiring information not available to you from your sources and methods—or information that will allow you to validate or open to question intelligence already in your possession. You may be able to acquire information, which because of your own budgetary or personnel limitations, you could not acquire on your own.

If sharing is working the way you want it to work, it may involve the use of intelligence as a commodity. One partner offers intelligence in return for a commodity other than intelligence from the other partner—in return for access to real estate for example. If sharing is working the way you want it to work, it not only can advance the nation's interests through favorable U.S. action in peace and war, it can also advance U.S. interests through the actions or the inactions of another nation or nations because of the information shared.

Intelligence sharing plays out in the relations between two nations—bilateral sharing. It also plays out in work among allies, and more recently, work among coalition partners or international organizations—multilateral sharing. The challenges abound. They can play out within the Intelligence Community out of the public eye. They can play out most publicly when differences arise between the U.S. Executive and Legislative Branches, or when differences arise between and among nations. These alternate outcomes will shape the remarks that follow.

BILATERAL SHARING: THE GOOD AND THE BAD

A few months after the beginning of the Second World War, 22 May 1940, with the U.S. still neutral, the British, building on French and Polish successes, broke a portion of the German ULTRA code created on the ENIGMA encryption machines. Exploitation of ULTRA was recognized by Prime Minister Churchill as both a crown jewel vital to the war effort and an intelligence source to be protected. He codenamed the intelligence BONIFACE and insisted on having credible human source cover for the signals intercepted traffic.[2] In the United States, U.S. codebreakers were having success breaking Japanese diplomatic traffic, codenamed MAGIC, and in replicating the MAGIC or PURPLE encryption machine.

As Churchill sought to bring President Roosevelt and the United States into the war, the British opened the door partially to their work on ULTRA, careful not to reveal the scope of their exploitation and the stunning importance of the resulting intelligence product. The British were troubled by what they saw as lax American security and weak intelligence organization. At the same time, the UK desperately needed the United States.

Limited cooperation on both the ENIGMA and MAGIC machines began. However, it was not until the beginning of 1943 that the British would accede to full intelligence sharing on the ULTRA traffic to include the cryptographic keys, the code to feed the code-cracking machines, and the resulting deciphered intelligence traffic.[3] From this work would emerge a program of bilateral U.S.-UK intelligence sharing and cooperation that would be dubbed the "special relationship."

The downside, the challenge of such full sharing, would appear just a few years later, early in the Cold War. Intelligence liaison officers were in both capitals. Intelligence doors were opened, and through these doors—at the State Department, the Defense Department, and the Central Intelligence Agency—the likes of Philby, Burgess, and Maclean, British officials spying for the Soviet Union, would pass; the most sensitive issues would be discussed, with a pulsing hemorrhage of U.S. national security secrets to the USSR.[4]

Bearing in mind both the benefits and the risks, bilateral intelligence relations—with allies of long standing, with other nations, indeed with former adversaries—have proven to be the preferred avenue for intelligence sharing. The relationships can be monitored both for the value of the information exchanged and the potential espionage and other counterintelligence problems. The relationships can be tailored to strengthen the broader fabric of the bilateral relationship on both intelligence and non-intelligence matters.

NATO

With the signing of the North Atlantic Treaty on 4 April 1949, the challenge of intelligence sharing entered the new realm of a standing, formal, multinational alliance, an alliance in which, under the terms of Article 5, "The Parties agree that an armed attack against one or more of them in Europe or North America shall be considered an attack

A. Denis Clift

against them all."[5] Nuclear deterrence and nuclear strike options were part of the responsibilities of the Alliance. Intelligence moved apace with new responsibilities in the nuclear age. Intelligence would become one of six operational planning divisions under the Director of NATO's International Military staff. A new security classification—SECRET Releasable to NATO—would be created.

As the number of NATO member nations grew from 12 to 15 and beyond, the risk of espionage, of theft of NATO secrets grew. The risk could manifest itself in unpredicted and high places—witness 1974 when West German Chancellor Willy Brandt's personal aide for several years, Gunter Guillaume, was arrested and confessed to being a spy for the East German Ministry of State Security and an officer in the East German Army.

The Cold War NATO challenge of intelligence sharing would be to balance the protection of sources and methods, and the determination of "who had the need to know" against the need for an Alliance militarily capable of handling either a conventional or nuclear attack.

COALITION PARTNERS

With the tearing down of the Berlin Wall, the coming of the 1990s, and the demise of the Soviet Union and Warsaw Pact, new dimensions of intelligence sharing would open in rapid succession. On 2 August 1990, Iraq invaded Kuwait. A coalition force would prepare in Operation DESERT SHIELD and fight in Operation DESERT STORM to drive Saddam Hussein's forces from Kuwait. Intelligence sharing with coalition partners played a new and important role in this military victory over Iraq.

In the Department of Defense's formal report to the Congress, entitled *The Conduct of the Persian Gulf War,* the Chairman of the Joint Chiefs, General Colin Powell, was quoted as saying, "No combat commander has ever had as full and complete a view of his adversary as did our field commander. Intelligence support to Operations Desert Shield and Desert Storm was a success story." General Norman Schwarzkopf, the Commander in Chief of Central Command, in turn stated, "The great military victory we achieved in Desert Storm and the minimal losses sustained by U.S. and Coalition forces can be directly attributed to the excellent intelligence picture we had on the Iraqis."[6]

The coalition included nations with whom the United States had had a longstanding intelligence relationship—for example, the United Kingdom. It also included nations with whom the United States had little if any intelligence dealings—Syria is one example.

Intelligence sharing in the coalition construct would have noteworthy particulars that have continued beyond DESERT STORM to contribute to more recent operations. The sharing would be for an unwritten contract period, that is, the length of the operation. For the length of that period, it would be important, while safeguarding sources and methods, to make as much actionable intelligence as possible available: first, to ensure military victory; second, to ensure to the maximum degree possible the protection of coalition forces, with absolute minimum loss of life; and third, to ensure the cohesion and effectiveness of the coalition at the government-to-government, political level.

Turning to this third point, first, the leaders of our coalition partners had to be persuaded—so that they in turn could assure their publics—that they had a clear and accurate picture of operations, that their troops had the best possible force protection, and that they were able to test media reports against intelligence reports and operational reports flowing from the theater.

Perhaps some of you remember the live TV images of coalition force cruise missiles winging their way past the Al Rashid Hotel en route to their targets in Baghdad. DESERT STORM was being fought in the era of live, 24-hour television coverage being broadcast to nations around the world. Television correspondents were on the ground in Iraq offering their interpretation of the action, including reports of bomb damage and the nature of the targets struck.

To provide the intelligence required to General Schwarzkopf and the coalition, the Dr. No's, the disclosure experts with the approval of their superiors took the lead in guiding the intelligence officers drafting reports on how to include as much information as possible, how to prepare and send intelligence to where it was needed in the coalition without compromising sources and methods. The concept of producing tear-sheet intelligence reports or perforated-line intelligence reports would emerge from the war in the Gulf. A report could be sent in its entirety at the most sensitive level for U.S. eyes only on a need-to-know basis. Or, part of the report could be stripped away and the key substance needed for action still transmitted without the more sensitive details. At the same time as the releasable U.S. intelligence was being sent to the theater of coalition operations, it was being provided to the ministries of defense in the capitals of the participating coalition nations.

BOSNIA

By the time of the mid-1990s, this intelligence-sharing technique would come of age and prove of great value in the Bosnian Peacekeeping Operations. In addition to his NATO forces, the Supreme Allied Commander Europe, General George Joulwan, had a Russian Brigade as a coalition partner. A Russian General Officer was assigned as Deputy to SACEUR as part of General Joulwan's staff, and the Brigade was integrated into the operation. To guide this new, post-Cold War construct, Joulwan and the Russians agreed to a set of principles for command, airspace management, and intelligence sharing.

It is important to bear in mind here that the Russian Federation had, to say the least, some experience in intelligence. The Russians had expertise on Serbia not to be found in the United States. There was intelligence to be shared. The tear-sheet methodology allowed the U.S. to exceed initial expectations in meeting its intelligence-sharing responsibilities.

A. Denis Clift

UNITED NATIONS

The end of the Cold War would see a blossoming of UN peacekeeping operations. The United Nations Secretary General and his senior secretariat would realize how desperately they needed more information not only for decisionmaking but just to keep abreast of events. The U.S. and other nations would assist the UN in developing a fledgling situation center to meet the intelligence requirements. The center worked to link with its Peacekeeping Forces in the field. The results have been checkered at best.

During the UNTAC operations, the United Nations Transitional Authority in Cambodia, in 1991-1993, many problems were encountered. Here I am drawing on the observations of Australian Army Major Peter Bartu who served as assistant to the UNTAC Commander:

- at the operational level, there was no formal intelligence structure;
- forces arriving in Cambodia depended on briefings they had received at their points of origin;
- UNTAC established a military information cell, staffed by a mix of nationalities, many with no intelligence training;
- the cell had no baseline for what constituted significant military activity; and
- there was no formal military information link between Phnom Penh and New York until mid-1993.[7]

The sharing of intelligence would evolve by the 1992-1994 United Nations Operation in Somalia II—and here I am indebted to Lieutenant Robert Allen, U.S. Navy, and his master's thesis research on the subject while at the Joint Military Intelligence College. The UN intelligence organization supporting some 24,000 troops from 32 countries was dominated by the United States. U.S. intelligence reports and analysis provided the bulk of the information flow.

While release procedures involved "judgment calls," U.S. intelligence officers were careful to edit out sensitive sources and methods information. And, to quote Lieutenant Allen, "The UN's lack of any adequate security system fostered concerns over leaks of information in Mogadishu as it had in New York. In the case of Somalia it has been charged that the 'intelligence network set up for the United Nations and the United States was rife with double agents.'"[8]

As U.S. intelligence sharing and intelligence involvement with the United Nations continued to grow in the early to mid-1990s, increasing alarms were sounded over leaks, unauthorized disclosures, and general mishandling by the UN of U.S. information. Congressional hearings were held, and the Congress clamped down in the Intelligence Authorization Act of 1997. Section 308 of that Act prohibits the provision of intelligence information to the UN absent certain presidential certifications. The statute imposes certain non-delegable duties upon the President and requires him to make semi-annual reports to the Congress.[9]

CONCLUSION

In concluding this survey of the issues bearing on intelligence sharing, I will avoid the urge to retrace the pros and cons I sketched at the beginning. What I would say is that these pros and cons will continue to shape the business of sharing in the future. It is a business of classic contradictions.

The U.S. Intelligence Community strives mightily to improve America's intelligence capabilities. An A Team and B Team are even now preparing their reports, findings, and recommendations on the subject in response to the taskings of President Bush's National Security Policy Directive, NSPD-5.

As U.S. technologies, methods, and capabilities continue to improve, the nation's security demands their safeguarding. There are methods we do not want to share, and there are Dr. No's in strength to guard against inappropriate disclosure. At the same time in the early 21st century, the demands on U.S. intelligence point up and down and across the entire globe. The set-piece USSR/Warsaw Pact target construct is long gone. U.S. intelligence needs to draw on the expertise of intelligence counterparts in regions and in nations we did not deal with before. That sharing can flow most easily from mutually beneficial bilateral relationships. Our need for the best possible intelligence will point to expanding such relationships.

CHAPTER 19
THE LEFT HAND OF CURIOSITY

In 1997, at the request of his host at a Harvard Seminar on Intelligence, Command, and Control, the author recounted lessons in his career, from New York Daily News *copy boy, to naval officer, to intelligence leader and college president. Information- and intelligence-gathering techniques, and the technological sophistication of the gathering tools, have changed dramatically since the 1950s. However, people still form the core, and they are being measured by a rising standard of personal accountability. The author examines this rising standard in the workings of intelligence, policy, and the exercise of power. Novelist John LeCarre said that "intelligence is the left hand of curiosity." Intelligence is indeed a vital part of the national decisionmaking body.*

"All things are relative in this world," Maxim Gorki wrote in his short story "Creatures That Once Were Men," "and a man cannot sink into a condition so bad that it could not be worse."[1]

For those entrusted with safeguarding American lives and the nation's well-being, the world continues to spin into a condition that is more and more exquisitely challenging if not worse. In this first of the post-Cold War decades, the watchstanders in the nation's command and intelligence centers do not sit and wait for the strategic Hot Line to ring. They are too busy taking the next 911 call. It is the role of the United States, President Clinton told Marines at Camp Lejeune two months ago, to be "the world's indispensable nation that must stand up to those who threaten international peace, whether they be Iraq's Saddam Hussein or China's Communist regime. Because of your example," he said, "people everywhere look to America for help and inspiration."[2]

"So it is proper"—to continue quoting—"that we assure our friends once again that, in the discharge of this responsibility, we Americans know and observe the difference between world leadership and imperialism; between firmness and truculence; between a thoughtfully calculated goal and spasmodic reaction to the stimulus of emergencies."[3]

I should note that in continuing my quote with the "so it is proper," I digressed from Clinton to Dwight D. Eisenhower, a sentence from his first inaugural address in January 1953. There were three reasons for doing so: First, your seminar chairman has invited me to discuss my experiences, formal and informal, throughout my career, and the chapters turned thus far in that career run from Eisenhower through Clinton; second, the soothing sense of flow between the two quotes serves to underscore Gorki's relativity; and third, our increasing ability to manipulate ever-greater amounts of information—indeed, going beyond the joining of two separate quotes—and to fire the results of our work around the world, must bring with it a recognized respect for the burden of our limitations and the weight of our accountability.

A. Denis Clift

Just over a month ago, *U.S. News & World Report* took a look at some of the Army's growing pains on the evolving high-tech battlefield as it plays its part in the indispensable nation's armed forces. The article described the big computer monitors in the field command center of an unfolding war game at Fort Hood, Texas. Closer to the frontline of the mock battle, the author reported:

> Inside a Bradley fighting vehicle, the keyboard for a $100,000 "militarized" PC is jammed behind the seat in the cramped turret. The crew is supposed to have used the PC to update the battle-tracking network, but their hands are full just trying to survive so they radio in their reports. And, one might ask, were the radio reports being captured on the computer monitors? [4]

And so, to indulge in another quote, I shall follow the practice of Aldous Huxley's Director of Hatcheries and Conditioning in the *Brave New World*—the D.H.C., as he was known: "'I shall begin at the beginning,' "said the D.H.C., and the zealous students recorded his intention in their notebooks: *Begin at the beginning.*"[5]

The early 1950s marked my first experiences in moving information, print and graphic, in a timely, accountable manner most useful to the consumer. Back then ocean liners were still more than holding their own with trans-Atlantic aircraft, and the hulking first-generation vacuum-tube computers were rare beasts dwelling in the main in defense and research laboratories. More importantly, it was an era in which the Brooklyn Dodgers, the New York Giants, and the New York Yankees all dwelled in New York City.

THE DAILY NEWS

A year and one-half after President Eisenhower delivered his first inaugural address, I began my first stint as a copyboy with the New York *Daily News*. The best part of the job was going to the ballparks—Yankee Stadium, the Polo Grounds, and Ebbetts Field—with the news photographers assigned to the games. The photographers still used the big Speed-Graphic glass-plate cameras complete with 24-inch zoom lenses five-to-six inches in diameter. The photographers were of the old school, heavy drinkers, dyspeptic, non-stop hilarious storytellers when they weren't cursing their lot. Their photographic gear was heavy, and the copyboy, first and foremost, was a useful beast of burden.

The photographers' boxes, hanging out from the face of the ballparks up behind homeplate, were the best free-beer seats in the house. The photographers would pivot their big cameras on stanchions, following the action and taking their shot. There would be a loud click of the thumb trigger when they did so. My job was to put down my beer and follow the swing of the camera, listen for the click, and write down the action—let's say a double play at second: the name of the shortshop, the name of the second baseman, the name of the runner out at second, the name of the second-base umpire, the name of the batter, the inning—top or bottom—the game, and the number of the glass plate exposed with the shot.

To meet deadlines, usually around the bottom of the fifth or top of the sixth inning I would stuff all of the exposed film plates and my rough caption materials into an envelope and catch a subway back to the *Daily News* building—the one with the big revolving globe in the lobby that *Superman* made famous. I would drop off the plates in the photo lab and deliver the captions to the news-floor captions department where grizzled veterans would turn my rough data into the slick captions of the nation's premier tabloid newspaper. Later that evening I would see the results of my work when the first edition of the next day's paper hit the newsstand. This has to be the most efficient collection, analysis, dissemination process I have ever had a hand in in my life.

NAVY YEARS

In the early spring of 1995, my secretary at the Joint Military Intelligence College buzzed me on the intercom to advise that there was a Gary Powers on the telephone. In fact, it was the son of the late U-2 pilot who was calling to invite me to be the speaker at the Smithsonian Air and Space Museum on the occasion of the formal inclusion of artifacts from his father's career into the museum's permanent collection.

I was a naval officer serving at the Fleet Intelligence Center, Pacific when Francis Gary Powers' U-2 was shot down over Sverdlovsk on 1 May 1960. With President Eisenhower providing quiet, determined leadership, the nation was racing to develop a far better source of information on the USSR's strategic ICBM and bomber forces. The allegation of a "missile gap" that would have the Soviets holding a 3-to-1 superiority in strategic nuclear forces by the early 1960s was figuring prominently in the Presidential campaign. To quote Arthur Schlesinger, Jr.: "By 1960, it was a staple of Democratic oratory."[6] With debate raging, the nation needed new ways, better information, harder analysis, better answers on the exact nature and capabilities of the USSR's forces for the shaping of our own strategic deterrent.

The downing of Powers' U-2 came just 110 days before the first successful recovery of a CORONA overhead satellite—the dawning of the space reconnaissance age. While I was not cleared into the CORONA program, I was privy to the gossip about the exotic missions being flown by Air Force twin-boom C-119 aircraft flying out of Hawaii, and then trailing trapezes designed to snag payload parachutes descending over the Pacific—payloads that I would learn were the first of the returning CORONA capsules. Here, I was witness to the birth of a film delivery system even more exotic than that which had involved me at the New York *Daily News*. Here, I was witness to one small facet of the immense pioneering enterprise and commitment that must accompany the accountability of power. "Aerial photos," the legendary photointerpreter Arthur Lundahl once said, "give crisp, hard information, like the dawn after long darkness."

In September 1960, freshly promoted from Ensign to Lieutenant Junior Grade, I headed south from Hawaii to Christchurch, New Zealand, en route to the first of two Antarctic expeditions—Operations DEEP FREEZE 60 and 61. In these operations, the thrill of a lifetime, there were important lessons on the usability of information and the accountability of man.

A. Denis Clift

September, spring down there, meant the launch of the first flights from New Zealand to the ice runway at McMurdo Sound more than 2,000 miles to the south across the unforgiving Southern Ocean, the pack ice, and the mountains, snow, and ice of the Antarctic landmass. The aircraft supporting the expedition were lineal descendants of Waldo Pepper's flying circus—the Marine Corps version of the DC-3, R4Ds with names like *Semper Shaftus,* fitted with skis and JATO (Jet-Assisted Takeoff) bottles; Navy P2V Neptunes, the photo-mappers; Air Force double-decker Globemasters hauling bulk cargo, people, helicopters, and fixed-wing Otters; Super Constellations; WILLIE VICTORs; and the new C-130 Hercules fitted with 7,500 pounds of snow skis.

Weather forecasts literally were vital to mission accomplishment. The task force commander had to rely on fragmentary information from three or four hopelessly separated ground stations and one lonely picket ship in trying to outguess potentially deadly headwinds, storms, and whiteouts. This would change within days of my arrival. I can picture clearly the first morning that the staff meteorologist, a Navy four-striper, strode into the morning operations and planning meeting, a smile from ear to ear, with the first take from the first weather bird, the first TIROS television and infrared observation satellite, in hand. There was awe, elation in the room. For the first time, the commander had a picture of the current and incoming weather over the entire route, from take-off to landing—a picture, I should note, to be checked against the data still flowing from ship and ground stations.

I would learn quickly in Antarctica that photography and imagery could meet only a limited part of the commander's need for usable information. There were no photo satellites able then to assist in the exploration and mapping of the continent. The mapping aircraft had limited range and were few in number. There were parts of the continent that you still had to explore if you wished to learn with certainty what was there. In 1961, I sailed on the Bellingshausen Sea Expedition aboard the icebreaker USS *Glacier* accompanied by the icebreaker USS *Staten Island,* a four-month odyssey during which our surveying parties would develop data that would lead to a redrawing of the world's maps of that part of the continent. In 1962, when I was reviewing the Rand McNally pageproofs of my book on Antarctica, I would have the pleasure of instructing that august publisher's cartographers to change Thurston Peninsula to Thurston Island.

The value of having the right people on scene, on site, on the ground in Antarctica was not limited to the requirements of exploration and research. Among my several responsibilities 37 years ago—1960—I was to become a frontline participant in the Cold War era's first successful treaty-based international on-site inspections.

In 1958, during the International Geophysical Year, President Eisenhower had proposed to the 11 nations engaged with the United States in scientific research on the Antarctic Continent that they enter into a treaty preserving the continent for such research and other peaceful purposes. That treaty was quickly negotiated and entered into force, giving treaty-state observers free access to any area to inspect all stations, installations, and equipment. Advance notice was required for all activities and for the introduction of military personnel.

Information derived "real-time" from on-site inspections has become an increasingly important source of usable information, information for which there can be accountability, in world politics. In the strategic arms negotiations and monitoring, we have moved beyond the near-total reliance we placed on satellites—or National Technical Means—from the 1960s through the mid-1980s. The Intermediate-Range Nuclear Forces (INF) Treaty ratified in May 1988 was the pathfinder, with Article XI and the 18-page protocol flowing from that article providing for on-site inspections.

The acceptability and expectation of on-site inspections has moved beyond U.S.-Soviet, NATO-Warsaw Pact, and U.S.-Russian arms agreements to enter the mainstream of international politics. To cite just one example, I have the greatest respect for the work of Chairman Ekeus and the UN Special Commission Team pursuing their on-site work in Iraq under UN Resolutions 606 and 687 until there is full and final disclosure that all capabilities for weapons of mass destruction have been eliminated—and that disclosure has been verified.

Before leaving Antarctica, I would also learn there that accurate, usable information can be subject to a major distortion and misinterpretation as it moves up and down the line of command. I had listened to President John F. Kennedy's inaugural address via the BBC at a friend's home in Wellington while the *Glacier* was in drydock fitting new propeller blades for our expedition. Once we were underway, I was responsible for the international visitors aboard. I was also the expedition's correspondent—the sole filing correspondent—and my news dispatches were beamed from the icebreakers to New Zealand and to the United States and began appearing in newspapers around the world. There were some exciting stories. At one point, the two ships were locked in by pack ice for several days. Winter was not far away; would the expedition have to winter over? The stories were being carried by the Associated Press and running in the *New York Times*. I would learn half a year later that the new President had taken a casual interest in the drama of the expedition and had asked his naval aide to keep him abreast of developments.

For those of you who have had the pleasure of serving in the Pentagon—or have dreamed of such a life—you can imagine how garbled and twisted this expression of interest would become as it moved down the line. Down at the bottom of the world, the *Glacier's* communicator would hand the expedition's commodore a message with a clipped order. He was told to extricate his ships from the ice immediately—immediately!—to avoid being trapped for the winter. We had been biding our time, as polar seamen must, awaiting a shift in the winds that would open leads, leads of water in the pack ice permitting us to steam north. But . . . an order was an order. Officers and men went over the side onto the ice with dynamite to blast a path to open water. The Keystone Cops couldn't have done it better. We blasted for more than a day with little effect. The masses of ice absorbed the explosive force in their elasticity. We paused to sleep. The winds shifted. The leads opened, and we were steaming free.

A. Denis Clift

THE NAVAL INSTITUTE

My tales of derring-do landed me a position first as Assistant Editor, then Editor of the *United States Naval Institute Proceedings*. The lesson I quickly learned and practiced was that if the information I published was to be useful to my professional readership, the essays had to be authoritative, the views of members of the sea services, of prime participants, of those with expert knowledge. The *Proceedings'* strength lay in the contributions of those with the best minds in the profession, not in the writings of the journal's staff. If we are to be accountable in these exquisitely challenging times, we must seek out the views of experts even if those views are not in vogue, even if they are not readily available for the mouse to command on our computer screen. In keeping with this preaching, I took myself off in 1966 to the marvelous bedlam of the London School of Economics to write and to receive my graduate degree.

THE WHITE HOUSE

From October 1967 through early 1981, I served continuously in the Executive Office of the President and the White House—the administrations of Presidents Johnson, Nixon, Ford, and Carter. The White House is a dispenser of lightning, with decisions that shape and shake the world coming down from the Oval Office and other lower power points within the institutional perimeter. The White House is a lightning rod, a place of extreme pressure, with the agencies of government, the Congress, the nation, and the world on the one hand vying for influence and favorable consideration and, on the other, seeking to bring the structure down. It is a place where information is guarded on a strict need-to-know basis as a priceless sought-after commodity. It is a place where accountability is at a premium as you collect, analyze, and act on information that literally within minutes can become national or international policy.

National Security Council Staff

My years on the staff of the National Security Council (NSC), 1971-1977, first as a member of the European staff, then as head of the Soviet and European staffs, were years of unmatched power for the NSC staff. The desktop computers and local area networks that one would learn so much about in the mid-1980s had not yet arrived. When Henry Kissinger or Brent Scowcroft had a communication for us, we were either summoned from the Old Executive Office Building (EOB) to the West Wing to receive it in person, or it was sealed in an envelope, placed in a pneumatic tube in the White House Situation Room, and sucked across to the NSC secretariat in the Old EOB to be hand-delivered to us by a member of the secretariat. Being a curator at heart, I've kept one of those envelopes: red tag stapled above "THE WHITE HOUSE" in the upper lefthand corner, "Secret" and "Exclusively Eyes Only" penned in Red and underlined, "Priority Action" penned in red and double underlined, Henry Kissinger's name lined out, my name penned in. It's heady stuff, and the White House is heady stuff.

One afternoon, in a meeting of the NSC senior staff in the Situation Room, Hal Saunders, who was heading Middle East affairs, said to Brent Scowcroft, who was in the chair, "I understand the need for close hold, but yesterday I received one of these sealed secret red-tagged envelopes from Henry marked for my eyes only, and I opened it up and it was empty . . . can you at least give me a hint as to what was on his mind?"

WHCA: Global Reach for Presidential Communications

"No one can experience with the President the glory and the agony of his office," Lyndon Johnson wrote. "[T]he President represents all the people and must face up to all the problems."[7] In serving on the staffs of Presidents dealing with all the problems, I became a student of and a participant in the extraordinary command, control, and communications systems supporting the President. I became an admirer of the White House Communications Agency (WHCA) and its seeming ability to put its hands on anyone, anytime, anywhere.

When I traveled with Nixon and Brezhnev to the Black Sea in 1974, I was quartered at a workers' paradise hotel, the Parus Sanatorium. To reach the beach, one descended by elevator 240 feet through a shaft cut in the granite cliff, then walked another hundred feet to the seaside face of the shaft's horizontal arm. Here, on a stand at the edge of the beach's worn and rounded granite rocks stood a telephone with the symbol of the White House Communications Agency and the words "Oreanda White House" on its dial. I complained to General Larry Adams, the WHCA Commander, later that day that he had forgotten the phone on the inflatable seahorse for us swimmers offshore.

In the early to mid-1970s, the Soviet Union took the occasion of the several U.S.-Soviet summits of détente to study at first hand the command and control support the United States was providing our Presidents. As in other fields of the superpower competition, they had a reputation for replicating, to the degree possible, the U.S. approach to the task at hand.

In November 1974, the Soviets had brought the best train in the entire USSR to the Far East for the 90-minute run from the fighter air base where Air Force One had just landed to the conference site of the Ford-Brezhnev Vladivostok summit. The President and the General Secretary rode in a dining car rich in paneling, oriental carpets, cut-glass, and crystal. I was one or two cars back, a staff car of continental layout—windowed compartments with sliding doors opening onto a corridor running the length of the carriage. My eye caught several cables on the floor's edge of the corridor. I followed them the length of the carriage, past the ajar door of the toilet compartment, where they plunged down through the open flap at the base of the toilet bowl before twisting and climbing like vines to the roof of the carriage.

Once again, the White House Communications Agency had preceded our summit party, giving the President secure communications leaping from the roof of the train to a global link of communications relays. In the years that followed, as the United States monitored the evolution of the USSR's rail-mobile command and control systems, I could never tell

A. Denis Clift

from National Technical Means whether their new cables went from the train's communications centers down through their toilet bowls up and out to the roof antennas!

WHCA's long reach rolled me out of bed between 2:00 and 3:00 a.m. on a night in June 1974. I was at my residence in Annapolis, Maryland. President Nixon was in Salzburg, Austria, en route to the Middle East and at the moment of the call was behind closed doors in conversation with Chancellor Bruno Kreisky. The Assistant White House Press Secretary came on the line, a sharp young character by the name of Diane Sawyer, to advise that she needed a text that the Press Secretary could draw on an hour later in reporting on the President's conversation to the awaiting, traveling press corps. It had been so easy to pick up that telephone in that staff room in Salzburg and say, "I need to speak to Denis Clift, NSC." It had been a bit harder to peel my eyes open and pound out some cogent highlights of the President's emerging conversation.

The global communications of the 1970s—I might as well be here before you marveling at the wonders of the steam engine. Now, day after day during the morning and evening commutes, the phones are to the ears. I do not know whether they are talking to Diane Sawyer or Brezhnev's ghost, but they have communications and they are communicating. We all have communications—global communications—with a difference. And that difference is that our ability to move information is outracing the accountability so central to national security affairs. This poses us with a nice challenge that has to be met for those in positions of trust, for those responsible for lives, for security beyond the moment and the immediate walls. It is a challenge that must be accepted as part of the core mission.

Travels with Mondale

Three more points on the White House years. Following the election of 1976, President-elect Carter took the decision to send his Vice President-elect on a mission to NATO Headquarters, major European capitals, and Japan in the first week of the new administration for face-to-face "getting-to-know-you" talks at the highest level. As a member of President Ford's NSC staff with a reputation as a scarred veteran of bilateral and multilateral summit travels, I was asked by the Vice President-elect to help organize and carry out his mission.

We launched three days into the new administration. Early in our whirlwind tour a member of the crew aboard Air Force II who had come to know me from earlier flights took me aside. "Sir," he said, "these guys are sending out every message FLASH—logistics stuff, who's to be in what car, you name it." Accountability—I had been unaware. Certainly the Vice President was unaware that well-intentioned members of his new staff fresh from the battles of the political campaign were slugging the most routine of communications FLASH. "Why not?" they thought. This was the Vice President of the United States. Why not? Beyond our winging airborne fuselage we were causing remarkable reverberations within the National Command structure. It was agreed by all that we would switch to ROUTINE with an occasional leavening of PRIORITY for such traffic.

We visited many capitals and traveled many miles in a very few days. I remember Strobe Talbott, when traveling with us as a correspondent for *Time*, showing me his calculations on the thousands of miles during the final leg of the mission from Tokyo to Washington. The pressures of the schedule had been such that we had been unable to include Portugal with its new democratically elected government on the itinerary. This was a source of concern, and to avoid even the hint of a slight, Vice President Mondale said he would call Prime Minister Soares from London and that we should have our traveling press party present to report on the conversation.

The call was placed from the Vice President's hotel suite. The Prime Minister was to be in our Ambassador's office in Lisbon for the occasion. Secretary-to-secretary connection had been made and the phone at the Vice President's end lay off the cradle at the ready on a coffee table. When word was received that our press was heading into the elevators, coming up to the suite, the Vice President's secretary again picked up the phone, and there was no one on the other end of the line. Shouting didn't fix the problem. I said "Hold the press." I was told, "Too late." For the Vice President to speak to Soares with press present would be a good event. For the Vice President to pick up the phone and have no reply . . . I'll leave it to you, a multiple-choice answer.

I ran down the hotel corridor to the Secret Service command post and had the agents use their circuit via Washington to Lisbon—instantaneously—to bring up Embassy Lisbon on another line. The Prime Minister and Ambassador Carlucci had been out on a balcony. Our press would have no more than a minute of pleasant light-hearted banter with the Vice President as the call went through: a splendid event, and it was so reported. If information is to be usable, if communications are to flow, there is nothing like immediate back-ups and work-arounds, multiple channels. This is a lesson we repeatedly work hard to forget.

At Camp David

Then again, *no* channel of communications may be the preferred answer. From 7 September through 17 September 1978, I would be sequestered in the Catoctin Mountains as a staff member of the Camp David Summit with President Carter, Prime Minister Begin, and President Sadat. Clearly that summit will stand as an enduring page in diplomatic achievement. It was an event made remarkable by the historical appreciation and the contributions to history that radiated from the Egyptian and Israeli leaders. It was an event that succeeded because of President Carter's clear understanding of the likely impact of communications from the Summit, and his imposition from the outset of a news blackout.

The participants at Camp David were genuine leaders, leaders who knew their nations, leaders able to frame and take the most important of decisions. The challenge the U.S. President faced was how to enable them and assist them in the taking of such decisions. President Carter knew in planning the summit that the slim chance of negotiating a peace agreement between Israel and Egypt would be eliminated if he, Begin, and Sadat were available to the press—or if members of their teams were available during the difficult negotiations. No matter what might be said, it would be subject to reporting, to different interpretations, to different reactions in each capital and elsewhere around the world. He knew that resultant pressures would build on the summit participants, requiring them to stand firm, blocking flexibility and the chance of compromise and progress. I witnessed the use of zero external communications as a remarkable tool in the hands of the Commander in Chief.

DEFENSE

The pictures that CNN's cameras caught of cruise missiles winging their way past the Al Rashid Hotel in Baghdad en route to their targets remain etched in my mind. This truly was picture collection and dissemination without benefit of any copyboy at all. What were their implications for the execution of U.S. policy?

As a nation, we had learned from certain of our experiences in Vietnam. In DESERT STORM, we knew that in the pursuit of our military and policy objectives, we would have to have our military and civilian leaders speak with authority and accountability live to the media, live on television on a regular basis—to provide the background and the information on which our policy and actions were based—if we were not to surrender the molding of international public opinion to the media.

For the preceding decade, returning to the thread of my Everyman's travels, I had had a considerable role to play in the molding of national and international public opinion in the terminal phase of the Cold War. As part of his participation in the NATO Defense Ministers' meeting in the spring of 1981, Secretary of Defense Caspar Weinberger had presented highly classified briefings on the breadth and rapidity of the Soviet Union's military build-up and capabilities. The late German Defense Minister Manfred Wörner had asked him to help make as much of this information as possible available to the public. Freshly arrived at the Pentagon from my White House years, I would become the founding Editor in Chief of *Soviet Military Power*. The first of 10 editions of the Department of Defense's annual report on Soviet military capabilities would be published in September 1981, the final edition in 1991. In 1990, when Secretary Cheney and Defense Minister Yazov dropped in on a committee of the Supreme Soviet in session, one of the Soviet members waved the most recent edition of our report in Yazov's face, yelling, "Why is it that we have to depend on the Americans for information on our forces?"

In producing *Soviet Military Power*, in providing the public with levels of detail about these forces never before presented in official open publications, the Department of Defense drew on the most authoritative information from classified sources and then formally reviewed and declassified the entire publication for release. The Soviet press labeled the first edition "99 Pages of Lies." However, the United States accepted full accountability for the information we were presenting. The report's stature as an authoritative document would grow with each new edition.

Soviet Military Power was so new and different a creature that Secretary Weinberger sent me to Brussels to brief the international Press Corps at NATO Headquarters at the same time that he was having his formal release press conference in Washington. One contentious area in the questions I received related to the first edition's use of paintings to depict various Soviet weapons systems either fielded or in development—the *Typhoon*-Class ballistic missile submarine, for example. Good unclassified photography was hard to come by in

1981; some excellent classified photography could not yet be declassified. Thus, we decided to use "combat art," if you will, illustrations derived from a number of sources.

The first good photo of the *Typhoon* would appear in the 1985 edition. I remember how pleased I was the following year when I headed off to Brussels for the 1986 edition's press conference that we were now able to move from artwork to the first releasable photos of the SS-20 intermediate-range ballistic missile system. The press conference began, and one of the first questions was, "Why do you have to have such poor photography of the SS-20 missile. Why can't you give us better photographs?" The pictures were grainy. They were stills from a TV broadcast of a night training film. I looked at the guy and said, "You know, if I drove an SS-20 right into this conference room, you would complain that the oil was dirty."

INTELLIGENCE, POLICY, AND THE EXERCISE OF POWER

Earlier this year, in a C-Span interview with George Plimpton, the novelist John LeCarre was asked whether he thought intelligence still had a useful role to play now that the Cold War is over. While generally decrying subversion and the darker side of covert operations, LeCarre said that "intelligence is the left hand of curiosity," that gathering, analyzing, and using information is a natural part of what we do if we are doing it well.

This year marks the 50th anniversary of the National Security Act of 1947, a truly remarkable act that created the National Security Council and the Central Intelligence Agency under Title I on the Coordination of National Security, and then went on to provide for the Secretary of Defense and the National Military Establishment under Title II.

The U.S. Intelligence Community has emerged with evolutionary adjustments from an intense 1995-1996 examination by a Presidential Commission and the oversight committees of the Congress. The Community and the Government more generally are exploring new and better ways for the left hand to meet the needs of a curious nation focused both on world leadership and survival. Of tremendous importance, intelligence is emerging from behind its fabled green door, the door that for decades had the sign that said, "We can't tell you. You are not cleared." We see this emergence, for example, in CIA's intelligence project with Harvard. We see it in the publications of the Director of Central Intelligence's Center for the Study of Intelligence. We see it in the Occasional Papers of the Joint Military Intelligence College and in the essays published in the College Foundation's *Defense Intelligence Journal.* More importantly, we see it in the emerging partnership among intelligence, policy, and operations.

When the late Chief of Naval Operations, Admiral Mike Boorda, met with my graduate students in 1995, he talked about the change in attitude, the new approach. He said that intelligence now had a seat with him at his table from start to finish on all major issues—a far cry from the days when the intelligence officer entered such a meeting, gave his briefing, and then was excused. Intelligence has come to recognize that in military affairs, for

A. Denis Clift

example, it is not there to support the commander. It is there as one of the commander's participants—it has a stake in the outcome—from start to finish, a full stake in the fight. Operations—the Commander—has come to recognize that the gifted, unique contributions of the left hand are essential to the effective functioning of the right. There is more than symbology in bricks and mortar and the disappearance thereof. A few years back, at the turn of the decade, the left hand and the right hand opened the Pentagon wall between the National Military Command Center and the National Military Intelligence Center—miracle of miracles.

We have come to recognize that intelligence properly shared to the fullest extent possible with other nations can make a major contribution to U.S. national security and foreign policy. We saw this in the coalition operations of DESERT STORM. Shared intelligence was important to the successes in the field, up and down the national command structures of each of the coalition partners. What was being said by the United States publicly could be confirmed, verified through other channels. The information they were receiving was good. It was usable. It was verifiable.

CONCLUSION: KNOWING WHAT THE LEFT HAND IS DOING

With the above said, I like to think we have followed the thread to the threshold of your field of seminar deliberations. On 4 December 1996, *Washington Post* staff writer Joel Achenbach published a piece entitled "Reality Check," which began "The Information Age has one nagging problem: Much of the information is not true. . . . There has always been bad information in our society," he continued, "but it moves faster now, via new technologies and a new generation of information manipulators."[8] College Presidents—small colleges, not Harvard perhaps—attend conferences of bodies such as the Commission on Higher Education. I did so in mid-December and heard one of the speakers, a college librarian, play on Achenbach's theme when she referred to the World Wide Web as an information dumpster.

At the Joint Military Intelligence College, I am working to provide our graduate students with improved computer and secure video and systems connectivity that will permit them to increase gaming and exercises with the War Colleges and the National Defense University, to open a new window of professional dialogue with staffs at commands around the world, and to increase sources available to them for their research. At the same time, I am increasing the priority we give to on-site research, to work overseas with principal players in the international security scene—to walk the land they are writing about, to meet eye-to-eye, to draw from living, interacting human beings insights that might not splash on a screen—travels to Japan, to Eastern Slavonia, to South Africa, to sit down with former African National Congress guerrillas now executive assistants to the Minister of Defense in researching the integration of former rival forces into the armed forces of South Africa. Going beyond the sources readily available—electronic, hard copy, or live human beings—developing multiple sources of information, some we might at first find hard to imagine, is not a new business. It is, however, a business that is more than ever central to the effective interaction between intelligence as the left hand of curiosity and the right hand as the exercise and accountability of power.

In his Foreword to *Short Stories,* Aldous Huxley said of Gorki's characters: "Their failings permit us to retain our self-esteem. We are all shorn lambs and, unless the wind were tempered for us, should feel extremely chilly for the blast."[9] We are at a point in the availability of information where first, the condition is not so bad that it could not be worse, and second, the standard of accountability is raised higher and higher. It is not a matter of others' failings permitting us to retain our self-esteem, rather a sobering reminder of our own vulnerability to failure and the larger cost that such failure may involve.

"People everywhere look to America for help and inspiration," the President told the Marines. This is true. I have seen it to be the case in humanitarian work I have been privileged to perform over the past five years, work as a U.S. Commissioner on a U.S.-Russian Joint Commission on Prisoners of War/Missing in Action created by the U.S. and Russian Presidents to help account for those still unaccounted for from World War II, Korea, the Cold War, Vietnam, and Afghanistan. I have traveled the length and breadth of Russia, traveled 13 of the 15 Soviet Republics, and without fail during the course of my meetings Presidents, generals, men, and women in each land, they grow misty-eyed, they weep, and they bless America for the example we are setting in our efforts to account for, to repatriate and to honor the missing and the dead. We are using and cross-checking multiple sources in this work: archival research here and abroad, interviews here and abroad, appeals on mass media for those with any information to come forward and assist.

I have a piece of Francis Gary Powers' U-2 in my office at the Joint Military Intelligence College, given to me by the Russian side of the Commission, General Volkogonov, the former Russian co-chair, and his deputy, General Volkov, both now dead. This small framed piece of aircraft skin serves to remind me of how high the left hand has soared, and at what peril, to meet the information needs essential to a full exercise and accountability of power.

CHAPTER 20
THE PLAY OF INTELLIGENCE
WITH PRESIDENTS AT THE SUMMIT

Whenever heads of state gather "at the summit" to decide matters of lasting importance to their respective nations, intelligence has a role. As the author points out in this chapter, originally an address to the Miller Center at the University of Virginia in April 2001, "intelligence is a complex variable in the summit dynamic." Here the author recounts some of the crucial roles played by intelligence in summit meetings from the 1940s through the 1990s. Included are his personal recollections from his own years in the White House, where he witnessed the play of intelligence by U.S. presidents and foreign heads of state at the summit.

On 5 January 1952, Prime Minister Winston Churchill arrived in Washington for talks with President Harry S. Truman. The two, accompanied by their delegations, boarded the Presidential yacht *Williamsburg* and, cruising the Potomac, discussed the problems of the world: China, Japan, Korea, the USSR, Iran, and Egypt. Seated at the cleared dining table, Churchill suggested that he follow the President's lead in the Far East and that the President follow his in the Middle East. "No wonder," Secretary of State Dean Acheson would write, "foreign ministers dislike meetings at the summit, where their chiefs are likely to take the bit in their teeth and have a gay canter across the country."[1]

Truman admired Acheson, but he had little time for the senior careerists at the State Department who felt that they, not he, should be making policy, and who had tried to block his recognition of the state of Israel three and one-half years earlier. He believed strongly in his role as policymaker and statesman at the summit.[2] In May 1951, Israel's Prime Minister David Ben-Gurion had come to the United States to raise Israel Bonds. He had met privately with the President, and then he had met at the CIA with Truman's Director of Central Intelligence General Walter Bedell Smith. From that meeting, a covert U.S.-Israeli connection grew. In the eyes of the Israelis, it was a counter to the reserved attitude of the State Department, "a major break in the Administration's stand-offish attitude toward Israel."[3]

INTELLIGENCE PREPARATION FOR THE SUMMIT

The Director of Central Intelligence is the President's intelligence adviser. The capabilities of the entire Intelligence Community are at the service of the President. The play of intelligence in the summit process—that is, the play of U.S. intelligence and foreign intelligence—for more than the past half century has figured prominently in the planning, the head-to-head talks, the follow-up in separate capitals. It has also figured almost not at all. The play has ranged from intelligence estimates to biographic studies, to current imagery, signals intelligence, and human reports flowing to the summit site—from covert actions designed to influence the summit to monitoring actions and commitments designed to reinforce summit agreements reached. Intelligence is a complex variable in the summit dynamic.

No one template shapes the way leaders draw on intelligence in preparing for summit meetings. President George H.W. Bush, who had served as Director of Central Intelligence in the Ford administration, would look to the Central Intelligence Agency for a steady flow of pre-summit papers and briefings. In the 1989 Malta Talks with President Mikhail Gorbachev aboard the cruise ship *Maxim Gorky*, Bush reviewed his hopes for progress on each of the priority arms control issues before them. To facilitate such progress, he asked the Soviet leader to follow the U.S. example by making public the details of military production, force levels, and budget, adding matter-of-factly, "As a former CIA man, I hope you got these from the KGB before our meeting."[4]

On 12 August 1941, President Franklin D. Roosevelt and Prime Minister Winston Churchill concluded their first summit talks off Newfoundland aboard the cruiser USS *Augusta* and the battleship *Prince of Wales*. The world would learn of the Atlantic Charter. Roosevelt's biographer James MacGregor Burns would write of the importance of the summit's chemistry—Roosevelt's fresh appreciation of Churchill's persuasiveness and persistence, Churchill's awareness of the difficulty of committing a President refusing to be cornered.[5] The intelligence dimensions of the summit would remain far from the public's eye.

Churchill was an absolute believer in the value of secret intelligence. In June 1940, one month after he had become Prime Minister, the British Government approved the recommendation of William Stephenson, the man called Intrepid, "that a British secret organization in the United States ... should undertake to do all that was not being done by overt means to assure sufficient aid for Britain and eventually to bring America into the war."[6] Stephenson and his newly formed British Security Coordination staff would immediately establish official liaison with FBI Director J. Edgar Hoover and begin sharing information with U.S. Army and Navy intelligence components. Of greater importance, they would cultivate people of influence close to the President: William Joseph "Wild Bill" Donovan, Vincent Astor, and Robert Sherwood. Astor, a close friend of the President's, served as his informal intelligence advisor. Sherwood, the playwright, had a hand in the President's speeches.

In July 1941, Donovan, who would become Roosevelt's Coordinator of Information and Director of the Office of Strategic Services, flew to London for an audience with the King, talks with Churchill, and an in-depth classified review of the war and British war needs. British Director of Naval Intelligence Rear Admiral John Godfrey arrived in the United States with his aide Lieutenant Commander Ian Fleming to promote closer intelligence sharing. They met with the President. With the stage thus set, "Churchill gave added momentum for intensified transatlantic intelligence exchanges in his first meeting with the President."[7] With the United States still neutral, Roosevelt would agree unofficially to patrol the U.S.-Iceland leg of the convoy route, with the sharing of intelligence that would be involved. While still aboard the *Prince of Wales*, Churchill cabled the Lord Privy Seal:

"Have reached satisfactory settlement about Naval Plan Number 4 (the United States Navy to take over the America-Iceland stretch of the Atlantic)."[8]

INTELLIGENCE AND THE COLD WAR SUMMITS

In the U.S.-Soviet superpower summits of the 1950s through early 1990s, intelligence figured extensively, sometimes prominently. On 1 May 1960, Francis Gary Powers' U-2 was shot down over Sverdlovsk, Russia. Two weeks later, President Dwight David Eisenhower would arrive in Paris for the Elysee Palace Four-Power Meeting among the USSR, France, Great Britain, and the United States. Nikita Khrushchev told the Summit host General Charles DeGaulle that Eisenhower would have to apologize for the U-2 overflight before the talks could proceed. Eisenhower politely refused, and the Soviet leader and his delegation stormed out of the conference room.

Eisenhower brought a strong belief in the importance of intelligence to his presidency. The United States needed to know the status of Soviet military research and development, the status of deployed strategic and conventional forces across the denied territory of one-sixth of the earth's land surface, the USSR. Early in his administration, he had approved planning for the development and deployment of the U-2 spy plane, as he had approved planning for Corona, the first reconnaissance satellite.[9] The Soviets had refused to agree to his Open Skies proposal. There would be no apology by the Chief of State for this intelligence program so essential to national security. The summit collapsed the next day.

At the end of his presidency, Eisenhower wrote a letter to Colonel Vernon A. "Dick" Walters. Walters, who as a Lieutenant General would serve as Deputy Director of Central Intelligence and joke that he spoke nine languages and made sense in none, was trained in defense intelligence. He would be posted as attaché to Rio, Rome, and Paris, and later be appointed U.S. Ambassador to Germany. He served often as Eisenhower's summit interpreter—as he had served as Truman's and would serve while on active duty with Kennedy, Johnson, Nixon, and Ford.

Upon Khrushchev's departure from the Elysee on day one of the 1960 summit, DeGaulle had come over to where the President and Colonel Walters were standing, taken them both by the arm a few steps aside, and said: "I do not know what Khrushchev is going to do, nor do I know what is going to happen, but whatever he does, I want you to know I am with you to the end."[10] Walters captured these important words. He brought a trained mind to the work of summits, and Eisenhower's letter would state in part, "The service you rendered me over a long period of time was invaluable—not only because you are so expert in the various languages at your command, but also because of your intelligent grasp of the problems and background of the various countries we together visited."[11]

In April 1974, Dick Walters and I would share adjoining seats on Air Force One as we flew home from Paris with President Nixon following the funeral for President Georges Pompidou. Shortly after we were airborne, he fished into a carry-on satchel for a book and began to read. A half-hour later he fished again for another. He had my wonderment and admiration, relaxing as he was reading foreign dictionaries.[12]

A. Denis Clift

Richard Nixon was a firm believer in the value of superpower summits, the value of a clearer understanding of the counterpart's interests and the limits on national actions that would have to be observed by both parties if conflict were to be avoided. Nixon also believed that there was "nothing like the deadline of a summit to knock heads together and to shape up a bureaucracy."[13]

President Ronald Reagan would agree. But in 1985, having experienced the deaths of Kosygin, Suslov, Brezhnev, Pelshe, Andropov, Ustinov and Chernenko since he had been elected President, Reagan said, "How can I be expected to make peace with them, if they keep dying on me?"[14]

BIOGRAPHIC INTELLIGENCE FOR THE SUMMIT

As we prepared for the summit meetings with President Brezhnev in the Nixon, Ford, and Carter administrations, information from the Intelligence Community updating the biographies of the Soviet leadership and information on the nature of Brezhnev's medical problems and the state of his declining health were an essential part of the staffing, as is biographic information for all summit talks. Psychological profiles, videos of foreign leaders in action, their mannerisms, their negotiating techniques are all part of the process.

In the late 1990s, Colonel General Dmitri Volkogonov would shed public light on Brezhnev's medical struggles, problems with his mouth and jaw, for example, which the U.S. had tracked far more discreetly years earlier. He would publish the entries in Brezhnev's diary of the gifts of game—whole wild boar—he had sent "to 'doctor Jakob from Bon' and 'doctor Ozinga from Diusendorf'[sic]" and, in 1976, Brezhnev's entry: "25 July. As usual no one around in morning Breakfast, shave, swim Today snoozed in rocker on bank. Today T. Nikolaevna went on cleaning teeth—and Muza examined the prosthesis Talked with Comrade Chernenko, K.U.—he's still not well, everything possible being done." As Brezhnev's health continued to decline, Volkogonov would write, "The shuffling gait, disjointed speech, wooden movements and complete inability to understand anything became the object of national pity and the butt of merciless jokes."[15]

ESTIMATES TO SUPPORT NEGOTIATIONS

He was, nonetheless, the Soviet leader. And, if biographic updates were useful, the collection, analysis, and flow of intelligence contributing to U.S. positions for the strategic arms negotiations with the Soviets were of central importance. The National Intelligence Estimates (NIEs), in turn, were the documents driving critical parts of the decisionmaking process. It is important to understand that not all NIEs had this stature and this potency. In my National Security Council and White House staff experience, most estimates were a voice contributing to the background Departmental chorus. They were relevant because I knew that the Intelligence Community was thinking about a particular subject; but more often than not they were irrelevant to my policy-level needs. If I wanted the best views in the community on a precise issue of the moment, I would go to the expert or experts most credible and valued.

Intelligence estimates on Soviet strategic forces were different. They helped to shape strategy at the same time that they were the summit negotiator's technical manual. They

> influenced debate and decision-making at the policy level regarding arms control, force structure, resource allocation, military procurement, and contingency planning for war. ... They provided a foundation for official U.S. public statements on Soviet military power and indirectly had a significant impact on the American population's understanding of the Soviet strategic threat as well.[16]

The estimates contributed importantly to the success of the SALT I Agreement, and to the Vladivostok nuclear arms accord signed by Brezhnev and President Gerald Ford. When the SALT II process began under President Jimmy Carter and the decision was made to set aside the best estimates of the Soviet leadership's negotiating tolerances and to seek deep arms cuts early in the new round of talks, the Soviets bitterly rejected the proposal. Foreign Minister Gromyko would label it a "cheap and shady maneuver." The Intelligence Community was ordered to produce an analysis of what had gone wrong. "We'd been left out of the huddle and then cut out of the play," bitterly remarked a high CIA official, "and now they were coming to us and demanding to know in this accusatory tone of voice why they'd dropped the ball."[17]

NATIONAL TECHNICAL MEANS

The play of intelligence at the summit would go well beyond the shaping of strategic arms negotiating positions to the declared responsibility for monitoring each side's compliance with the arms accords. The term "National Technical Means" was coined for this purpose, to embrace the role to be played by orbiting satellites, seismometers, and telemetry collectors.

When the SALT II Agreement would be signed by Brezhnev and Carter in 1979, Article XV—following SALT precedent—would provide that each side would use the national technical means of verification at its disposal, consistent with international law, to monitor compliance, that there would be no interference with such national technical means, and that there would be no deliberate concealment measures impeding verification by such means.

When I was in Moscow with Secretary Henry Kissinger in October 1974 preparing for the Vladivostok summit, Brezhnev would complain that the United States was deliberately concealing operational activities at one of our ICBM complexes. Kissinger explained that there had been recent construction and that the area in question had been covered while the concrete was drying. The General Secretary half-playfully kept returning to the issue as these talks in the Kremlin continued, at one point saying "I don't think we should argue about one rocket here, 17 there where the cement dries quicker—yours doesn't seem to dry at all." And, at another: "Poor Comrade Dobrynin having to write reports about Comrade Kissinger having a net over his house." And then when it came time for a toast, he watched one member of our delegation down his drink and said, "That's an honest man; all the others

A. Denis Clift

have nets over their glasses." Then turning to another he asked, "Are you the guy who puts the nets over the missiles?"[18]

MONITORING THE MIDDLE EAST

For several decades, intelligence has played in the monitoring of compliance of Middle East summit agreements, and in the security and confidence-building measures accompanying such agreements. With the outbreak of the October 1973 war, high-altitude, U.S. SR-71 reconnaissance flights monitored the military action between Israel and Syria on the Golan Heights and Israel and Egypt along the Suez Canal.[19] When on 17 January 1974 the Israeli-Egyptian troop disengagement was achieved, President Nixon would give full credit to Secretary Kissinger for the success of his shuttle diplomacy. Israeli Prime Minister Golda Meir and President Anwar Sadat in turn would praise both Nixon and Kissinger.[20] The disengagement agreement documents signed by the parties would include "a number of Presidential letters to both sides containing assurances or statements of intention regarding passage through waterways and rebuilding of the Canal cities."[21]

As part of the assurances provided, U.S. U-2 reconnaissance aircraft would begin flying monitoring missions over the demilitarized zones in the Sinai and the Golan Heights. The resulting photography documenting the disposition of forces would be provided by the United States to the parties as one of the agreement-implementation confidence-building measures.[22] I would have the privilege of being at Camp David throughout the 1978 summit talks to watch this process of confidence-building measures continue.

Over the past few years, with the Middle East still fragile, still volatile and violent, still in search of peace, the role of U.S. intelligence in the summit process has increased in profile as it has evolved. Following the 1998 Wye River summit, Director of Central Intelligence George Tenet would be assigned by President Bill Clinton to take the lead in trilateral security talks aimed at improving communication on security between the Israeli Government and the Palestinian Authority, and aimed at improving the professional capabilities of security forces on the West Bank and Gaza. In this information age, the presence of the DCI at Middle East talks would become familiar to television and Internet viewers around the world.

Former Director of Central Intelligence Richard Helms would state: "This has been a significant departure, because Director Tenet has taken on a policy-making role that has nothing to do with the intelligence-making business."[23] DCI Tenet would be on record as stating that the CIA was not making policy but helping to carry it out, that the CIA was uniquely qualified to deal with the Israelis and Palestinians on security matters, that the CIA was keeping American policymakers informed about the implementation of the summit accords.[24] On 22 March 2001, at the time of Prime Minister Ariel Sharon's visit to Washington, the media would report that the George W. Bush administration had ended this role for the Director of Central Intelligence.[25]

INTELLIGENCE AT THE SUMMIT

Intelligence operations before, during, and after summits abound just as most continue to reside in unpublicized galaxies of their own. There are glimpses, to cite two examples, that remind of the breadth of these galaxies. When President Jimmy Carter and President Park Chung Hee met in Seoul, South Korea in 1979, agreement was reached that U.S. troop levels would not be reduced if, in turn, Korean defense expenditures were increased and if there were to be a demonstrable improvement in Korean human rights. Within days, as part of the implementation of that accord, Korean CIA Director Kim would call on the U.S. ambassador with a message for President Carter advising that 180 political prisoners would be released over the next six months.[26]

With the Cold War still in full sway, to quote former DCI Robert Gates:

In November 1985, CIA pulled out all the stops to make Gorbachev feel unwelcome in Geneva when he had his first meeting with President Reagan. CIA mobilized its assets to participate in a wide range of anti-Soviet demonstrations, meetings, exhibits, and other such activities in Geneva. [The] first major effort to publicize the Soviet role in Cambodia was in Geneva at this time, and drew broad media coverage.[27]

If I began with the play of intelligence including side talks that led to secret intelligence cooperation between the United States and Israel, I will conclude with a summit that led to secret cooperation between the United States and the People's Republic of China. In January 1979, Vice Chairman Deng Xiaoping would fly to Washington for talks with President Carter. The visit would be recorded as an important step in the normalization of relations process. The barriers to the granting of Most Favored Nation status would be discussed. The Chinese leader would advise of his country's plans to teach the Vietnamese a lesson, with limited military strikes across the border into Vietnam. Carter would recommend against this action, to no avail, and U.S. intelligence would subsequently monitor the military action, as it would monitor the Soviet reaction.

In his memoirs, President Carter would record that he and Deng covered "several more issues, a few of them highly confidential."[28] One of those issues, it would later be revealed, dealt with the coming of the revolutionary government of Iran and the closing of U.S. intelligence stations collecting Soviet missile test range data. While in Washington, Deng would offer to cooperate on talks aimed at new intelligence collection facilities in western China to fill the Soviet missile test gap. In late December 1980, Director of Central Intelligence Stansfield Turner would travel to Beijing to complete the intelligence collection and sharing arrangements.[29]

INTELLIGENCE: ESSENTIAL TO NATIONAL SECURITY

Since the signing of the National Security Act of 1947, eleven Presidents have exercised the nation's intelligence capabilities in their dealings with foreign leaders and in the summit

A. Denis Clift

agreements they have entered so as to advance the interests of the nation. Those intelligence capabilities are the subject of continuing review as a part of the remarkable checks and balances of our democracy.

In 1961, a Senate Subcommittee chaired by Senator Henry M. "Scoop" Jackson charged with examining Presidential policymaking in the era of the national security system, wrote in its report that: "The free world needs intelligence activities to assure its survival. Intelligence is as important as armed strength. In this age of pushbutton weapons, intelligence is more than ever our first line of defense."[30]

> Twenty years later, in 1981, Presidential Executive Order 12333 stated anew that:
>
> Timely and accurate information about the activities, capabilities, plans, and intentions of foreign powers, organizations, and persons, and their agents is essential to the national security of the United States. All reasonable and lawful means must be used to ensure that the United States will receive the best intelligence available.[31]

With each new administration, the ways in which the best intelligence available has served Presidents at the summit have continued to evolve, more often than not with remarkable results of great benefit to the nation. With the inauguration of President George W. Bush in 2001, we turn a fresh chapter in the play of intelligence with Presidents at the summit.

CHAPTER 21
E PLURIBUS UNUM MMII

The attack on the American homeland on September 11, 2001 served to strengthen our resolve to fight terrorism at home and abroad. Our national motto, E Pluribus Unum— *from many, one—takes on added significance in these early years of the 21st century. Addressing students and faculty at Trinity College in Washington, DC, on 31 January 2002, the author points out some other examples of treason, espionage, and sabotage in United States history, showing that the need for vigilance today is rooted in the past and will be ever more crucial in the years ahead. The looming challenges posed by the Internet and information technology make our task even more demanding, as do the challenges of balancing individual freedoms with enhanced security. It is, in the words of Dame Rebecca West, "equivalent to walking a tight-rope over an abyss." But, as ably demonstrated by the research and writing of Joint Military Intelligence College students in their master's theses, there are new and innovative ways of uniting against the threat.*

On 29 October 1940, Secretary of War Henry Stimson, blindfolded with cloth cut from a chair used at the signing of the Declaration of Independence, drew an encapsulated number from a glass bowl and handed it to President Franklin Delano Roosevelt. The President opened the capsule. "One fifty eight," he announced. Across the nation, the 6,000 men holding that number received orders to report for military service.[1] In a process that was bringing our motto *E Pluribus Unum*—from many one—once again into play, the nation took a first step to prepare for mounting challenges from totalitarian powers in Europe and Asia, this despite strong longings for peace and deep opposition to involvement in foreign wars on the part of the majority of America's citizens.

As we embark as a nation on the year 2002, we have taken first steps to address mounting new challenges—the shocking terrorist attacks of September 11, 2001 on the American homeland and the broader menace of international terrorism. And, in the process, we are again demonstrating a remarkable resilience—truly unique to the United States of America among the world's nation states—a resilience that goes beyond our counterterrorist actions, a resilience that is sharpening the focus of our broader sense of purpose, and that is heightening our awareness of our responsibilities as well as our rights as citizens of this land.

When President Pat McGuire of Trinity College suggested several weeks ago that it would be good if I were to discuss the challenges of this new era with an audience at Trinity, I said, "Yes, of course." President McGuire is a very persuasive individual, and she is also a member of my College's Board. I say yes whenever possible to members of my Board. In fact, when she extended the invitation, I was taking fresh inspiration from reading a remarkable work by Dame Rebecca West, a book entitled *The Meaning of Treason.*

During her illustrious writing career, Rebecca West covered the Nuremberg trials at the end of World War II and then, at the invitation of *The New Yorker* magazine, the trial of William Joyce, the British traitor known as Lord Haw Haw during his years of broadcasts from Nazi Germany. As she reflected on spying and treason, she wrote with eloquence and passion on the importance of safeguarding civil rights, the full rights of each individual:

> But there is a case against the traitor. It has been put with classic simplicity by the law: If a state gives a citizen protection it has a claim to his allegiance, and if he gives it his allegiance it is bound to give him protection. Moreover, there are now other reasons for regarding treachery with disfavor, which grow stronger every year.[2]

As we act against treachery—evil today embracing acts of terrorism at home and abroad—and as we act to bring greater protection to all who pledge their allegiance, we should bear in mind the experiences of this nation many decades ago, in the first half of the 20th century.

TREACHERY ROOTED IN HISTORY

From 1915 through America's entry into World War I, Germany mounted a major espionage and sabotage operation in the United States. More than 40 American factories were sabotaged; cargoes in ships with supplies bound for the allies were destroyed. In July 1916, two million pounds of dynamite were detonated at the major transshipment point of Black Tom Island in New York Harbor, destroying windows across Jersey City and Manhattan, a detonation heard as far as 100 miles away. Pro-German Americans were organized to oppose U.S. involvement in the conflict. A spy scare swept the nation, fueled by the parallel actions of the Industrial Workers of the World, and the pronouncement of their leader W. D. Haywood: "Sabotage—sabotage means to push back; pull out or break off the fangs of capitalism."[3]

The Congress passed statutes dealing with espionage and sabotage, including an amendment to the Espionage Act dealing with "seditious utterances." The Department of Justice's Bureau of Investigation—predecessor to today's FBI—was only 300 strong. Americans organized volunteer citizens' organizations. The Council for Defense in Henry County, Missouri, issued warnings to anyone speaking or acting in a disloyal way—first a white card, then a blue card, and then a red card. In March 1917, a Chicago advertising executive suggested that a citizens volunteer group, the American Protective League, should be organized to assist the Bureau of Investigation. The Department of Justice gave its blessing. In less than a year, 250,000 Americans were wearing badges emblazoned "American Protective League: Secret Service Division." By the time of the League's disbandment in 1919, the nation had learned that there was no place for vigilantism and amateur sleuthing even in times of greatest national emergency.[4]

The terror continued. On a late evening in June 1919, Assistant Secretary of the Navy Franklin Roosevelt and his wife Eleanor had parked their car in the garage at 2131 R Street in Northwest Washington, and were climbing the steps to the front entrance of their home, when a tremendous explosion tore off the front of Attorney General A. Mitchell Palmer's residence across the street. Pieces of the suicide bomber landed at the Roosevelts' feet.

Leaflets were nearby proclaiming "class war is on and cannot cease but with a complete victory for the international proletariat."[5]

The unsolved Wall Street terrorist bombing came a little more than a year later, September 16, 1920. A driver brought a horse and wagon to a halt opposite the J.P. Morgan building and walked away. "And then the object in the old wagon exploded." Here I am quoting author Don Whitehead:

> It was a bomb made of dynamite and cast-iron window weights. The metal rods were hurled like shrapnel through the narrow street. Men and women were mowed down in bloody, screaming heaps. Thirty were killed and three hundred were injured. The House of Morgan was damaged...other financial houses were badly damaged.[6]

ACTIONS TO MEET THE THREAT

In 1924, a young attorney named J. Edgar Hoover was named Acting Director, then Director of Department of Justice's Bureau of Investigation. The Bureau would be renamed the Federal Bureau of Investigation in 1935. As war in Europe loomed again in the 1930s, President Franklin Roosevelt, deeply mindful of the espionage, sabotage, and terrorism of 20 years before, gave Director Hoover full authority to guard against and to act against fifth columnists, saboteurs, and spies on U.S. soil and throughout the western hemisphere. New laws were passed requiring re-registration of all aliens and further strengthening federal law enforcement.

Roosevelt was encouraged in these actions by the British, who mounted their own overt and covert intelligence operations against Germany in the United States. Roosevelt, a great believer in intelligence, was similarly encouraged by Prime Minister Winston Churchill to create a more effective U.S. intelligence organization, in addition to the intelligence branches of the Army and Navy. His actions would lead first to the office of Coordinator of Information and then the Office of Strategic Services (OSS), which would evolve into today's Central Intelligence Agency with the enactment of the National Security Act of 1947.

As an aside, I would note that Churchill not only believed devoutly in secret intelligence but also had a passion for innovative ideas. In his book *Roosevelt and Churchill: Men of Secrets,* David Stafford describes the Prime Minister's reading of John Steinbeck's 1942 novel *The Moon is Down,* a fictional story of invaders occupying a small foreign town— clearly patterned on Germany's invasion of Norway, the defiance and sabotage by the townspeople, and then flights from Great Britain dropping thousands of small explosive devices gathered like Easter eggs from the snow by the town's adults and children for use against the invaders. Churchill urged his secret intelligence service to create such devices to be dropped to the citizens of the Nazi-occupied countries of Europe. He was quietly deterred, given the broader strategic planning underway.[7]

A. Denis Clift

There are two other actions taken by President Roosevelt during World War II that we should bear in mind when considering the actions that the United States is taking today to meet the 21st century terrorist challenge. In February 1942, the President drew on the precedent of the Alien Enemies Act of 1789 in issuing Executive Order 9066, the order that would see the internment of more than 100,000 Japanese-Americans.[8] Then in June 1942, the FBI captured eight German saboteurs who had come ashore from U-boats off Long Island and Florida. Roosevelt, determined to prevent further such attempts, immediately appointed a military tribunal to hear the case. All eight were found guilty. In early August, six were sent to the electric chair and two were given lengthy prison sentences.[9]

CONTINUING THREATS: THE COLD WAR AND BEYOND

Following these stark actions in the heat of World War II, the United States entered into an entirely new challenge with the 46-year superpower rivalry of the Cold War. With the collapse of the Soviet Union we turned still another chapter, entering the post-Cold War era in 1991. The signs of a mounting terrorist menace grew and multiplied: the 1993 attacks on the World Trade Center, the terrorist bombings of our embassies in Tanzania and Kenya, the terrorist attack on the destroyer USS *Cole*.

Experts testified as to the growing menace; experts wrote and published on the subject. In 1998, President Clinton announced that he would appoint a National Coordinator for Security, Infrastructure Protection and Counter-Terrorism. To launch this work, he signed Presidential Decision Directive 63 establishing a national goal of protecting critical infrastructures including telecommunications, energy, banking and finance, transportation, water systems, and emergency services within five years. In March 2001, the Hart-Rudman Commission stated on the first page of its excellent report, *Road Map for National Security: Imperative for Change:* "The combination of unconventional weapons proliferation with the persistence of international terrorism will end the relative invulnerability of the U.S. homeland to catastrophic attack."[10]

When President George W. Bush took office, his new administration intensified government actions aimed at protecting the homeland and identifying and thwarting planned terrorist actions. But this was not the focus of the nation—until September 11, 2001. September 11 was the day we as a nation entered the war on terrorism. In this war, we have deployed our Armed Forces—land, sea, and air—to the Indian Ocean, the South Asian Theater, and the mountains of Afghanistan. We have ended Taliban rule of that nation, and we are in pursuit of the al Qaeda terrorists who used that nation as their safe haven and training base for their horrific acts.

An Office of Homeland Security has been created, and its Director former Governor Tom Ridge and his staff are working with urgency with the Departments of Government, the State and local levels of government, and the Congress to help us as a nation identify the steps we must take if we are to enhance our security at the same time we safeguard freedoms we cherish as a democracy. In December 2001, Director Ridge announced that a national coordination center would soon be opened allowing law enforcement organizations at the national, state, and local levels to share fused threat and operational information with each other, with immigration, customs, public health, and other homeland security sectors.

STEPS TOWARD HOMELAND SECURITY

The Executive Branch and the Congress have acted and continue to act with new legislation and stricter standards for improved airline and airport security. The Congress has acted to give our law enforcement and intelligence agencies enhanced authority they need to act more effectively against terrorists at home and abroad. To look at one part of this, in the years preceding the attacks on the World Trade Center and the Pentagon, there had been a great reluctance on the part of some in the nation to having intelligence officials deal with foreigners considered unsavory, criminal, or unfit for U.S. contact. This is changing. The world of terrorism can be an unsavory criminal world, and that is where the most important information may be found.

Here, Dame Rebecca West's voice as expressed in *The Meaning of Treason* again provides sage advice:

> Not till the Earthly Paradise is established, and man regains his innocence, can a power which has ever been at war be blamed if it accepts information regarding the military strength of another power, however this may be obtained; and of course it can be blamed least of all if the information comes to it from traitors, for then it is likely to touch on the truly secret.[11]

These are the first steps in a national journey toward improved homeland security that will extend beyond this year to the foreseeable future. We have realized in recent months that the society we had shaped for ourselves—a society increasingly centered on the individual "me," on individual comforts, on costumer-oriented efficiencies, a society in the new web era where the notion of community was fading as the Internet was progressing from second- to third-generation powers of service—was not the society we wanted in the face of the world's stark, new threats. There is a bond, however subtle, going beyond the flags on buildings and cars, that is developing across the land, a bond of resolve and common purpose—and with good reason.

A COMPLEX PROBLEM

We are a nation that is, in the vernacular, wide open. "Over $8.8 billion worth of goods, over 1.3 million people, over 340,000 vehicles, and over 58,000 shipments are processed daily at entry points and ... Customs can inspect one to two percent of all inbound shipments."[12] The United States is dependent on international shipping for the vast majority of our commerce. More than 165 million containers are on the move across the world's oceans annually, millions coming to our seaports and from our seaports to our trains, trucks, and inland destinations. And we are with a sense of urgency examining security at our ports, working hard on the challenge of determining that there is no devastating harm awaiting the nation in even one of those millions of containers.

A. Denis Clift

Given the porousness of our borders, we are addressing the need for increased security against radiological, biological, and chemical attack. In a June 2000 exercise named DARK WINTER, several U.S. research centers and universities explored the impact on the nation if terrorists arriving in three U.S. cities by commercial airline flights were to introduce a biological weapon, the contagious pathogen smallpox. Given the contagious nature of the pathogen and the high mobility of the U.S. population, the results produced by the exercise were devastating—in part, and in brief:

> An attack on the United States with biological weapons could threaten vital national security interests—massive civilian casualties, breakdown in essential institutions, violation of democratic processes, civil disorder ... no surge capability in the US health care and public health systems, or in the pharmaceutical and vaccine industries.[13]

INFORMATION TECHNOLOGY: FRIEND AND FOE

It is instructive to read news accounts of the use of the Internet by those implicated in the September 11 attacks, from the booking of airline tickets, to the researching of flight training schools, to dipping the vast array of information available to anyone—friend or foe—with access to a computer, from the most humble personal laptop to a public library terminal anywhere in the land. The Internet era has also become the era of cyber terrorism, cyber security, and network infrastructure protection. The amount of detailed information on seemingly the most sensitive of subjects that one can gain from skilled searching of the web is extraordinary. The amount of havoc that one can wreak from skilled attacks on unprotected networks has not yet been fathomed.

The Federal Reserve System and the nation's banking system depend on information technology. Indeed, the nation's financial center has led the implementation of private-sector data encryption in the United States. In times of crisis and attack—the attacks of September 11, for example—the Fed needs emergency relocation centers, the capability of emergency power to run the computers, and emergency water to cool the computers. Following the attacks, as the Fed again reviewed its security, it examined the enormous amount of Federal Reserve System information that could be extracted from the Internet, even including information about the relocation sites and photographs of the buildings. As it again moved to upgrade security, it acted on these findings.[14]

If information of use to a foe abounds on the Internet, the ingredients of weapons of mass destruction are just a mail order away. In an article entitled "Better Killing through Chemistry" in the December 2001 *Scientific American,* the author describes how a chemist at Rice University a little more than a year ago ordered all of the chemicals needed to make the nerve agent sarin—the poison gas used by a cult in the mid-1990s Tokyo subway attacks. In went his order and back the chemicals came the next day in a nice, big, customer-friendly overnight delivery box. Following the September 11, 2001 attacks, the staff of *Scientific American* placed another order for the sarin precursors, and the chemicals arrived a few days later.[15]

CONTRIBUTING TO THE NATION'S SECURITY

We are addressing these challenges as America, the sleeping giant, again awakens. And there is an opportunity for each of us to play a part bearing in mind the strength that we can derive from our common resolve, from many acting as one. Earlier this year, the Associated Press reported that more than half of Maryland's practicing physicians have joined an e-mail registry that can be used to send them updated clinical advice during bioterrorist attacks. This is part of a far broader registration by physicians across the nation.[16]

At much the same time that this news was appearing, the President was announcing the priority his administration would give to public health issues in this new year. These actions are occurring against the background of the weaknesses demonstrated in the public health system in the Bioterrorism exercise DARK WINTER. When we think about the role that each of us might play, how each of us can contribute our energies, the field of public health stands as noble service.

When we consider other fields of worthy service, I again refer to the findings of the 2001 Hart-Rudman Commission mentioned earlier. There were three principal Commission findings: the imperative of an effective homeland defense; the imperative of an improved American educational system, with focus on science and technology; and the imperative of a national campaign to reinvigorate and enhance the prestige of both civil and military service to the nation.

The dimensions of teaching in this new age, from earliest schooling through university, embrace the ethical, social, and security dimensions of the computer, as well as the incredible spectrum of substantive capabilities we develop and build on in the cyber era. The Internet arrived; the Internet spread around the world; the Internet, in many ways, is like the earlier centuries' wide-open range. For those interested in teaching, the world of the web— correct, ethical use of the web—is an important part of such teaching if we are to contribute to cyber integrity and the cyber security of the nation.

When we consider the nobility of public service, both civilian and military, I would cite the examples of research by two of my students at the Joint Military Intelligence College— two of the men and women, military officers, non-commissioned officers, and civilians working and studying in the field of intelligence. Ms. Lisa Krizan received her Master's degree in 1996. Her Master's thesis was entitled "Benchmarking the Intelligence Process for the Private Sector." Building on this research, she would write the monograph entitled *Intelligence Essentials for Everyone,* published by the College in 1999. In her prologue, she wrote:

> The widespread trend toward incorporating government intelligence methodology [in the business sector] was a primary impetus for publishing this document ... Educators in business and academia are following suit inserting BI [business intelligence] concepts into professional training and college curricula.[17]

A. Denis Clift

Ms. Krizan's work is used as a text for training and education throughout the Intelligence Community. It was selected for distribution to Government Printing Office stores across the United States. It was discovered by *Newsweek* magazine. It is a fundamentally valuable contribution to an understanding of intelligence processes in the government and private sectors.

Marine Lieutenant Colonel Doman McArthur, Class of '98, wrote his thesis on key issues to be addressed when dealing with the challenge of rogue nations such as Iraq and its development of weapons of mass destruction. One of his findings was the weakness in U.S. export control policies and procedures. He offered his recommendations for improved procedures. Those findings and recommendations became law of the land as part of the Proliferation Prevention Enhancement Act of 1999. McArthur's thesis was published by the College last year with a Foreword by Senator Arlen Specter.[18]

To those of you interested in service to the nation in the field of intelligence, I say it is a most rewarding field. The Defense Intelligence Agency offers a select number of highly competitive scholarships to undergraduates interested in entering the field upon graduation—scholarships that enable those selected to spend their first year of federal service earning their Master of Science of Strategic Intelligence degree.

To those of you who have had enough of study, but who are thinking long and hard about the need for enhanced security against the balance of protecting our cherished liberties as a democracy, I would close by again returning to the words of Dame Rebecca West: "Our task," she wrote, "is equivalent to walking a tight-rope over an abyss. But history proves that, if man has a talent, it is for tight-rope walking."[19]

CHAPTER 22
FROM SEMAPHORE TO PREDATOR: INTELLIGENCE IN THE INTERNET ERA

Intelligence and its supporting communications technologies have made quantum advances from the days of semaphore signals to modern unmanned aerial surveillance vehicles. In this address to Yale University's International Security Studies Conference on 27 April 2002, the author points out how today's "Internet era" poses special opportunities and difficulties for intelligence professionals. One way the Intelligence Community has met the challenges has been in developing and implementing its own advanced, classified intranet, known as Intelink, which provides instant communications connectivity among national, theater, and tactical levels of government and military operations. In addition, the Central Intelligence Agency in 1999 created a private, not-for-profit company known as In-Q-Tel to spur the development of innovative information technologies for safeguarding national security. To provide swift, efficient, and expert connectivity to deployed field commanders during operations or crises, the Joint Chiefs of Staff have fielded National Intelligence Support Teams composed of representatives from CIA, NSA, DIA, and NIMA. It is an era laden with challenges, but the Intelligence Community is rising to the task by setting aside old practices in favor of dramatically new ways of doing business. Decisionmakers, policymakers, and military commanders realize that good intelligence—today more than ever before—is essential to the nation's security.

During the Napoleonic Wars, the French revolutionized land-based communications with the erection of semaphore towers bearing rotating arms to fashion coded signals that could speed line-of-sight from tower to tower along the coast and across the country at some 200 miles an hour. The British quickly followed suit in this new era of signals intelligence. Theft of the enemy's semaphore code books became an important part of the business of war.[1]

During the war on terrorism in Afghanistan, Predator unmanned aerial vehicles have been flying lengthy missions at heights of some 25,000 feet providing multi-hour surveillance of designated geography, installations, and activity. Tasking to the Predator and electro-optical video and infrared images collected by its cameras move near-instantaneously—which is to say real-time—to and from the area being surveilled and in-theater commanders and Washington. Communications and the resulting data stream flow through a network of ground stations and satellites with part of the product traveling through the secure medium of Intelink, the classified Internet counterpart.[2]

The episodic, manned U-2 photography missions of the 1950s and the periodic, evolutionary satellite photography missions proceeding from the 1960s have now been joined by the current generation of surveilling UAV eyes. Imaging collection, analysis, and decisionmaking that once proceeded in distinct, often lengthy sequential steps are now the business of simultaneity. To leap thus across the centuries and the more recent decades is to realize in a glimpse the incredible dynamic involved in the world of intelligence and its

---

supporting communications technologies. Actionable information from wherever on the face of the globe is today the air we breathe, essential to our national security and survival.

The Internet era is a dynamic with an on-rush of changes both revolutionary and far more subtle to the work of intelligence: changes in the doctrine and practice of collection, analysis, and dissemination; and changes in the relationship and the mindset between intelligence and law enforcement, intelligence and the policymaker, and intelligence and the military commander.

ARPANET

In 1957, the communications signals from the beeping Soviet satellite Sputnik I would sound the beginning of the highly visible superpower space race. That race would produce some remarkable by-products — from cordless power tools and Teflon, to CAT Scanners and Magnetic Resonance Imaging technology. Out of the public eye, the orbiting Sputnik would launch other races by U.S. scientists and engineers. The United States realized that it must surge in its science programs. The Office of Science Adviser was added to the White House. In 1958, President Eisenhower created the Advanced Project Research Office, and that office as one of its earliest priorities tackled the challenge of linking research centers with one another and with their important sponsor, the Department of Defense.

As this research evolved, the computer's initial role as arithmetic engine would be joined by the computer as communications medium. Pioneers in the work of data networking and packet switching would bring their talents to the goal of the government-supported computer data network — ARPANET. Those pioneering the first network of the late 1960s — sites at UCLA, Stanford Research Institute, University of California Santa Barbara, and the University of Utah — could not imagine their work would spawn the global Internet of today, to include the World Wide Web browser of the early 1990s.[3]

This early ARPANET linkage work led to attention to another critical problem. If the Soviets could orbit Sputnik, who was to say that they were not now proceeding to develop the capability for space-based missile attack? A principal U.S. concern lay in the vulnerability of the nation's strategic communications infrastructure. If a nuclear attack destroyed key command and control centers, it would eliminate our ability to assess the impact of the attack and to decide on and deliver the strategic response. Attention would subsequently turn to fashioning a survivable computer network linking the Pentagon and the national decisionmakers in Washington, with the Cheyenne Mountain nuclear command and control center, and the Headquarters of the Strategic Air Command.[4]

The Chairman of my College's Board of Visitors, Dr. Anthony Oettinger, has written of the Information Technology/Internet era:

> What it all boils down to is that faster, smaller, cheaper electro-optical digital technologies have put into our hands enormously powerful and varied yet increasingly practical and economical means for information processing, means that stimulate us to re-examine everything we do to information and

with information, and then choose to do nothing, to reinforce the old ways, to modify them, or to abandon them altogether in favor of altogether new ways.[5]

For U.S. intelligence, it is increasingly an era of modifications and altogether new ways. The technologies supporting U.S. intelligence develop in Web years, with three months to the Web year. The year 2010 is 32 Web years away.

INTELINK AND IN-Q-TEL

If we are to consider key aspects of the play of intelligence in the Internet era, we should bear in mind at the outset that the U.S. Intelligence Community has developed and implemented its own highly advanced, ever-evolving Intelink intranet, a secure collection of networks employing Web-based technology, using standard Web browsers such as *Navigator* and Internet *Explorer*. Intelink uses advanced network technology and applies it across the work of the departments and agencies of the Intelligence Community to the collection, analysis, production, and dissemination of classified and unclassified multimedia data.[6]

In the assessment of the former Deputy Director of Central Intelligence, Admiral William O. Studeman:

> Application of evolving Internet technologies to intelligence applications in the form of Intelink has been a transcendent and farsighted strategy. ... Its future application requirements parallel those of the global Internet, so that there is the expectation that, for continuing modest investment, intelligence can continue to ride the wave of Internet growth, with commensurate access to amazing and relevant commercial off-the-shelf (COTS) developments.[7]

The Intelink intranet provides connectivity to national, theater, and tactical levels of government and military operations. Taking into account the sensitivity of some of the intelligence data involved, the sensitivity of the sources and methods for acquiring such data, the resulting "need to know" of those logging on the system, Intelink provides several separate classification families, or instantiations of services. These range from:

- Intelink-SCI, which operates at the top secret, compartmented intelligence level;
- to the Intelink-PolicyNet, run by the Central Intelligence Agency as CIA's sole-source link to the White House and other high-level intelligence consumers;
- to Intelink-S, the SIPRnet at the secret level — the main communications link for the military commands and those operating on land, at sea, and in the air; and
- Intelink Commonwealth, or Intelink-C, linking the United States, United Kingdom, Canada, and Australia.[8]

A steadily evolving suite of Intelink support services, such as collaboration tools, search tools, and search engines, are available. Intelink security policy and practice reserving the intranet for authorized users are multi-layered and comprehensive, from encryption, to passwords, to user certifications and audits.

A. Denis Clift

In positioning itself for the Internet era, the Intelligence Community has gone beyond innovative use of the World Wide Web and its engines, to CIA's creation in 1999 of a private, not-for-profit company, In-Q-Tel, dedicated to spurring the development of information technologies to be used in the safeguarding of national security. As stated on its web page:

> [T]he blistering pace at which the IT [information technology] economy is advancing has made it difficult for any government agency to access and incorporate the latest in information technology. In-Q-Tel strives to extend the Agency's access to new IT companies, solutions, and approaches to address their priority problems.[9]

In investing in technologies that can benefit CIA and the rest of the U.S. Intelligence Community at the same time that they will become available commercially, In-Q-Tel underscores that in this new era, underlying information technologies of importance to commerce are of importance to intelligence—IT functions such as data warehousing and mining, the profiling of search agents, statistical data analysis tools, imagery analysis and pattern recognition, language translation, strong encryption, data integrity, and authentication and access control. The work of In-Q-Tel, unclassified work with commercial potential, is giving initial attention to such issues as secure receipt of Internet information, non-observable surfing, hacker resistance, intrusion detection, data protection, and multimedia data fusion and integration.[10]

NEW STRENGTHS FOR NEW CHALLENGES

What are the goals being set for U.S. intelligence with this on-rushing development and implementation of information technology? For the Director of Central Intelligence, it is the goal of an Intelligence Community providing a decisive information advantage to the President, the military, diplomats, law enforcement, and the Congress. For the Chairman of the Joint Chiefs of Staff, as stated in *Joint Vision 2010,* it is, in parallel, the emerging importance of information superiority, "the capability to collect, process, and disseminate an uninterrupted flow of information while exploiting or denying an adversary's ability to do the same."[11]

The need for information advantage, information superiority is in many instances causing U.S. intelligence to pursue dramatically new ways. The Internet era has become the Intelligence Community's new strength and its new challenge. The 46-year Cold War assumptions driving intelligence doctrine and practice—collection and analysis against closed society targets and subject matter in the superpower rivalry with the Soviet Union— are assumptions of the past.

If the semaphore was the signals intelligence breakthrough at the time of Napoleon, the Internet and its communications channels are at the forefront of signals intelligence challenges in this new century. With new transnational adversaries—the international terrorist foremost among them—with the flood of new information technologies, the easing of encryption export controls, and global access to the web, the National Security Agency is charting new directions in the ways it identifies, gains access to, and successfully exploits target communications. NSA is also pursuing new ways of charting our information security, given the openness of our society early in the cyber era, the global dimensions of that openness, and the enhanced exploitation capabilities that information technology and the Internet give our adversaries.

The Director of NSA, Lieutenant General Michael Hayden, has placed this challenge in the following context:

> Forty years ago, there were 5,000 stand-alone computers, no fax machines and not one cellular phone. Today, there are over 180 million computers—most of them networked. There are roughly 14 million fax machines and 40 million cell phones and those numbers continue to grow, the telecommunications industry is making a $1 trillion investment to encircle the world in millions of high bandwidth fiber-optic cable.[12]

At the same time, General Hayden reminds, the new information technologies are an enhancement and an enabler, as NSA seeks outs and exploits the current era's targets.

The web and the new information technologies are an incredible enabler and at the same time a challenge to the intelligence analyst with a thousand different shadings depending on the specific work of the analyst and the consumer being served. To cite an example drawing on my own career experience as a policy-level consumer of intelligence, from 1974 to 1977, I was the head of President Ford's National Security Council staff for the Soviet Union and Eastern and Western Europe. As we pursued our nation's agenda with the USSR and Warsaw Pact, we were dealing with closed societies. There was no World Wide Web. The information being volunteered by the USSR was usually not the information we required. Intelligence collection, analysis, and dissemination were geared toward ascertaining the current state of play and toward estimating future developments behind the Iron Curtain. The role of the Intelligence Community's sovietologists, the analysts expert on the USSR, was central. Not only could they divine the significance of any changes in the renowned line-up of the Soviet leadership atop Lenin's tomb, they often were the only source of information on developments of importance inside the Soviet Union.

The sources of information available to today's policy-level consumer—whether dealing with the Russian Federation or with any of the current closed societies—are far, far greater than a quarter century ago. It is almost a given that today's policy-level consumer of intelligence is quite well-informed in his or her area of interest and not dependent on an analyst for a continuing stream of routine, updating information. The analyst no longer sets the pace of the information flow. The web, the media, electronic and hard-copy, U.S. and foreign, the telephone, the fax, the interaction with U.S. and foreign colleagues in the field, and intelligence reporting available at the touch of the Intelink keyboard all play a part.

Today's analyst must not only have a sense of his or her consumer's level of continuing information and knowledge. To provide value-added analysis, today's analyst must focus more sharply on the specific needs and the timing of meeting those needs for the policy-level consumer, seek specific tasking, analyze feedback from analysis already provided, and invite and tackle the consumer's hard questions demanding answers.[14]

NIST AND THE JOINT INTELLIGENCE
VIRTUAL ARCHITECTURE

If the policy-level consumer is demanding, in this new era, the military commander has, since the time of the late 1990s operations in the Balkans, been expecting the information superiority envisioned in *Joint Vision 2010*. The requirement, from mission planning through mission execution, is for intelligence to be able to locate and to surveil targets either stationary or mobile, either exposed or hidden—to be able to obtain and provide to the commander a continuing picture of his entire field of operations in all its dimensions.

This extraordinary challenge requires intelligence to move fluidly to and from the national level, the theater commanders in chief and the tactical commanders on land, at sea, and in the air. For any given requirement, the broadest capabilities of U.S. intelligence are considered potentially available to contribute to the solution. The challenge posed by today's commander requires a complex harnessing of collection, analysis, and dissemination across the disciplines of intelligence—imagery, measurements and signatures, signals intelligence, human-source intelligence—to provide an as-valuable-as-possible all-source intelligence product when and where needed.

To say the least, this commander's challenge to intelligence has not been universally met. Like Mount Everest, the challenge is there, and U.S. intelligence is ascending month after month, year after year with no little success. Since the mid-1980s, the global reach of U.S. intelligence has been strengthened by Intelink, by the accessibility of growing amounts of information in cyber databases, and by the near-real-time links of communications satellites. These capabilities have helped bring into being the Joint Worldwide Intelligence Communications System (JWICS) and the companion desktop analyst's Joint Deployable Intelligence Support System (JDISS). The JWICS system allows video teleconferencing, imagery transfer, electronic data transfer, publishing, and video broadcasting—all up to the highest levels of classification. The system, first tested in 1991, is now installed at more than 125 defense and intelligence locations worldwide.

National Intelligence Support Teams, NIST teams, were born as a lesson learned from the U.S. participation in the DESERT STORM coalition that expelled Iraq from Kuwait. The teams belong to the Chairman of the Joint Chiefs of Staff's Director of Intelligence. When they deploy they are attached to the commander in the field. The idea is to provide the Joint Task Force commander with the ability to reach back swiftly, efficiently, and expertly to national agencies for answers to questions unanswerable in the field, and to receive warnings of threats that otherwise could not be received. NIST teams are fast-response, rapidly deployable intelligence cells made up of personnel from CIA, NSA, DIA, and the National Imagery and Mapping Agency (NIMA). Using its light-weight, high-technology multi-media communications flowing via Intelink and satellite, the NIST team is able to link via voice, soft- and hard-copy word and imagery to bring the very best intelligence available to the commander in the field.[15] Truly, NIST is a remarkable advance in intelligence doctrine and methodology in the Internet era.

I have spoken more than once of the national, theater, and tactical levels. The world of the analyst in the Internet era is one in which collection and development of the analytic product, and its dissemination, are no longer limited to flow up and down hierarchical lines but move horizontally and diagonally to selected nodes of the global intranet. The expert at the Joint Intelligence Center Pacific in Hawaii, for example, in the development of analysis may be routinely and matter-of-factly in Intelink contact with carrier battle group counterparts in the Indian Ocean and at the National Military Joint Intelligence Center at the Pentagon.

Collaborative information technology tools, using commercial web technologies, are being developed through the Joint Intelligence Virtual Architecture program to assist today's analyst in locating and accessing valuable data wherever it may be found, in assessing such data, in producing an informed analytic product, and in moving that product to where it will be of value. To cite a few examples, such tools are designed to provide search and discovery protocols allowing mining of data not only of what the analyst knows is important but also of—while unthought-of by the analyst—what might be of importance. Such tools will allow automatic extraction of relevant data from classified and unclassified sources. Such tools will support the analyst in making rapid assessments and developing time-critical reporting of streaming media—video and audio, for example.

Adding the enabling strengths of web-based information technology to the analyst's kit is of importance for military intelligence if the commander is to have the continuing picture of the entire field of operations in all its dimensions. Such tools are of vital importance for analysts addressing asymmetric threats such as terrorism, where the disparate data must be located and mined not only from classified and unclassified intelligence sources, but also from worldwide open sources, and all in new and correct collaboration with the FBI, the INS, Customs—law enforcement both U.S. and international.

In 1899, Commissioner of Patents Charles Duell urged President William McKinley to abolish the Patent Office, saying, "Everything that can be invented has been invented." Those fearless words have always appealed to me, as have those of Dr. Dionysus Lardner, who in 1823 advised that "Rail travel at high speed is not possible because passengers, unable to breathe, would die of asphyxia."[16]

I quote these gentlemen to remind that we cannot begin to imagine or comprehend where the onward march of discovery and technology will take us in the decades ahead. My words have offered a snapshot of the remarkable doors the Internet has opened and the formidable new challenges the Internet era has posed for the work of intelligence. It is an era in which the U.S. Intelligence Community continues to set aside old practices in favor of dramatically new ways of doing business. This comes at a time when both decisionmakers and military commanders recognize the heightened priority and the central importance of good intelligence in providing for the wellbeing, the security, and the defense of the United States.

Biography
A. Denis Clift
President
Joint Military Intelligence College

A. Denis Clift was appointed President of the Joint Military Intelligence College in 1994. The College, in the Department of Defense, is the nation's only accredited academic institution awarding the Master of Science of Strategic Intelligence degree and the Bachelor of Science in Intelligence degree. In 1999, in his role as president of the college, Mr. Clift was elected to serve as a Commissioner on the Commission on Higher Education of the Middle States Association of Colleges and Schools for the term 2000-2002. Since 1992, he has also served as a U.S. Commissioner on the U.S.-Russia Joint Commission on Prisoners of War/Missing in Action, a commission created by Presidents Bush and Yeltsin with the humanitarian goal of accounting for servicemen still missing from past conflicts. In 2002, he was named a member of the Board of Trustees, Consortium of Universities of the Washington Metropolitan Area.

Mr. Clift was born in New York City, New York. He was educated at Friends Seminary, Phillips Exeter Academy (1954), Stanford University (B.A. 1958), and The London School of Economics and Political Science, University of London (M.Sc. 1967). He began a career of public service as a naval officer in the Eisenhower and Kennedy administrations and has served in military and civilian capacities in 10 administrations, including 13 successive years in the Executive Office of the President and The White House. From 1971-1976, he served on the National Security Council staff. From 1974-1976, he was head of President Ford's National Security Council staff for the Soviet Union and Eastern and Western Europe. From 1977-1981 he was Assistant for National Security Affairs to the Vice President of the United States. From 1991-1994, he was Chief of Staff, Defense Intelligence Agency, following service as an Assistant Deputy Director and Deputy Director for External Relations of the Agency. He is a veteran of two Antarctic expeditions, including the 1961 Bellingshausen Sea Expedition. From 1963-1966, he was Editor, United States Naval Institute *Proceedings*.

His awards and decorations include the President's Rank of Distinguished Executive, awarded by President George W. Bush in 2001; the President's Rank of Meritorious Executive, awarded by President Ronald Reagan in 1986; the Department of Defense Medal for Distinguished Public Service; the Department of Defense Distinguished Civilian Service Medal; the Secretary of Defense's Meritorious Civilian Service Medal; the Secretary of the Navy's Commendation for Achievement; the Oceanographer of the Navy's Superior Achievement Award; and the Director of Central Intelligence's Sherman Kent Award and Helene L. Boatner Award. He directed the production of the film "Portrait of Antarctica" screened at the Venice Film Festival. His published fiction and nonfiction include the novel *A Death in Geneva* (Ballantine Books of Random House), *Our World in Antarctica* (Rand McNally), and *With Presidents to the Summit* (George Mason University Press).

A. Denis Clift

Biography
Samuel V. Wilson
Lieutenant General, United States Army (Retired)
President Emeritus, Hampden-Sydney College,
Hampden-Sydney, Virginia

Lieutenant General Samuel V. Wilson retired from the United States Army in 1977 after a distinguished 37-year career that culminated in a tour as Director of the Defense Intelligence Agency in 1976-1977. His military service included a tour with "Merrill's Marauders" in the 1944 North Burma Campaign and extensive service behind the Iron Curtain as a Russian Foreign Area Specialist. Other assignments included tours in special operations, conventional forces, and intelligence positions.

In July 1992 he became the 22nd President of Hampden-Sydney College in Virginia, serving in that post until 2000. He remains active, however, having been elected President Emeritus of the College in 2000, and he serves as the James C. Wheat Professor of Leadership. Hampden-Sydney College honored General Wilson upon his retirement by naming its Wilson Center for Leadership in the Public Interest after him.

NOTES

Chapter 1: "Intelligence Education for Joint Warfighting"

1. David Stafford, *Churchill and Secret Service* (Woodstock & New York: The Overlook Press, 1997), 190.

2. Dmitri Volkogonov, *Autopsy for an Empire* (New York: The Free Press, 1998), 114, 351, and 353.

3. *Eye in the Sky*, eds. Dwayne A. Day, John M. Logsdon, and Brian Latell (Washington, DC: Smithsonian Institution Press, 1998), 173 and 283.

4. Harold P. Ford, *CIA and the Vietnam Policymakers: Three Episodes 1962-1968* (Washington, DC: Center for the Study of Intelligence, Central Intelligence Agency, 1998), 151.

5. Daniel S. Gressang, "The Role of Perceptions and Beliefs of U.S. Policymakers in the Decision-making Process," *Joint Military Intelligence College Newsletter 5*, no. 1 (June 1998): 15.

6. William O. Studeman, "Leading Intelligence Along the Byways of our Future: Acquiring C4ISR Architectures for the 21st Century," *Defense Intelligence Journal 7*, no. 1 (Spring 1998): 47-48.

7. Wilhelm von Humboldt, quoted in Gerhard Casper, "Teaching and Research," *Stanford Today*, March/April 1998, 27.

8. Perry L. Pickert and Russell G. Swenson, Editors, *Intelligence for Multilateral Decision and Action* (Washington, DC: Joint Military Intelligence College, 1997).

9. Mark G. Marshall, *The Nature of Imagery Analysis and its Place Beside Intelligence Analysis* (Washington, DC: Joint Military Intelligence College, 1998).

10. *Report to the Faculty, Administration, Board of Visitors and Students of the Joint Military Intelligence College,* by an Evaluation Team representing the Commission on Higher Education of the Middle States Association of Colleges and Schools, 14 April 1998, 3.

11. Honorable Ike Skelton (D-MO), "Intelligence and U.S. Military Policy," address to the "Leading Intelligence in the 21st Century" Conference, 25 June 1998 (Washington, DC: Joint Military Intelligence College, 1998), 2.

A. Denis Clift

Chapter 2: "From Roe, Sims, and Thomas to You"

1. Immo Starbreit, Ambassador to the United States from the Federal Republic of Germany, Remarks at the Ceremony Commemorating the 10th Anniversary of the Defense Intelligence Analysis Center, Washington, DC, 23 May 1994.

2. A. Denis Clift, Letter to Lt Gen Lincoln Faurer, USAF (Ret.), 28 October 1994.

3. Corey Ford, *A Peculiar Service*, quoted in *Great True Spy Stories,* ed. Allen Dulles (New York: Harper and Row, Publishers, 1968), 104.

4. *Great True Spy Stories,* ed. Allen Dulles (New York: Harper and Row, publishers, 1968), 101.

5. Lyman Kirkpatrick, *The Real CIA* (New York: The Macmillan Co., 1968), 205-206.

Chapter 3: "The San Cristobal Trapezoid"

1. Robert F. Kennedy, *Thirteen Days* (New York: W.W. Norton & Company, Inc., 1969), 14.

2. NIE 85-2-62, *The Situation and Prospects in Cuba,* 1 August 1962.

3. CIA Fact Sheet, *Soviet Forces in Cuba,* 5 February 1963.

4. SNIE 85-3-62, *The Military Buildup in Cuba,* 19 September 1962.

5. CIA Fact Sheet.

6. SNIE 11-19-62, *Major Consequences of Certain U.S. Courses of Action on Cuba,* 20 October 1962.

7. Newsletter, *Light Photographic Squadron Sixty-Two (VPF-62),* February 1963.

8. Kennedy, 198-199.

9. Kennedy, 15-16.

10. Kennedy, 203.

11. *Public Papers of the Presidents of the United States: John F. Kennedy, 1962* (Washington, DC: U.S. Government Printing Office, 1963), 832-833.

12. CIA Fact Sheet.

13. Statement on Cuba by the DCI, 6 February 1963.

Chapter 4: "The Knotted Stick of History"

1. Graham Greene, *The Quiet American* (New York: The Viking Press, 1956).

2. Ezer Weizman, *On Eagles' Wings* (London: Weidenfeld and Nicholson, 1976), 22.

3. Moshe Dayan, *Living With The Bible* (New York: William Morrow & Company, Inc., 1978), 13.

4. A. Denis Clift, *With Presidents to the Summit* (Fairfax, VA: George Mason University Press, 1993), 169.

5. R. D. Heinl, Jr., "The Right to Fight," *United States Naval Institute Proceedings,* September 1962, 27.

6. Kemp Tolley, "The Strange Assignment of USS Lanikai," *United States Naval Institute Proceedings,* July 1966, 44.

7. E. B. Potter, "Chester William Nimitz 1885-1966," *United States Naval Institute Proceedings,* July 1966, 44.

8. Potter, 44.

9. Harry S. Truman, *Memoirs, Vol. One: Year of Decisions* (Garden City, NY: Doubleday and Company, Inc., 1955), 337.

10. Truman, 402.

11. Michael Warner, ed., *The CIA Under Harry Truman* (Washington, DC: Central Intelligence Agency, 1994), 1.

12. Thomas F. Troy, *Donovan and the CIA* (Frederick, MD: Aletheia Books, 1981), 321.

13. *Report of the Commission on the Roles and Capabilities of the United States Intelligence Community* (Washington, DC: Government Printing Office, 1996), 149.

14. John A. Cash, John Albright, and Allan W. Sandstrum, *Seven Firefights in Vietnam* (New York: Bantam Books, 1985), 175.

15. Cash, Albright, and Sandstrum, Foreword.

16. Robert S. McNamara, *In Retrospect* (New York: Times Books Random House, 1995), 32.

17. Harold P. Ford, "An Analyst's View: Why Were CIA Analysts so Pessimistic About Vietnam?" paper presented to 63rd Annual Meeting, Society for Military History, 1996, 5.

18. Ronnie E. Ford, *Tet 1968: Understanding the Surprise* (London: Frank Cass, 1995), 4.

19. Oscar W. Koch, G-2: *Intelligence for Patton* (Philadelphia: Whitemore Publishing Co. 1971), 165.

A. Denis Clift

20. B. J. Shwedo, *Patton's ULTRA System and Its Employment on the European Battlefield,* MSSI Thesis, Joint Military Intelligence College, August 1995.

Chapter 5: "The Dinkum Oil"

1. *Sherman Kent and the Board of National Estimates: Collected Essays,* ed. Donald P. Steury (Washington, DC: Center for the Study of Intelligence, Central Intelligence Agency, 1994), 14.

2. *Kent: Collected Essays,* 14.

3. *Kent: Collected Essays,* 22.

4. Obituary, *Palo Alto Times,* Palo Alto, CA, 23 August 1972, 2.

5. Chilton R. Bush, *Newspaper Reporting of Public Affairs* (New York: Appleton-Century-Crofts, Inc., 1951), dedication page.

6. Bush, 1-3.

7. Thomas O'Toole, *The Washington Post,* 28 December 1968, A1.

8. James Harney, *Daily News,* 25 April 1986, 3.

9. Ernest Hemingway, "The Spanish War," *Fact*, July 1938, 65.

10. Matthew Halton, *Ten Years to Alamein* (London: Lindsay Drummond Ltd., 1944), 76.

11. *Kent: Collected Essays*, 10.

12. Duane R. Clarridge, *A Spy for All Seasons* (New York: Scribner, 1997), 9.

13. Clarridge, 11.

14. Clarridge, 72.

15. Clarridge, 184.

16. Clarridge, 303.

17. Clarridge, 412.

18. *Intelligence for Multilateral Decision and Action,* eds. Perry L. Pickert and Russell G. Swenson (Washington, DC: Joint Military Intelligence College, 1997), xxiv.

19. *Intelligence for Multilateral Decision and Action,* 294-295.

Chapter 6: "Safecrackers: The Past, Present, and Future of U.S. Intelligence"

1. Ron Shaffer, *The Washington Post,* 12 February 1998, D6.

2. Office of the Secretary of Defense, "Proliferation: Threat and Response" (Washington, DC: Government Printing Office, November 1997), iii.

3. Joseph Conrad, *The Secret Agent,* in *A Conrad Argosy* (Garden City, NY: Doubleday, Doran & Company, Inc., 1942), 359.

4. David Williams, "Justice Finally Catches up with the Jackal," *Daily Mail* (London), 28 December 1997.

5. Clair Rosemberg, "Has-been Revolutionary Carlos laps up Limelight at Trial," Agence France Presse, Paris, 28 December 1997.

6. Helmut Raether, "No Precise Information on Iraq's Weapons of Mass Destruction," Deutsche Presse-Agenture, 13 February 1998.

7. National Public Radio, Inc., Transcript # 98021709-212, "All Things Considered," 17 February 1998.

8. AP Online, 5 February 1998.

9. Robert D. Walpole, "Lessons Learned: Intelligence Support on Chemical and Biological Warfare During the Gulf War and on Veterans' Illnesses Issues" (Washington, DC: Director of Central Intelligence's Persian Gulf War Illnesses Task Force, December 1997), 8.

10. Ewen Montagu, *The Man Who Never Was* (Philadelphia: J. P. Lippincott Company, 1954), 25.

11. Montagu, 45.

12. Captain Neal D. Norman, U.S. Army, *British Intelligence and Information Superiority at the Battle of Alam Halfa: Turning the Tide in North Africa,* Master of Science of Strategic Intelligence Thesis (Washington, DC: Joint Military Intelligence College, 1997), 78-80.

13. Tim Weiner, "Master Creator of Ghosts Is Honored by CIA," *The New York Times,* 19 September 1997, A24.

14. National Security Agency, Center for Cryptologic History, "Introductory History of VENONA and Guide to the Translations" (Fort George G. Meade, MD: National Security Agency), 1996, 1.

15. NSA, 2-3.

A. Denis Clift

16. Kevin C. Ruffner, "CORONA: America's First Satellite Program" (Washington, DC: Center for the Study of Intelligence, Central Intelligence Agency, 1995), 19.

17. Colonel Philip A. Rowe, Jr., USAF (Ret.), "The Star Catchers," *Air Force Magazine,* Washington, DC, 1995, 75.

18. "Safecracker Eddie Chapman Dies: Spy for Britain in WW II," *The Washington Post,* 17 December 1997.

19. "Safecracker."

20. Dwight D. Eisenhower, *Crusade in Europe* (Garden City, NY: Doubleday & Co., Inc., 1948), 32.

21. Herbert S. Parmet, *George Bush: The Life of a Lone Star Yankee* (New York: Scribner, 1997), 194.

22. Stansfield Turner, *Secrecy and Democracy* (Boston: Houghton Mifflin Company, 1985), 206-207.

23. Joseph Conrad, *A Personal Record* (Garden City, NY: Doubleday, Page & Co., 1924), xii.

Chapter 7: "In His Own Time a Man Is Always Very Modern"

1. Norman R. Augustine, "Socio-engineering (And Augustine's Second Law Thereof)," Lecture presented at the University of Colorado Engineering Centennial Convocation, 1 October 1993, 1.

2. CDR John Alden, USN (Ret.), "USS Brooklyn," *United States Naval Institute Proceedings* 92, no. 4 (April 1966): 112-129.

3. Augustine: 1.

4. RADM Thomas R. Wilson, USN, "Joint Intelligence and UPHOLD DEMOCRACY," *Joint Force Quarterly,* no. 7 (Spring 1995): 57-58.

5. CPT (P) Erich V. Boerner, USA, *National Intelligence Support to the Warfighters: An Analysis of an Office in Transition,* MSSI Thesis (Washington, DC: Joint Military Intelligence College, May 1994), 10.

6. Boerner, 9.

7. Department of Defense, *Conduct of the Persian Gulf War, Final Report of the Department of Defense to Congress pursuant to Title V of the Persian Gulf Conflict Supplemental Authorization and Personnel Benefits Act of 1991* (Public Law 102-25),

Annex C (April 1992): 333. Reprinted from *United States Naval Institute Proceedings* with permission, copyright 1991, U.S. Naval Institute.

8. *New York Times,* 8 May 1991.

9. Diana D. Rueb, *The Joint Worldwide Intelligence Communications System (JWICS): Increased Utilization of JWICS Video Teleconferencing will Augment Defense Intelligence Agency Mission Requirements,* MSSI Thesis (Washington, DC: Joint Military Intelligence College, July 1993).

10. Steven Schanzer, "Information Systems/Information Technology: What is Their Value?" Address to Mitre Corporation Government Executives Seminar, Williamsburg, Virginia, 22 February 1994.

11. George Heilmeier, "Educating Tomorrow's Engineers," *ASEE Prism,* May/June 1995.

12. T.E. Lawrence, *The Seven Pillars of Wisdom* (New York: Doubleday & Company, Inc., 1935), 193.

13. Jeffrey B. White, "Thoughts on Irregular Warfare," unpublished manuscript accepted for publication in *Studies in Intelligence.*

14. R. Jeffrey Smith, "Expansion of Covert Action Eyed," *The Washington Post,* 13 September 1995, A8.

15. Lt Gen Kenneth A. Minihan, USAF, address to Army Intelligence Ball, Alexandria, Virginia, 23 September 1995, 5.

16. The Hon. Richard Riley, address to the Fifth National Science Bowl Competition (Associated Press/AP Online, 2 May 1995).

17. ADM Charles R. Larson, USN, "The Military Officer of the 21st Century," address to the Parent's Club of San Francisco, 15 June 1995.

18. In November 1997 the President signed legislation that gives the JMIC the authority to grant the BSI degree. The first graduates received their degrees in June 1998.

Chapter 8: "FA34 + MSSI/2000> = JV 2010"

1. Theodore Roosevelt, Address to Hamilton Club, Chicago, 10 April 1899, quoted in *A Treasury of the World's Great Speeches,* ed. Houston Peterson (New York: Simon and Schuster, 1954), 657-658.

2. Roosevelt Address.

3. Lawrence Friedman, "Revolutions in Military Affairs," The Ivan Bloch Commemorative Conference, St. Petersburg, Russia, February 1999, 2.

A. Denis Clift

4. Statement by Director of Central Intelligence George J. Tenet before the Senate Armed Services Committee, Washington, DC, 2 February 1999, 1.

5. General Sir Michael Rose, "Address," The Ivan Bloch Commemorative Conference, St. Petersburg, Russia, February 1999, 4.

6. Gen. John M. Shalikashvili, Chairman of the Joint Chiefs of Staff, *Joint Vision 2010* (Washington, DC: GPO, 1997), 28.

7. Major Richard A. Paquette, U.S. Army, *Ethnic Conflict: Kosovo and the Next Balkan War,* MSSI Thesis (Washington, DC: Joint Military Intelligence College, August 1998).

8. Captain David H. Foglesong, U.S. Air Force, *Intelligence, Dominant Battlespace Knowledge and the Warfighter,* MSSI Thesis (Washington, DC: Joint Military Intelligence College, August 1998), 106.

9. Captain Chris N. Carver, U.S. Army, *Square Peg, Round Hole: Why Military Intelligence is Unprepared for Operations Other Than War,* MSSI Thesis (Washington, DC: Joint Military Intelligence College, August 1998), 3-4 and 51-52.

10. Captain Peter J. Don, U.S. Army, *The Awakening: Developing Military Intelligence Professionals to Support United States Army Special Forces,* MSSI Thesis (Washington, DC: Joint Military Intelligence College, August 1998).

11. Captain Christian H. Veeris, U.S. Marine Corps, *Concrete Hamlet: Using a Vietnam Model for Tactical Information Gathering in Future Urban Environments,* MSSI Thesis (Washington, DC: Joint Military Intelligence College, July 1998).

12. Captain Michael P. McCrane, U.S. Marine Corps Reserve, *Time-Sensitive Document Exploitation: Lessons Learned from the Vietnam Conflict Applicable to Drug Law Enforcement,* MSSI Thesis (Washington, DC: Joint Military Intelligence College, August 1998).

13. Staff Sergeant Robert P. Ives II, U. S. Army, *The National Security Implications of the Space Launch Industry,* MSSI Thesis (Washington, DC: Joint Military Intelligence College, August 1998).

14. Second Lieutenant Darin L. Hoenle, U.S. Air Force, *Emptying a Bucket with a Spoon: Commercial Satellite Support for Unmanned Aerial Vehicle Video,* MSSI Thesis (Washington, DC: Joint Military Intelligence College, August 1998).

15. First Lieutenant Jean M. Lewis, U.S. Army Reserve, *Biotechnology: New Possibilities for Biological Warfare,* MSSI Thesis (Washington, DC: Joint Military Intelligence College, August 1998).

16. Frederick Thomas Martin, *TOP SECRET INTRANET: How U.S. Intelligence Built INTELINK—The World's Largest, Most Secure Network* (Saddle River, NJ: Prentice Hall, 1999).

17. Alvin H. Bernstein, "The Academic Researcher and the Intelligence Analyst: How and Where the Twain Might Meet," in *Military Intelligence and the Universities: A Study of an Ambivalent Relationship* (Boulder, CO: Westview Press, 1984), 40.

18. Marjorie W. Cline, ed., *Intelligence in the Mid-1980s* (Washington, DC: National Intelligence Study Center, 1985), iii.

19. David Stafford, *Churchill and Secret Service* (New York: The Overlook Press, 1997), 27.

Chapter 9: "The Commander's Kit"

1. Jerome S. Rubin and Janet Wikler, "Publishing as a Creature of Technology," in *The Information Resources Policy Handbook,* eds. Benjamin M. Compaine and William H. Read (Cambridge, MA: MIT Press, 1999), 301.

2. R. James Woolsey, Major General Doyle Larson, and Linda Zall, "Honoring Two World War II Heroes," *Studies in Intelligence* 38, no. 5 (1995): 33.

3. Winston S. Churchill, *Their Finest Hour* (Boston: Houghton Mifflin Company, 1949), 383.

4. R. V. Jones, *The Wizard War* (New York: Coward, McCann & Geoghegan, Inc., 1978), 100-102.

5. Jones, 108.

6. Woolsey, Larson, and Zall, 33.

7. Jones, 67.

8. Sean J. Cantrell, "Integrated Intelligence Operations: The Key to Force Protection," Tractate submitted to the U.S. Air Force Institute for National Security Studies, January 2000, ii.

9. Cantrell, 34-35.

10. As quoted by General Sir Michael Rose, "Address," The Ivan Bloch Commemorative Conference, St. Petersburg, Russia, February 1999, 4.

11. Lieutenant General Michael V. Hayden, USAF, "Warfighters and Intelligence: One Team-One Fight," *Defense Intelligence Journal* 4, no. 2 (Fall 1995): 18.

12. Lieutenant General Michael V. Hayden, Address to the Nixon Center, Washington, DC, 12 November 1999, 5.

13. George J. Tenet, Oscar Iden Lecture, Georgetown University, 18 October 1999, 3.

14. Vice Admiral Thomas R. Wilson, U.S. Navy, "Military Threats and Security Challenges Through 2015," Statement for the Record, Senate Select Committee on Intelligence, Washington, DC, 2 February 2000, 7.

Chapter 10: "Semper Proteus"

1. James A. Reed, "Renaissance of the Coast Guard," *United States Naval Institute Proceedings* 91, no. 8 (August 1965): 34.

2. Reed, 39.

3. "A Nice Catch-for Customs," Associated Press, 14 July 2000.

4. General Anthony C. Zinni, USMC, "A Commander Reflects," *United States Naval Institute Proceedings* 126, no. 7 (July 2000): 34.

5. U.S. President, Executive Order 12333, "United States Intelligence Activities," 4 December 1981.

6. Office of Naval Intelligence and Coast Guard Intelligence Coordination Center, *Threats and Challenges to Maritime Security 2020* (Washington, DC: GPO, March 1999).

7. Interagency Task Force, "A Coast Guard for the 21st Century," *Report of the Interagency Task Force on U.S. Coast Guard Roles and Missions,* December 1999, 2-7.

8. Interagency Task Force, 2-118 through 2-122.

9. Rear Admiral Lowell E. Jacoby, USN, "Intelligence Support to Military Operations-Implications for Joint Vision 2010," unpublished manuscript, February 2000, 3.

10. Jacoby, 28.

11. Lieutenant Eric S. Ensign, USCG, *Intelligence in the Rum War at Sea, 1920-1933,* MSSI Thesis (Washington, DC: Joint Military Intelligence College, 1998), 75.

12. Ensign, 31-33.

13. Lieutenant Commander William J. Quigley, USCG, "Driftnet Fishery Enforcement: A New Intelligence Problem," in *Intelligence for Mutililateral Decision and Action,* ed. Perry L. Pickert (Washington, DC: Joint Military Intelligence College, 1997), 509-514.

14. President John F. Kennedy, "Remarks Aboard the Coast Guard Training Barque Eagle," 15 August 1962, *Public Papers of the Presidents of the United States* (Washington, DC: GPO, 1963), 618.

Chapter 11: "Two If By Sea, Three If By Cyberspace"

1. President Bill Clinton, Commencement Address, U.S. Naval Academy, Annapolis, Maryland, 22 May 1998.

2. The White House, *Presidential Decision Directive 63,* Appendix B (Washington, DC: GPO, 22 May 1998), 176-177.

3. Office of Naval Intelligence and Coast Guard Intelligence Coordination Center, National Maritime Intelligence Center, *Threats and Challenges to Maritime Security 2020* (Washington, DC: National Maritime Intelligence Center, March 1999), ii. Cited hereafter as Threats and Challenges.

4. *Threats and Challenges,* III-27.

5. Roberto Suro, "Coast Guard Tactics Boost Drug Seizures," *The Washington Post,* 30 September 1999, A6.

6. "132 Chinese Found Hidden Aboard Ship in Georgia Port," Reuters, *The Washington Post,* 14 August 1999, A5.

7. "Ship Drops 150 Asians on Canadian Beach," Associated Press, *The New York Times,* 12 August 1999, A4.

8. Louis J. Freeh, *The Threat to the United States Posed by Terrorists,* Statement for the Record by the Director, Federal Bureau of Investigation, before the Senate Committee on Appropriations, Subcommittee for the Departments of Commerce, Justice, and State, the Judiciary, and Related Agencies, Washington, DC, 4 February 1999, 18.

9. George J. Tenet, Commencement Address, Joint Military Intelligence College, Washington, DC, 3 September 1999, 9.

10. Captain Stephen W. Magnan, U.S. Air Force, *Information Operations: Are We Our Own Worst Enemy?* Master's Thesis (Washington, DC: Joint Military Intelligence College, August 1998).

11. Lieutenant Jay Wylie, U.S. Navy, *Naval Intelligence Support to Surface Warfare: Is the Surface Navy Missing the Boat?* Master's Thesis (Washington, DC: Joint Military Intelligence College, August 1999).

12. Captain James M. Lose, U.S. Marine Corps, "The National Intelligence Support Teams," *Studies in Intelligence* 42, no. 1 (1998): 29-38.

13. Paul Leverkuehn, *German Military Intelligence* (New York: Frederick A. Praeger, Inc., 1954), 55-56.

14. Thomas E. Mahl, *Desperate Deception: British Covert Operations in the United States, 1939-44* (Washington and London: Brassey's, 1998), 14.

15. George D. Sanders, "Containers and Containerships," *U. S. Naval Institute Proceedings,* April 1963, 60-61.

16. LCDR Arthur E. Hammonland, U.S. Navy, and LCDR David L. Cooper, U.S. Navy, "The Largest Tankers," *U.S. Naval Institute Proceedings,* July 1964, 89-101.

17. Noel Mostert, *Supership* (New York: Alfred A. Knopf, 1974), 30.

18. "1970 - Report of the United States Delegation to the Conference on Pollution of the Sea by Oil Spills, Committee on the Challenges of Modern Society North Atlantic Treaty Organization, Brussels, Belgium, November 2-6, 1970," submitted to the President: The Honorable John F. Volpe, Chairman of Delegation, The Honorable Daniel P. Moynihan, Vice Chairman of Delegation, prepared by A. Denis Clift, Secretary of Delegation, 42.

19. A. Denis Clift and John T. Hughes, "The San Cristobal Trapezoid," *Studies in Intelligence* 36, no. 5 (1992), 61.

20. The White House, "U.S. Foreign Policy for the 1970's: Shaping a Durable Peace," A Report to Congress by Richard Nixon, President of the United States, Washington, DC, 3 May 1973, 35.

21. Joseph P. Harahan, *On-Site Inspections Under the INF Treaty* (Washington, DC: Department of Defense, 1993), 85.

22. Admiral Jay Johnson, "International Sea Power Symposium Address," Naval War College, Newport, Rhode Island, 1997.

23. Federal Maritime Commission, *Annual Report for Fiscal Year 1998* (Washington, DC: GPO, 1999) 68-69.

24. Department of Defense, *Conduct of the Persian Gulf War,* Report to the Congress (Washington, DC: DoD, April 1992), 418.

25. DoD, *Conduct of the Persian Gulf War,* 421.

26. Department of Transportation, Maritime Administration, *1998 Annual Report* (Washington, DC: GPO, May 1999), 1-2.

27. Daniel Y. Coulter, "Global Commercial Maritime Environment," (Washington, DC: Office of Naval Intelligence, 1999).

28. John Markoff, "High-Tech Advances Push C.I.A. Into New Company," *The New York Times,* 29 September 1999, A14.

29. U.S. Customs, Intelligence Division, "The HINT Alliance Marine Containers Industry Project," (Washington, DC: GPO, 12 August 1999).

Chapter 12: "The Emerging Butterfly"

1. William Perry, Secretary of Defense, Remarks to the Corps of Defense Attachés, Washington, DC, 28 February 1996.

2. Stanley L. Falk and Theodore W. Bauer, *The National Security Structure* (Washington, DC: Industrial College of the Armed Forces, 1972), 2.

3. Letter from General George Washington to Colonel Elias Dayton, 26 July 1777, Pforzheimer Collection of Intelligence Literature, Washington, DC.

4. James Van Wagenen, "Congressional Oversight: A Look Back," paper by DIA Chair, Joint Military Intelligence College, to be published 1996.

5. National Security Act of 1947, Eighteenth Congress of the United States of America, 26 July 1947.

6. U.S. President, Executive Order 12333, §2.5.

7. Benjamin Wittes, "Inside America's Most Secretive Court," *Legal Times,* Washington, DC, week of 19 February 1996, 21.

8. Van Wagenen, 6.

9. Van Wagenen, 8.

Chapter 13: "The Role of Defense Intelligence"

1. Caspar Weinberger, Citation to DIA, Speech at the Defense Intelligence Analysis Center, 1 October 1996.

2. Dwight D. Eisenhower, *Crusade in Europe* (New York: Doubleday and Company, Inc., 1948), 32.

3. For a detailed "first-person" account of the early days of that crisis, see Chapter 3, "The San Cristobal Trapezoid."

4. U.S. President, Executive Order 12333, "United States Intelligence Activities," 4 December 1981, in U.S. Congress, House Permanent Select Committee, *Compilation of Intelligence Laws and Executive Orders of Interest to the National Intelligence Community,* 99th Congress, 1st session, 1985, Committee Print, 361. Hereafter cited as EO 12333.

5. EO 12333, 1.1(b), 361.

6. EO 12333, 1.12(a), 367.

7. Boren Hearings for Webster's confirmation as DCI, Senate Select Committee on Intelligence, 8 April 1987.

8. Congressman Louis Stokes (D-OH), Remarks to the Graduating Class at the Defense Intelligence College, Bolling Air Force Base, Washington, DC, 11 September 1987.

9. Stokes, Remarks, 11 September 1987.

10. William Casey, remarks on the 25th anniversary of DIA, Defense Intelligence Analysis Center, Washington, DC, 26 September 1986.

11. John LeCarre, *Tinker, Tailor, Soldier, Spy* (New York: Alfred A. Knopf, 1974), 23.

12. Frederick Forsyth, *The Fourth Protocol* (New York: Viking, 1984), 72.

13. Graham Greene, *The Human Factor* (New York: Simon and Schuster, 1978), 46-47.

Chapter 14: "National Security/Open Sources"

Chapter 14 had no endnote citations.

Chapter 15: "The Five-Legged Calf"

1. A.M. Rosenthal, "On My Mind: Profiles in Terrorism," *New York Times,* 10 February 1989, A35.

2. Ambassador Charles Whitehouse, remarks at the Pentagon Release of "Profiles in Terrorism," Washington, DC, February 1989.

3. Robert Gates, Testimony in Joint Session of the Subcommittees of Senate Armed Services and Appropriation Committees, quoted in *The Washington Post,* 17 June 1985.

4. Robert S. McNamara, press conference, Department of State, 6 February 1963.

5. NATO Foreign Ministers' Statement, Brussels, May 1981.

6. "U.S. Study on Soviet Power Welcomed by NATO," *New York Times,* 4 October 1981, A16.

7. Edward R. Murrow, testimony as Director of USIA before the Subcommittee of the Committee on Appropriations, United States Senate, 20 September 1962.

8. Secretary General Joseph Luns, North Atlantic Treaty Organization's report, *NATO and the Warsaw Pact: Force Comparisons,* Brussels, 1982, Foreword.

9. "Down Madisonsky Avenue," *The Economist,* 6 February 1982, 45.

10. President Ronald Reagan, White House Statement on the Release of *Soviet Military Power,* March 1983.

11. Preface to the 1983 edition of *Soviet Military Power,* by Federal Defense Minister Manfred Wörner, Bonn, 1983.

12. Secretary General Joseph Luns, North Atlantic Treaty Organization's report, *NATO and the Warsaw Pact: Force Comparisons,* Brussels, 1984, Foreword.

13. Secretary of Defense Caspar Weinberger, Preface to the 1987 edition of *Soviet Military Power,* 24 March 1987.

14. Editorial, *New York Times,* 30 April 1987, A30.

15. H.L. Mencken, *The American Language, Supplement 1* (New York: Alfred A. Knopf, 1962), 282.

Chapter 16: "The Strategic Balance in Very Odd Times"

1. Address of the President of the Czechoslovak Republic to a Joint Session of the United States Congress, Washington, DC, 21 February 1990.

2. *The Wall Street Journal,* 28 March 1991, 10.

3. *Bulletin of the Atlantic Council of the United States* 2, no. 3, 29 March 1991.

4. *The New York Times,* 30 May 1991, 12.

5. Opening Statement by George Kott, Director, Office of Soviet Analysis, Central Intelligence Agency, to the Technology and National Security Subcommittee of the Joint Economic Committee, Congress of the United States, 16 May 1991, 1 and 2.

6. Address by President George Bush to the Aspen Institute Symposium, 2 August 1990, reprinted in *Report of the Secretary of Defense to the President and the Congress,* Appendix E (Washington, DC: Government Printing Office, January 1991), 132.

7. Remarks by General Colin L. Powell, Chairman of the Joint Chiefs of Staff, to the American Stock Exchange Washington Conference, Mayflower Hotel, Washington, DC, 15 October 1990, 5.

8. Department of Defense, *Soviet Military Power 1990* (Washington, DC: Government Printing Office, September 1990, 51-56.

9. Department of Defense, *Report of the Secretary of Defense to the President and the Congress* (Washington, DC: Government Printing Office, January 1991), 51-56.

10. Hearing of Senate Armed Services Committee on Strategic and Space Force Posture, 23 April 1991.

11. "Collective Defense in the Post-Cold War Era," speech delivered by John Jorgen Holst, Minister of Defense of Norway, to the Atlantic Council of the United States, 20 March 1991, 7 and 9.

12. "Collective Defense," 133.

A. Denis Clift

13. Statement of Secretary of Defense Dick Cheney, Senate Armed Services Committee, in connection with the FY 1992-93 Budget for the Department of Defense, 21 February 1991, 7.

14. Janne E. Nolan, *Trappings of Power* (Washington, DC: The Brookings Institution, 1991), 5.

15. TASS, Mikhail Gorbachev, Nobel Lecture, Oslo, Norway, 5 June 1991.

Chapter 17: "Intelligence in Partnership"

1. Lyndon Baines Johnson, *The Vantage Point* (New York: Holt, Rinehart and Winston, 1971), 479.

2. *Treaty between the United States of America and the Union of Soviet Socialist Republics on the Limitation of Strategic Offensive Areas,* Article XV, Vienna, 18 June 1979.

3. *The New York Times,* 8 May 1991.

4. Annex, Declaration of the Heads of States and Governments participating in the meeting of the Northern Atlantic Council held at NATO Headquarters, Brussels, 11 January 1994.

5. The conference proposed by Clift in his remarks did in fact take place on 26-27 June 1997 at the Defense Intelligence Analysis Center in Washington, DC. Hosted by the Joint Military Intelligence College, the "Intelligence in Partnership" Conference welcomed intelligence professionals from around the world who met in a spirit of cooperation and sharing information. One product of that conference was a book, by JMIC adjunct faculty member Dr. Perry L. Pickert, entitled *Intelligence for Multilateral Decision and Action* (Washington, DC: JMIC, 1997). JMIC faculty member Dr. Russell G. Swenson edited the book, which is a compilation of work done by MSSI candidates at the College.

Chapter 18: "Through the Prism of National Security"

1. Stephen E. Ambrose, *Band of Brothers* (New York: Simon and Schuster, 2001).

2. David Stafford, *Churchill and Secret Service* (New York: The Overlook Press, 1997), 193.

3. Stephen Budiansky, *Battle of Wits* (New York: The Free Press, 2000), 239.

4. Edward R.F. Sheehan, "The Rise and Fall of a Soviet Agent," in *Great True Spy Stories,* edited by Allen Dulles (New York: Harper and Row Publishers, 1968), 55-56.

5. NATO Information Service, *NATO Facts and Figures* (Brussels: NATO, 1971), 22-23.

6. Department of Defense, *Conduct of the Persian Gulf War,* Final Report to Congress (Washington, DC: DoD, 1992), 333.

7. Peter Bartu, "Lessons from Cambodia," in *Intelligence in Partnership Conference Proceedings* (Washington, DC: Joint Military Intelligence College, 1997), 22-23.

8. Robert J. Allen, "Intelligence Theory and Practice in Somalia," in *Intelligence for Multilateral Decision and Action* (Washington, DC: Joint Military Intelligence College, 1997), 168-170.

9. H.R. Report No. 104-832, accompanying H.R. 3259 (*Intelligence Authorization Act for Fiscal Year 1997*) (1996).

Chapter 19: "The Left Hand of Curiosity"

1. Maxim Gorki, *A Book of Short Stories* (New York: Henry Holt and Company, 1939), 101.

2. Peter Baker, "Pitching Globalism to Marines," *The Washington Post,* 24 December 1996, A4.

3. Dwight D. Eisenhower, First Inaugural Address, 20 January 1953, in *Great Speeches,* ed. Houston Peterson (New York: Simon and Schuster, 1954), 829.

4. Richard J. Newman, "Ready! Aim! Reboot!" *U.S. News & World Report,* 20 January 1997, 45.

5. Aldous Huxley, *Brave New World* (Garden City, NY: The Sun Dial Press, 1932), 3.

6. Arthur M. Schlesinger, Jr., *A Thousand Days* (Boston: Houghton Mifflin Company, 1965), 499.

7. Lyndon B. Johnson, *The Vantage Point* (New York: Holt, Rinehart and Winston, 1971), ix.

8. Joel Achenbach, *The Washington Post,* 4 December 1996.

9. Gorki, *A Book of Short Stories,* x.

Chapter 20: "The Play of Intelligence with Presidents at the Summit"

1. Dean Acheson, *Present at the Creation* (New York: W.W. Norton & Company, Inc., 1969), 599.

2. Harry S. Truman, *Memoirs by Harry S. Truman, Volume Two: Years of Trial and Hope* (Garden City, NY: Doubleday & Company, Inc., 1956), 164-165.

A. Denis Clift

3. Hagai Eshed, *Reuven Shiloah: The Man Behind the Mossad* (London: Frank Cass, 1997), 168.

4. George Bush and Brent Scowcroft, *A World Transformed* (New York: Vintage Books, 1998), 163.

5. James MacGregor Burns, *Roosevelt: The Soldier of Freedom* (New York: Harcourt Brace Jovanovich, Inc., 1970), 131.

6. *British Security Coordination: The Secret History of British Intelligence in the Americas, 1940-1945,* Introduction by Nigel West. (New York: Fromm International, 1999), xxvi-xxvii.

7. David Stafford, *Churchill and Secret Service* (Woodstock & New York: The Overlook Press, 1998), 229.

8. Winston S. Churchill, *The Grand Alliance* (Boston: Houghton Mifflin Company, 1950), 441.

9. *Eye in the Sky: The Story of the Corona Spy Satellites,* edited by Dwayne A. Day, John M. Logsdon, and Brian Latell (Washington, DC: Smithsonian Institution Press, 1998), 173.

10. LtGen Vernon A. Walters, "General De Gaulle in Action," *Studies in Intelligence* 38, no. 5 (1995): 125.

11. Vernon A. Walters, *Silent Missions* (Garden City, NY: Doubleday & Company, Inc., 1978), 310.

12. A. Denis Clift, *With Presidents to the Summit* (Fairfax, VA: George Mason University Press, 1993), 63.

13. *The Reagan Foreign Policy,* edited by William G. Hyland (New York: A Meridian Book, 1987), 125.

14. Edmund Morris, *Dutch: A Memoir of Ronald Reagan* (New York: Random House, 1999), 517.

15. Dmitri Volkogonov, *Autopsy for an Empire: The Seven Leaders Who Built the Soviet Regime* (New York: The Free Press, 1998), 310, 315, 324.

16. *Intentions and Capabilities: Estimates on Soviet Strategic Forces, 1950-1983,* ed. Donald P. Steury (Washington, DC: Center for the Study of Intelligence, Central Intelligence Agency, 1996), vii.

17. Strobe Talbott, *End Game: The Inside Story of SALT II* (New York: Harper & Row Publishers, 1979), 24-25.

18. *The Kissinger Transcripts,* Edited by William Burr (New York: The New Press, 1998), 349 and 353.

19. Charles P. Wilson, *Strategic Reconnaissance in the Near East* (Washington, DC: The Washington Institute for Near East Policy, 1999), 59.

20. Richard Nixon, *RN: The Memoirs of Richard Nixon* (New York: Gross & Dunlap, 1978), 982.

21. Henry Kissinger, *Years of Upheaval* (Boston: Little, Brown and Company, 1982), 840.

22. Wilson, 60.

23. Elaine Sciolino, "Violence Thwarts C.I.A. Director's Unusual Role in Middle Eastern Peacemaking," *The New York Times,* 13 November 2000, A-10.

24. George J. Tenet, "What 'New' Role for CIA?" *The New York Times,* 27 October 1998, A23.

25. Alan Sipress and Vernon Loeb, "Bush Ends CIA's Role as Middle East Broker," *The Washington Post,* 22 March 2001, A25.

26. William H. Gleysteen, Jr., *Massive Entanglement, Marginal Influence* (Washington, DC: Brookings Institution Press, 1999), 50.

27. Robert M. Gates, *From the Shadows* (New York: Simon & Schuster, 1996), 358.

28. Jimmy Carter, *Keeping Faith* (New York: Bantam Books, 1982), 210.

29. Gates, 122-123.

30. "Intelligence and National Security," in *Organizing for National Security,* U.S. Congress, Senate Committee on Government Operations, Subcommittee on National Policy Machinery, 3 volumes, (Washington, DC: Government Printing Office, 1961), 1-483.

31. U.S. President, Executive Order 12333, "United States Intelligence Activities," 4 December 1981.

Chapter 21: "E Pluribus Unum MMII"

1. Joseph E. Persico, *Roosevelt's Secret War* (New York: Random House, 2001), 47-48.

2. Rebecca West, *The Meaning of Treason* (London: Phoenix Press, 2000), 414.

3. Don Whitehead, *The FBI Story* (New York: Random House, 1956), 27-32.

4. Whitehead, 33-39.

5. Persico, 32.

6. Whitehead, 46-47.

7. David Stafford, *Roosevelt and Churchill: Men of Secrets* (New York: The Overlook Press, 1999), 162-163.

8. Persico, 168.

9. William Breuer, *Hitler's Undercover War* (New York: St. Martin's Press, 1989), 278-283.

10. United States Commission on National Security/21st Century, *Road Map for National Security: Imperative for Change,* (Washington, DC: GPO, 2001), xiii.

11. West, 192.

12. United States Commission on National Security/21st Century, 15.

13. ANSER Institute for Homeland Security, *Dark Winter,* URL: <http://www.Homelandsecurity. org/darkwinter/index.cfi>.

14. Stephen R. Malphrus, Staff Director for Management, Board of Directors of the Federal Reserve System, Remarks at the Homeland Defense Training Conference, Washington, DC, 18 December 2001.

15. George Musser, "Better Killing through Chemistry," *Scientific American* 285, no. 6 (December 2001): 16.

16. "Doctors to Combat Bioterrorism," *The Capital* (Annapolis, MD), 3 January 2002, B2.

17. Lisa Krizan, *Intelligence Essentials for Everyone,* Occasional Paper Number Six, Joint Military Intelligence College (Washington, DC: Defense Intelligence Agency, 1999), 1.

18. LtCol Doman McArthur, United States Marine Corps Reserve, *Intelligence and Policy: Venturing a Structured Analysis of Iraqi Weapons of Mass Destruction,* Discussion Paper Number Eleven, Joint Military Intelligence College (Washington, DC: Defense Intelligence Agency, 2001).

19. West, 420.

Chapter 22: "From Semaphore to Predator: Intelligence in the Internet Era"

1. Stephen E. Maffeo, *Most Secret and Confidential* (Annapolis, MD: Naval Institute Press, 2000), 68-69.

2. General Atomics Aeronautical Systems, Inc., "Predator: A Global Option," Fact Sheet (San Diego, CA: General Atomics Aeronautical Systems, Inc.), n.d.

3. Leonard Kleinrock, "The Birth of Internet," updated 27 August 1996, URL: <http// www.lk.cs.ucla.edu/ LK/Inet/birth.html>, accessed 2 May 2002.

4. "DARPA," in *The Living Internet,* URL: <http.//www.livinginternet.com/?i/ ii_darpa.htm>, accessed 2 May 2002.

5. *The Information Resources Policy Handbook,* Eds. Benjamin M. Compaine and William H. Read (Cambridge, MA: The MIT Press, 1999), 22.

6. Fredrick Thomas Martin, *Top Secret Intranet: How U.S. Intelligence Built Intelink—The World's Largest, Most Secure Network* (Upper Saddle River, NJ: Prentice-Hall, Inc., 1999), 6-7.

7. Martin, xliii.

8. Martin, 53-56.

9. "About In-Q-Tel," URL: <http.//www.In-Q-Tel.com/about.htm>, accessed 2 May 2002.

10. Rick E. Yannuzzi, "In-Q-Tel: A New Partnership Between the CIA and the Private Sector," *Defense Intelligence Journal* 9, no. 1 (Winter 2000): 29-30.

11. Chairman of the Joint Chiefs of Staff, *Joint Vision 2010* (Washington, DC: Joint Chiefs of Staff, 1996), 16.

12. Michael V. Hayden, Lieutenant General, USAF, Address to Kennedy Political Union of American University, Washington, DC, 17 February 2000, 2.

13. See Carmen A. Medina, "What to Do When Traditional Models Fail," *Studies in Intelligence* 45, no. 4 (2001): 35-40.

14. James M. Lose, "National Intelligence Support Teams," *Studies in Intelligence,* Unclassified Edition (Winter 1999-2000): 87-88.

15. Norman R. Augustine, "Socio-engineering (And Augustine's Second Law Thereof)," lecture presented at the University of Colorado Engineering Centennial Convention, 1 October 1993, 1.

A. Denis Clift

WORKS CITED

"132 Chinese Found Hidden Aboard Ship in Georgia Port." Reuters. *The Washington Post*, 14 August 1999, A5.

"1970 – Report of the United States Delegation to the Conference on Pollution of the Sea by Oil Spills, Committee on the Challenges of Modern Society North Atlantic Treaty Organization, Brussels, Belgium, November 2-6, 1970." Submitted to the President: The Honorable John F. Volpe, Chairman of Delegation, The Honorable Daniel P. Moynihan, Vice Chairman of Delegation. Prepared by A. Denis Clift, Secretary of Delegation.

"About In-Q-Tel." URL: <http.//www.In-Q-Tel.com/about.htm>. Accessed 2 May 2002.

Achenbach, Joel. "Reality Check." *The Washington Post,* 4 December 1996, C1+.

Acheson, Dean. *Present at the Creation.* New York: W.W. Norton & Company, Inc., 1969.

Alden, John, CDR, USN (Ret.). "USS Brooklyn." *United States Naval Institute Proceedings* 92, no. 4 (April 1966): 112-129.

"All Things Considered." Transcript # 98021709-212. National Public Radio, Inc., 17 February 1998.

Allen, Robert J. "Intelligence Theory and Practice in Somalia." In *Intelligence for Multilateral Decision and Action.* Washington, DC: Joint Military Intelligence College, 1997.

Ambrose, Stephen E. *Band of Brothers.* New York: Simon and Schuster, 2001.

ANSER Institute for Homeland Security. *Dark Winter.* URL: <http://www.Homelandsecurity. org/darkwinter/index.cfi>.

Augustine, Norman R. "Socio-engineering (And Augustine's Second Law Thereof)." Lecture presented at the University of Colorado Engineering Centennial Convocation, 1 October 1993.

Baker, Peter. "Pitching Globalism to Marines." *The Washington Post,* 24 December 1996, A4.

Bartu, Peter. "Lessons from Cambodia." In *Intelligence in Partnership Conference Proceedings.* Washington, DC: Joint Military Intelligence College, 1997.

Bernstein, Alvin H. "The Academic Researcher and the Intelligence Analyst: How and Where the Twain Might Meet." In *Military Intelligence and the Universities: A Study of an Ambivalent Relationship.* Boulder, CO: Westview Press, 1984.

Boerner, Erich V., CPT(P), USA. *National Intelligence Support to the Warfighters: An Analysis of an Office in Transition.* MSSI Thesis. Washington, DC: Joint Military Intelligence College, May 1994.

Breuer, William. Hitler's *Undercover War.* New York: St. Martin's Press, 1989.

British Security Coordination: The Secret History of British Intelligence in the Americas, 1940-1945. Introduction by Nigel West. New York: Fromm International, 1999.

Budiansky, Stephen. *Battle of Wits.* New York: The Free Press, 2000.

Bulletin of the Atlantic Council of the United States 2, no. 3 (29 March 1991).

Burns, James MacGregor. *Roosevelt: The Soldier of Freedom.* New York: Harcourt Brace Jovanovich, Inc., 1970.

Bush, Chilton R. *Newspaper Reporting of Public Affairs.* New York: Appleton-Century-Crofts, Inc., 1951.

Bush, George, and Brent Scowcroft. *A World Transformed.* New York: Vintage Books, 1998.

Cantrell, Sean J. "Integrated Intelligence Operations: The Key to Force Protection." Tractate submitted to the U.S. Air Force Institute for National Security Studies, January 2000.

Carter, Jimmy. *Keeping Faith.* New York: Bantam Books, 1982.

Carver, Chris N., Captain, U.S. Army. *Square Peg, Round Hole: Why Military Intelligence is Unprepared for Operations Other Than War.* MSSI Thesis. Washington, DC: Joint Military Intelligence College, August 1998.

Casey, William. Remarks on the 25th anniversary of DIA. Defense Intelligence Analysis Center, Washington, DC, 26 September 1986.

Cash, John A., John Albright, and Allan W. Sandstrum. *Seven Firefights in Vietnam.* New York: Bantam Books, 1985.

Central Intelligence Agency. *Soviet Forces in Cuba.* Fact Sheet. Washington, DC: CIA, 5 February 1963.

Chairman of the Joint Chiefs of Staff. *Joint Vision 2010.* Washington, DC: Joint Chiefs of Staff, 1996.

Cheney, Dick. Secretary of Defense. Statement to the Senate Armed Services Committee, in connection with the FY 1992-93 Budget for the Department of Defense, 21 February 1991.

Churchill, Winston S. *Their Finest Hour.* Boston: Houghton Mifflin Company, 1949.

The CIA Under Harry Truman. Ed. Michael Warner. Washington, DC: Central Intelligence Agency, 1994.

A. Denis Clift

_____. *The Grand Alliance.* Boston: Houghton Mifflin Company, 1950.

Clarridge, Duane R. *A Spy for All Seasons.* New York: Scribner, 1997.

Clift, A. Denis. Address to the Naval Postgraduate School, Monterey, California, 1995. Published as the President's Column in *Defense Intelligence Journal* 4, no. 2 (Fall 1995): 107-121, and reprinted here by permission.

_____. Address to the Romanian Institute for Higher Military Studies, Bucharest, Romania, 25 March 1996.

_____. Address to the Symposium on National Security and National Competitiveness, 1 December 1992. It originally appeared in print in *American Intelligence Journal* (Spring/Summer 1993): 25-28, a publication of the National Military Intelligence Association, www.nmia.org. It is reprinted here by permission.

_____. "The Commander's Kit." Address to the World Affairs Council, San Antonio, Texas, 6 April 2000.

_____. "The Dinkum Oil." Address to the Patterson School of Diplomacy and International Commerce at the University of Kentucky, Lexington, KY, 26 September 1997.

_____. *"E Pluribus Unum MMII."* Address to Trinity College, Washington, DC, 31 January 2002.

_____. "The Five-Legged Calf: Bringing Intelligence to the National Security Debate." *American Intelligence Journal* (Winter 1989-1990): 24-30. *American Intelligence Journal* is a publication of the National Military Intelligence Association, www.nmia.org. The article cited is reprinted here by permission.

_____. "From Semaphore to Predator: Intelligence in the Internet Era." Address delivered to the International Security Studies Conference, Yale University, 27 April 2002.

_____. "Intelligence Education for Joint Warfighting." Essay originally published in *Joint Force Quarterly*, no. 21 (Spring 1999): 96-99. *JFQ* is a professional military journal published for the Chairman of the Joint Chiefs of Staff by the Institute for National Strategic Studies, National Defense University, Washington, DC. The article is reprinted here by permission.

_____. "The Knotted Stick of History." Banquet Address at the 63rd Annual Meeting of the Society for Military History, 20 April 1996.

_____. "The Left Hand of Curiosity." Address delivered to a Seminar on Intelligence, Command, and Control at Harvard University, 27 February 1997. Originally published in an Incidental Paper, *Program on Information Resources Policy,* Cambridge, MA: Center for Information Policy Research, Harvard University, Spring 1997. It is reprinted here by permission.

_____. "The Play of Intelligence: With Presidents at the Summit." Address to the Miller Center, University of Virginia, Charlottesville, Virginia, 30 April 2001.

_____. Letter to Lieutenant General Lincoln Faurer, USAF (Ret.), 28 October 1994.

_____. "Remarks at the Smithsonian Air and Space Museum." Originally published in *Defense Intelligence Journal* 4, no. 1 (Spring 1995): 5-10, and reprinted here by permission.

_____. "From Roe, Sims, and Thomas to You." *Defense Intelligence Journal* 3, no. 2 (Fall 1994): 105-113. The essay is reprinted here by permission.

_____. "Safecrackers: The Past, Present, and Future of U.S. Intelligence." Address delivered to the Georgia Institute of Technology, Atlanta, GA, 29 April 1998.

_____. "Semper Proteus." Address to the United States Coast Guard Academy, New London, Connecticut, 20 October 2000.

_____. "Through the Prism of National Security: The Challenge of Intelligence Sharing." Address to the Kennedy School, Harvard University, 27 August 2001.

_____. "Two If By Sea ... Three If By Cyberspace." Address to the U.S. Merchant Marine Academy, Kings Point, New York, 30 November 1999.

_____. *With Presidents to the Summit.* Fairfax, VA: George Mason University Press, 1993.

Conrad, Joseph. *A Personal Record.* Garden City, NY: Doubleday, Page & Co., 1924.

_____. "The Secret Agent." *In A Conrad Argosy.* Garden City, NY: Doubleday, Doran & Company, Inc., 1942.

Coulter, Daniel Y. "Global Commercial Maritime Environment." Washington, DC: Office of Naval Intelligence, 1999.

"DARPA." *In The Living Internet.* URL: <http.//www.livinginternet.com/?i/ii_darpa.htm>. Accessed 2 May 2002.

Dayan, Moshe. *Living With The Bible.* New York: William Morrow & Company, Inc., 1978.

Declaration of the Heads of States and Governments participating in the meeting of the Northern Atlantic Council. Annex. Brussels, Belgium: NATO Headquarters, 11 January 1994.

Department of Defense. *Conduct of the Persian Gulf War.* Final Report of the Department of Defense to Congress pursuant to Title V of the Persian Gulf Conflict Supplemental Authorization and Personnel Benefits Act of 1991. Washington, DC: Government Printing Office, April 1992.

A. Denis Clift

_____. *Report of the Secretary of Defense to the President and the Congress.* Washington, DC: Government Printing Office, January 1991.

Department of Transportation, Maritime Administration. *1998 Annual Report.* Washington, DC: GPO, May 1999.

"Doctors to Combat Bioterrorism." *The Capital* (Annapolis, MD), 3 January 2002, B2.

Don, Peter J., Captain, U.S. Army. *The Awakening: Developing Military Intelligence Professionals to Support United States Army Special Forces.* MSSI Thesis. Washington, DC: Joint Military Intelligence College, August 1998.

"Down Madisonsky Avenue." *The Economist.* Review, "Whence the Threat to Peace," 6 February 1982.

Eisenhower, Dwight D. *Crusade in Europe.* Garden City, NY: Doubleday & Co., Inc., 1948.

Ensign, Lieutenant Eric S., USCG. *Intelligence in the Rum War at Sea,* 1920-1933. MSSI Thesis. Washington, DC: Joint Military Intelligence College, 1998.

Eshed, Hagai. *Reuven Shiloah: The Man Behind the Mossad.* London: Frank Cass, 1997.

Eye in the Sky. Eds. Dwayne A. Day, John M. Logsdon, and Brian Latell. Washington, DC: Smithsonian Institution Press, 1998.

Falk, Stanley L., and Theodore W. Bauer. *The National Security Structure.* Washington, DC: Industrial College of the Armed Forces, 1972.

Federal Maritime Commission. *Annual Report for Fiscal Year 1998.* Washington, DC: GPO, 1999.

Foglesong, David H., Captain, U.S. Air Force. *Intelligence, Dominant Battlespace Knowledge and the Warfighter.* MSSI Thesis. Washington, DC: Joint Military Intelligence College, August 1998.

Ford, Harold P. "An Analyst's View: Why Were CIA Analysts so Pessimistic About Vietnam?" Paper presented to 63rd Annual Meeting, Society for Military History, 1996.

_____. *CIA and the Vietnam Policymakers: Three Episodes 1962-1968.* Washington, DC: Center for the Study of Intelligence, Central Intelligence Agency, 1998.

Ford, Ronnie E., CPT, U.S. Army. *Tet 1968: Understanding the Surprise.* London: Frank Cass, 1995.

Forsyth, Frederick. *The Fourth Protocol.* New York: Viking, 1984.

Freeh, Louis J. *The Threat to the United States Posed by Terrorists.* Statement for the Record by the Director, Federal Bureau of Investigation, before the Senate Committee on Appropriations, Subcommittee for the Departments of Commerce, Justice, and State, the Judiciary, and Related Agencies, Washington, DC, 4 February 1999.

Friedman, Lawrence. "Revolutions in Military Affairs." Paper presented to the Ivan Bloch Commemorative Conference. St. Petersburg, Russia, February 1999.

Gates, Robert M. *From the Shadows.* New York: Simon & Schuster, 1996.

————. Quoted in *Washington Post*, 17 June 1985.

General Atomics Aeronautical Systems, Inc. "Predator: A Global Option." Fact Sheet. San Diego, CA: General Atomics Aeronautical Systems, Inc., n.d.

Gleysteen, William H. Jr. *Massive Entanglement, Marginal Influence.* Washington, DC: Brookings Institution Press, 1999.

Gorbachev, Mikhail. Nobel Lecture. Oslo, Norway, 5 June 1991. Reported in TASS.

Gorki, Maxim. *A Book of Short Stories.* New York: Henry Holt and Company, 1939.

Great Speeches. Ed. Houston Peterson. New York: Simon and Schuster, 1954.

Great True Spy Stories. Ed. Allen Dulles. New York: Harper and Row, Publishers, 1968.

Greene, Graham. *The Human Factor.* New York: Simon and Schuster, 1978.

————. *The Quiet American.* New York: The Viking Press, 1956.

Gressang, Daniel S. "The Role of Perceptions and Beliefs of U.S. Policymakers in the Decisionmaking Process," *Joint Military Intelligence College Newsletter* 5, no. 1 (June 1998): 15.

Halton, Matthew. *Ten Years to Alamein.* London: Lindsay Drummond Ltd., 1944.

Hammarskjold, Dag. Former Secretary-General of the United Nations. Quoted by General Sir Michael Rose in "Address." The Ivan Bloch Commemorative Conference, St. Petersburg, Russia, February 1999.

Hammonland, Arthur E., LCDR, U.S. Navy, and LCDR David L. Cooper, U.S. Navy. "The Largest Tankers." U.S. Naval Institute *Proceedings*, July 1964, 89-101.

Harahan, Joseph P. *On-Site Inspections Under the INF Treaty.* Washington, DC: Department of Defense, 1993.

Harney, James. *Daily News,* 25 April 1986, 3.

Havel, Vaclav. President of the Czechoslovak Republic. Address to a Joint Session of the United States Congress. Washington, DC, 21 February 1990.

Hayden, Michael V., Lieutenant General, USAF. "Warfighters and Intelligence: One Team-One Fight." *Defense Intelligence Journal* 4, no. 2 (Fall 1995).

————. Address to Kennedy Political Union of American University, Washington, DC, 17 February 2000.

A. Denis Clift

_____. Address to the Nixon Center, Washington, DC, 12 November 1999.

Heilmeier, George. "Educating Tomorrow's Engineers." *ASEE Prism,* May/June 1995.

Heinl, R. D. Jr. "The Right to Fight." *United States Naval Institute Proceedings,* September 1962, 27.

Hemingway, Ernest. "The Spanish War." *Fact*, July 1938, 65.

Hoenle, Darin L., Second Lieutenant, U.S. Air Force. *Emptying a Bucket with a Spoon: Commercial Satellite Support for Unmanned Aerial Vehicle Video.* MSSI Thesis. Washington, DC: Joint Military Intelligence College, August 1998.

Holst, John Jorgen. Minister of Defense of Norway. "Collective Defense in the Post-Cold War Era." Speech delivered to the Atlantic Council of the United States, 20 March 1991.

H.R. Report No. 104-832, accompanying H.R. 3259. *Intelligence Authorization Act for Fiscal Year 1997* (1996).

Hughes, John T., with A. Denis Clift. "The San Cristobal Trapezoid." *Studies in Intelligence* 36, no. 5 (1992): 55-71. Copyright 1992 by John T. Hughes. Used by permission of Mrs. John T. Hughes.

Huxley, Aldous. *Brave New World.* Garden City, NY: The Sun Dial Press, 1932.

The Information Resources Policy Handbook. Eds. Benjamin M. Compaine and William H. Read. Cambridge, MA: MIT Press, 1999.

Intelligence in the Mid-1980s. Ed. Marjorie W. Cline. Washington, DC: National Intelligence Study Center, 1985.

Intelligence for Multilateral Decision and Action. Ed. Perry L. Pickert and Russell G. Swenson. Washington, DC: Joint Military Intelligence College, 1997.

Intentions and Capabilities: Estimates on Soviet Strategic Forces, 1950-1983. Ed. Donald P. Steury. Washington, DC: Center for the Study of Intelligence, Central Intelligence Agency, 1996.

Interagency Task Force. "A Coast Guard for the 21st Century." Report of the Interagency Task Force on U.S. Coast Guard Roles and Missions, December 1999.

Ives, Robert P. II, Staff Sergeant, U. S. Army. *The National Security Implications of the Space Launch Industry.* MSSI Thesis. Washington, DC: Joint Military Intelligence College, August 1998.

Jacoby, Rear Admiral Lowell E., USN. "Intelligence Support to Military Operations—Implications for Joint Vision 2010." Unpublished manuscript, February 2000.

Johnson, Jay, Admiral, U.S. Navy. "International Sea Power Symposium Address." Naval War College, Newport, Rhode Island, 1997.

Clift Notes

Johnson, Lyndon Baines. *The Vantage Point.* New York: Holt, Rinehart and Winston, 1971.

Jones, Reginald V. *The Wizard War.* New York: Coward, McCann & Geoghegan, Inc., 1978.

Kennedy, President John F. "Remarks Aboard the Coast Guard Training Barque *Eagle.* 15 August 1962. *Public Papers of the Presidents of the United States.* Washington, DC: GPO, 1963.

Kennedy, Robert F. *Thirteen Days.* New York: W.W. Norton & Company, Inc., 1969.

Kirkpatrick, Lyman. *The Real CIA.* New York: The Macmillan Co., 1968.

Kissinger, Henry. *Years of Upheaval.* Boston: Little, Brown and Company, 1982.

The Kissinger Transcripts. Edited by William Burr. New York: The New Press, 1998.

Kleinrock, Leonard. "The Birth of Internet." Updated 27 August 1996. URL: <http// www.lk.cs.ucla.edu/ LK/Inet/birth.html>. Accessed 2 May 2002.

Koch, Oscar W. *G-2: Intelligence for Patton.* Philadelphia: Whitemore Publishing Co. 1971.

Kott, George. Director, Office of Soviet Analysis, Central Intelligence Agency. Opening Statement to the Technology and National Security Subcommittee of the Joint Economic Committee, Congress of the United States, 16 May 1991.

Krizan, Lisa. *Intelligence Essentials for Everyone.* Occasional Paper Number Six. Joint Military Intelligence College. Washington, DC: Defense Intelligence Agency, 1999.

Larson, Charles R., ADM, USN. "The Military Officer of the 21st Century." Address to the Parent's Club of San Francisco, 15 June 1995.

Lawrence, T.E. *The Seven Pillars of Wisdom.* New York: Doubleday & Company, Inc., 1935.

LeCarre, John. *Tinker, Tailor, Soldier, Spy.* New York: Alfred A. Knopf, 1974.

Leverkuehn, Paul. *German Military Intelligence.* New York: Frederick A. Praeger, Inc., 1954.

Lewis, Jean M., First Lieutenant, U.S. Army Reserve. *Biotechnology: New Possibilities for Biological Warfare.* MSSI Thesis. Washington, DC: Joint Military Intelligence College, August 1998.

Lose, James M., Captain, U.S. Marine Corps. "The National Intelligence Support Teams." *Studies in Intelligence* 42, no. 1 (1998): 29-38.

_____. "National Intelligence Support Teams." *Studies in Intelligence,* Unclassified Edition (Winter 1999-2000).

A. Denis Clift

Luns, Joseph. NATO Secretary General. Foreword to the North Atlantic Treaty Organization's report, *NATO and the Warsaw Pact: Force Comparisons,* April 1982.

Maffeo, Stephen E. *Most Secret and Confidential.* Annapolis, MD: Naval Institute Press, 2000.

Magnan, Stephen W., Captain, U.S. Air Force. *Information Operations: Are We Our Own Worst Enemy?* Master's Thesis. Washington, DC: Joint Military Intelligence College, August 1998.

Mahl, Thomas E. *Desperate Deception: British Covert Operations in the United States, 1939-44.* Washington and London: Brassey's, 1998.

Malphrus, Stephen R. Staff Director for Management, Board of Directors of the Federal Reserve System. Remarks at the Homeland Defense Training Conference, Washington, DC, 18 December 2001.

Markoff, John. "High-Tech Advances Push C.I.A. Into New Company." *The New York Times,* 29 September 1999, A14.

Marshall, Mark G. *The Nature of Imagery Analysis and its Place Beside Intelligence Analysis.* Washington, DC: Joint Military Intelligence College, 1998.

Martin, Frederick Thomas. *Top Secret Intranet: How U.S. Intelligence Built INTELINK—The World's Largest, Most Secure Network.* Saddle River, NJ: Prentice Hall, 1999.

McArthur, Doman, LtCol, United States Marine Corps Reserve. *Intelligence and Policy: Venturing a Structured Analysis of Iraqi Weapons of Mass Destruction.* Discussion Paper Number Eleven. Joint Military Intelligence College. Washington, DC: Defense Intelligence Agency, 2001.

McCone, John A. Director of Central Intelligence. Statement on Cuba, 6 February 1963.

McCrane, Michael P., Captain, U.S. Marine Corps Reserve. *Time-Sensitive Document Exploitation: Lessons Learned from the Vietnam Conflict Applicable to Drug Law Enforcement.* MSSI Thesis. Washington, DC: Joint Military Intelligence College, August 1998.

McNamara, Robert S. *In Retrospect.* New York: Times Books Random House, 1995.

————. Press Conference, U.S. Department of State, 6 February 1963.

Medina, Carmen A. "What to Do When Traditional Models Fail." *Studies in Intelligence* 45, no. 4 (2001): 35-40.

Mencken, H.L. *Supplement 1* to *The American Language.* New York: Alfred A. Knopf, 1962.

Minihan, Kenneth A., Lt Gen, USAF. Address to Army Intelligence Ball. Alexandria, Virginia, 23 September 1995.

Montagu, Ewen. *The Man Who Never Was.* Philadelphia: J. P. Lippincott Company, 1954.

Morris, Edmund. *Dutch: A Memoir of Ronald Reagan.* New York: Random House, 1999.

Mostert, Noel. *Supership.* New York: Alfred A. Knopf, 1974.

Murrow, Edward R. Testimony as Director of USIA before the Subcommittee of the Committee on Appropriations, United States Senate, 20 September 1962.

Musser, George. "Better Killing through Chemistry." *Scientific American* 285, no. 6 (December 2001).

National Intelligence Council. National Intelligence Estimate (NIE) 85-2-62. *The Situation and Prospects in Cuba.* Washington, DC, 1 August 1962.

————. Special National Intelligence Estimate (SNIE) 85-3-62, *The Military Buildup in Cuba,* 19 September 1962.

————. SNIE 11-19-62, *Major Consequences of Certain U.S. Courses of Action on Cuba,* 20 October 1962.

National Security Act of 1947. Eighteenth Congress of the United States of America, 26 July 1947.

National Security Agency, Center for Cryptologic History. "Introductory History of VENONA and Guide to the Translations." Fort George G. Meade, MD: National Security Agency, 1996.

Newman, Richard J. "Ready! Aim! Reboot!" *U.S. News & World Report,* 20 January 1997, 45.

New York Times, 8 May 1981; 4 October 1981; 30 April 1987; 8 May 1991; and 30 May 1991.

"A Nice Catch-for Customs," Associated Press, 14 July 2000.

Nixon, Richard. *RN: The Memoirs of Richard Nixon.* New York: Gross & Dunlap, 1978.

Nolan, Janne E. *Trappings of Power.* Washington, DC: The Brookings Institution, 1991.

Norman, Neal D., Captain, U.S. Army. *British Intelligence and Information Superiority at the Battle of Alam Halfa: Turning the Tide in North Africa.* MSSI Thesis. Washington, DC: Joint Military Intelligence College, 1997.

North Atlantic Treaty Organization (NATO). Foreign Ministers' Statement. Brussels, Belgium, May 1981.

A. Denis Clift

_____. *NATO and the Warsaw Pact: Force Comparisons.* Brussels, Belgium: NATO, April 1982.

Office of Naval Intelligence and Coast Guard Intelligence Coordination Center. *Threats and Challenges to Maritime Security 2020.* Washington, DC: GPO, March 1999.

Office of the Secretary of Defense. "Proliferation: Threat and Response." White Paper. Washington, DC: Government Printing Office, November 1997.

O'Toole, Thomas. *The Washington Post,* 28 December 1968, A1.

Palo Alto Times. Obituary. Palo Alto, CA, 23 August 1972, 2.

Paquette, Richard A., Major, U.S. Army. *Ethnic Conflict: Kosovo and the Next Balkan War.* MSSI Thesis. Washington, DC: Joint Military Intelligence College, August 1998.

Parmet, Herbert S. *George Bush: The Life of a Lone Star Yankee.* New York: Scribner, 1997.

Perry, William. Secretary of Defense. Remarks to the Corps of Defense Attachés. Washington, DC, 28 February 1996.

Persico, Joseph E. *Roosevelt's Secret War.* New York: Random House, 2001.

Potter, E.B. "Chester William Nimitz 1885-1966." *United States Naval Institute Proceedings,* July 1966, 44.

Powell, Colin L., General, U.S. Army. Chairman of the Joint Chiefs of Staff. Remarks to the American Stock Exchange Washington Conference. Washington, DC: Mayflower Hotel, 15 October 1990.

Powers, Francis Gary. *Operation Overflight.* New York: Holt, Rinehart, and Winston, 1970.

Public Papers of the Presidents of the United States: John F. Kennedy, 1962. Washington, DC: GPO, 1963.

Quigley, Lieutenant Commander William J., USCG. "Driftnet Fishery Enforcement: A New Intelligence Problem." In *Intelligence for Mutililateral Decision and Action.* Ed. Perry L. Pickert. Washington, DC: Joint Military Intelligence College, 1997, 509-514.

Raether, Helmut. "No Precise Information on Iraq's Weapons of Mass Destruction." Deutsche Presse-Agenture, 13 February 1998.

The Reagan Foreign Policy. Edited by William G. Hyland. New York: A Meridian Book, 1987.

Reed, James A. "Renaissance of the Coast Guard." *United States Naval Institute Proceedings* 91, no. 8 (August 1965).

Report of the Commission on the Roles and Capabilities of the United States Intelligence Community. Washington, DC: Government Printing Office, 1996.

Report to the Faculty, Administration, Board of Visitors and Students of the Joint Military Intelligence College. Evaluation Team representing the Commission on Higher Education of the Middle States Association of Colleges and Schools. 14 April 1998.

Riley, The Hon. Richard, Secretary of Education. Address to the Fifth National Science Bowl Competition. Associated Press, *AP Online,* 2 May 1995.

Rose, General Sir Michael. Address to the Ivan Bloch Commemorative Conference. St. Petersburg, Russia, February 1999.

Rosemberg, Clair. "Has-been Revolutionary Carlos Laps up Limelight at Trial." Agence France Presse, Paris, 28 December 1997.

Rosenthal, A.M. "On My Mind: Profiles in Terrorism." *New York Times,* 10 February 1989, A35.

Rowe, Philip A. Jr., Colonel, USAF (Ret.). "The Star Catchers." *Air Force Magazine,* Washington, DC, 1995, 75.

Rueb, Diana D. *The Joint Worldwide Intelligence Communications System (JWICS): Increased Utilization of JWICS Video Teleconferencing Will Augment Defense Intelligence Agency Mission Requirements.* MSSI Thesis. Washington, DC: Joint Military Intelligence College, July 1993.

Ruffner, Kevin C. "CORONA: America's First Satellite Program." Washington, DC: Center for the Study of Intelligence, Central Intelligence Agency, 1995.

"Safecracker Eddie Chapman Dies: Spy for Britain in WW II." Obituary in *The Washington Post,* 17 December 1997, B6.

Sanders, George D. "Containers and Containerships." U. S. Naval Institute *Proceedings,* April 1963, 60-61.

Schanzer, Steven. "Information Systems/Information Technology: What is Their Value?" Address to Mitre Corporation Government Executives Seminar. Williamsburg, Virginia, 22 February 1994.

Schlesinger, Arthur M. Jr. *A Thousand Days.* Boston: Houghton Mifflin Company, 1965.

Sciolino, Elaine. "Violence Thwarts C.I.A. Director's Unusual Role in Middle Eastern Peacemaking." *The New York Times,* 13 November 2000, A-10.

Shaffer, Ron. *The Washington Post,* 12 February 1998, D6.

Shalikashvili, John M., Gen., U.S. Army, Chairman of the Joint Chiefs of Staff. *Joint Vision 2010.* Washington, DC: GPO, 1997.

Sheehan, Edward R.F. "The Rise and Fall of a Soviet Agent." *In Great True Spy Stories,* edited by Allen Dulles. New York: Harper and Row Publishers, 1968.

A. Denis Clift

Sherman Kent and the Board of National Estimates: Collected Essays. Ed. Donald P. Steury. Washington, DC: Center for the Study of Intelligence, Central Intelligence Agency, 1994.

"Ship Drops 150 Asians on Canadian Beach." Associated Press. *The New York Times,* 12 August 1999, A4.

Shwedo, B. J. *Patton's ULTRA System and Its Employment on the European Battlefield.* MSSI Thesis. Washington, DC: Joint Military Intelligence College, August 1995.

Sipress, Alan, and Vernon Loeb. "Bush Ends CIA's Role as Middle East Broker." *The Washington Post,* 22 March 2001, A25.

Skelton, Ike, Representative (D-MO). "Intelligence and U.S. Military Policy." Address to the "Leading Intelligence in the 21st Century" Conference, 25 June 1998. Washington, DC: Joint Military Intelligence College.

Smith, R. Jeffrey. "Expansion of Covert Action Eyed." *The Washington Post,* 13 September 1995, A8.

Soviet Military Power. Department of Defense Report. Washington, DC: Government Printing Office. Various editions, 1981-1990.

Stafford, David. *Churchill and Secret Service.* New York: The Overlook Press, 1998.

_____. *Roosevelt and Churchill: Men of Secrets.* New York: The Overlook Press, 1999.

Starbreit, Immo. Ambassador to the United States from the Federal Republic of Germany. Remarks at the Ceremony Commemorating the 10th Anniversary of the Defense Intelligence Analysis Center. Washington, DC, 23 May 1994.

Stokes, Louis, Representative (D-OH). Address to the Graduating Class, Joint Military Intelligence College, 11 September 1987. Washington, DC: Bolling AFB.

Studeman, William O. "Leading Intelligence Along the Byways of our Future: Acquiring C4ISR Architectures for the 21st Century," *Defense Intelligence Journal* 7, no. 1 (Spring 1998): 47-48.

Suro, Roberto. "Coast Guard Tactics Boost Drug Seizures." *The Washington Post,* 30 September 1999, A6.

Talbott, Strobe. End Game: *The Inside Story of SALT II.* New York: Harper & Row Publishers, 1979.

Tenet, George J. Director of Central Intelligence. Commencement Address. Joint Military Intelligence College, Washington, DC, 3 September 1999.

_____. Oscar Iden Lecture. Georgetown University, 18 October 1999.

Clift Notes

N

_____. Statement before the Senate Armed Services Committee, Washington, DC, 2 February 1999.

_____. "What 'New' Role for CIA?" *The New York Times,* 27 October 1998, A23.

Tolley, Kemp. "The Strange Assignment of USS *Lanikai." United States Naval Institute Proceedings,* July 1966, 44.

A Treasury of the World's Great Speeches. Ed. Houston Peterson. New York: Simon and Schuster, 1954.

Treaty between the United States of America and the Union of Soviet Socialist Republics on the Limitation of Strategic Offensive Areas. Article XV. Vienna, 18 June 1979.

Troy, Thomas F. *Donovan and the CIA.* Frederick, MD: Aletheia Books, 1981.

Truman, Harry S. *Memoirs, Vol. One: Year of Decisions.* Garden City, NY: Doubleday and Company, Inc., 1955.

_____. *Memoirs, Vol. Two: Years of Trial and Hope.* Garden City, NY: Doubleday & Company, Inc., 1956.

Turner, Stansfield. *Secrecy and Democracy.* Boston: Houghton Mifflin Company, 1985.

United States Commission on National Security/21st Century. *Road Map for National Security: Imperative for Change.* Washington, DC: GPO, 2001.

U.S. Congress, Senate Armed Services Committee. *Hearings on Strategic and Space Force Posture.* April 1991.

U.S. Congress, Senate Committee on Government Operations, Subcommittee on National Policy Machinery. *Organizing for National Security.* 3 volumes. Washington, DC: Government Printing Office, 1961.

U.S. Congress, Senate Select Committee on Intelligence. *Hearings on the Nomination of William Webster as Director of Central Intelligence.* May 1987.

U.S. Customs, Intelligence Division. "The HINT Alliance Marine Containers Industry Project." Washington, DC: GPO, 12 August 1999.

U.S. Navy. Light Photographic Squadron Sixty-Two (VPF-62) *Newsletter,* February 1963.

U.S. President (George Bush). Address to the Aspen Institute Symposium, 2 August 1990. Reprinted in *Report of the Secretary of Defense to the President and the Congress,* Appendix E. Washington, DC: Government Printing Office, January 1991.

U.S. President (Bill Clinton). Commencement Address. U.S. Naval Academy, Annapolis, Maryland, 22 May 1998.

A. Denis Clift

U.S. President (Ronald Reagan). Executive Order 12333. "United States Intelligence Activities." 4 December 1981.

————. Statement on the release of *Soviet Military Power.* March 1983.

Van Wagenen, James. "Congressional Oversight: A Look Back." Unpublished paper by DIA Chair, Joint Military Intelligence College, 1996.

Veeris, Christian H., Captain, U.S. Marine Corps. *Concrete Hamlet: Using a Vietnam Model for Tactical Information Gathering in Future Urban Environments.* MSSI Thesis. Washington, DC: Joint Military Intelligence College, July 1998.

Volkogonov, Dmitri. *Autopsy for an Empire: The Seven Leaders Who Built the Soviet Regime.* New York: The Free Press, 1998.

von Humboldt, Wilhelm. Quoted in Gerhard Casper, "Teaching and Research." *Stanford Today,* March/April 1998, 27.

The Wall Street Journal, 28 March 1991, 10.

Walpole, Robert D. "Lessons Learned: Intelligence Support on Chemical and Biological Warfare During the Gulf War and on Veterans' Illnesses Issues." Washington, DC: Director of Central Intelligence's Persian Gulf War Illnesses Task Force, December 1997.

Walters, Vernon A., LTG, USA (Ret.). "General De Gaulle in Action," *Studies in Intelligence* 38, no. 5 (1995).

————. *Silent Missions.* Garden City, NY: Doubleday & Company, Inc., 1978.

Washington, George, General. Letter to Colonel Elias Dayton, 26 July1777. Pforzheimer Collection of Intelligence Literature, Washington, DC.

Washington Post, 17 June 1985 and 13 June 1989.

Weinberger, Caspar. Secretary of Defense 1981-1987. Citation for the Defense Intelligence Agency's Meritorious Unit Award, 1 October 1986.

Weiner, Tim. "Master Creator of Ghosts Is Honored by CIA." *The New York Times,* 19 September 1997, A24.

Weizman, Ezer. *On Eagles' Wings.* London: Weidenfeld and Nicholson, 1976.

West, Rebecca. *The Meaning of Treason.* London: Phoenix Press, 2000.

White, Jeffrey B. "Thoughts on Irregular Warfare." Unpublished manuscript accepted for publication in *Studies in Intelligence.*

Whitehead, Don. *The FBI Story.* New York: Random House, 1956.